THOMAS B. SEARIGHT'S

THE OLD PIKE

An illustrated narrative of The National Road

EDITED, DESIGNED & ILLUSTRATED

WITH OVER 230 PHOTOGRAPHS, PRINTS AND ILLUSTRATIONS

by

JOSEPH E. MORSE

& R. DUFF GREEN

Produced & Published by

GREEN TREE PRESS

Library of Congress

Catalog Card Number 70-182366

© *1971 by Green Tree Press, Orange, Virginia*

printed in United States of America

The MAN

T. B. Searight

The BOOK

Thomas Brownfield Searight was born February 20, 1827, with Old Pike blood in his veins. His father and grandfather both owned taverns on the National Road, and during Searight's early life his father became a Road contractor and later a Road commissioner.

Searight studied law at Washington (and Jefferson) College on the National Road at Washington, Pennsylvania, graduating in 1848. Admitted to the bar in 1850, he served as Clerk of the Court in Uniontown and until the Civil War began, edited a publication entitled "Genius of Liberty".

Work, for a time, carried him away from the Pike, first to Harrisburg, Pennsylvania for two terms with the State Legislature in the 1860's, then to the territory of Colorado in 1873 where by appointment of President Grant he served as Surveyor General.

After his return to Uniontown, Searight began a vigorous and voluminous correspondence campaign throughout the country seeking information and confirmation of persons, places and events connected with the National Road. It was an olympian effort to preserve and document an eyewitness history of our National Road before knowledge and memories faded irretrievably into the past.

Searight's work first appeared as a series of articles in his hometown newspaper, "The Jeffersonian Democrat", then in 1894 emerged between hard covers as The Old Pike. In his opening chapter the lawyer turned historian humbly prefaced his work to the reader:

The author of this work was born and reared on the line of the road, and has spent his whole life amid scenes connected with it. He saw it in the zenith of its glory, and with emotions of sadness witnessed its decline. It was a highway at once so grand and imposing, an artery so largely instrumental in promoting the early growth and development of our country's wonderful resources, so influential in strengthening the bonds of the American Union, and at the same time so replete with important events and interesting incidents, that the writer of these pages has long cherished a hope that some capable hand would write its history and collect and preserve its legends, and no one having come forward to perform the task, he has ventured upon it himself, with unaffected diffidence and a full knowledge of his inability to do justice to the subject.

Thomas Searight died in 1899 a few short years away from the automobile and a renewed national interest in his beloved Old Pike.

EDITORS' PREFACE

The National Road from Cumberland, Maryland into southwestern Pennsylvania criss-crossed an old trail blazed by Col. Thomas Cresap and his Indian guide Nemacolin for the Ohio Company in 1751. This trail was also the ill-fated route of Lt. Col. George Washington to Fort Necessity in 1754 and General Braddock enroute to Fort Duquesne the following year.

To our fledgling Congress of the early 1800's a portage link between the Potomac River at Cumberland and the Ohio River at Wheeling Creek was considered the most advantageous route to the new Northwest Territory. Thus in 1811 the National or Cumberland Road, roughly following this already historic trail, began a tortuous 10-year trek west across the Alleghenies to Wheeling. And for 30 colorful years thereafter the Old Pike was a bustling artery of east-west travel and commerce.

By 1852 the railroads had pushed west to the Ohio and the National Road along with other eastern roads slipped into a decline that prevailed for half a century. The Pike by the 1890's was in such bad repair that signs were posted warning the traveler to "proceed at your own risk." Shacks and sheds had sprung up along with weeds on unused parts of the roadbed. It was during this low ebb in Pike history that Searight published his book.

After almost a century of quiet the mounting cry for good roads was soon echoing about the walls of Congress. Profiting by its past mistakes with the Old National Road, Congress, through the Federal Government and State governments, entered into a new era of road building. The Old Pike, revitalized in the 1920's, became part of the National Old Trails Road. Then after WWII it was incorporated with U. S. Route 40 as an ocean to ocean highway.

Hale and hardy today the National Road, superseded in part by Interstate Route 70, patiently endures the ravages of time and travel to retain its hard-earned role as one of America's most historic highways—still in service.

CONTENTS

acknowledgments

Many persons have assisted and encouraged the editors in preparing this present work. To them we are indeed grateful. We are particularly indebted to Alderman Library at the University of Virginia for the use of Searight's book and related material; and for the use of visual material selected from the files of Oglebay Mansion Museum in Wheeling, West Virginia; the Mount Washington Tavern Museum of the National Park Service at Farmington, Pennsylvania; the Washington and Jefferson College in Washington, Pennsylvania; and the Department of Transportation and Smithsonian Institution in Washington, D. C.

NATIONAL ROAD

Our first national road; fathered by Albert Gallatin. Begun in 1811 at Cumberland, Md.; completed to Wheeling in 1818. Toll road under State control, 1835-1905. Rebuilt, it is present U. S. Route 40.

PENNSYLVANIA HISTORICAL AND MUSEUM COMMISSION 1948

U. S. PRESIDENTS AND THE NATIONAL ROAD

Chronological list of National Road appropriations and the President holding office at time of approval.

Thomas Jefferson
Mar. 29, 1806

James Madison
Feb. 14, 1810
Mar. 3, 1811
Feb. 26, 1812
May 6, 1812
Mar. 3, 1813
Feb. 14, 1815
Apr. 16, 1816

James Monroe
Apr. 14, 1818
Mar. 3, 1819
Apr. 11, 1820
May 15, 1820
Feb. 28, 1823
Mar. 3, 1825

John Quincy Adams
Mar. 14, 1826
Mar. 25, 1826
Mar. 2, 1827
Mar. 2, 1827
May 19, 1828
Mar. 2, 1829
Mar. 3, 1829
Mar. 3, 1829

Andrew Jackson
May 31, 1830
Mar. 2, 1831
July 3, 1832
Mar. 2, 1833
June 24, 1834

Road ownership returned to the individual States by Congress. Since portions of the Road were still under construction, the Federal Government was obligated to fund its completion.

Mar. 3, 1835
Mar. 3, 1835
July 2, 1836
Mar. 3, 1837

Martin Van Buren
June 27, 1837
May 25, 1838

John Tyler
Mar. 3, 1843
June 17, 1844

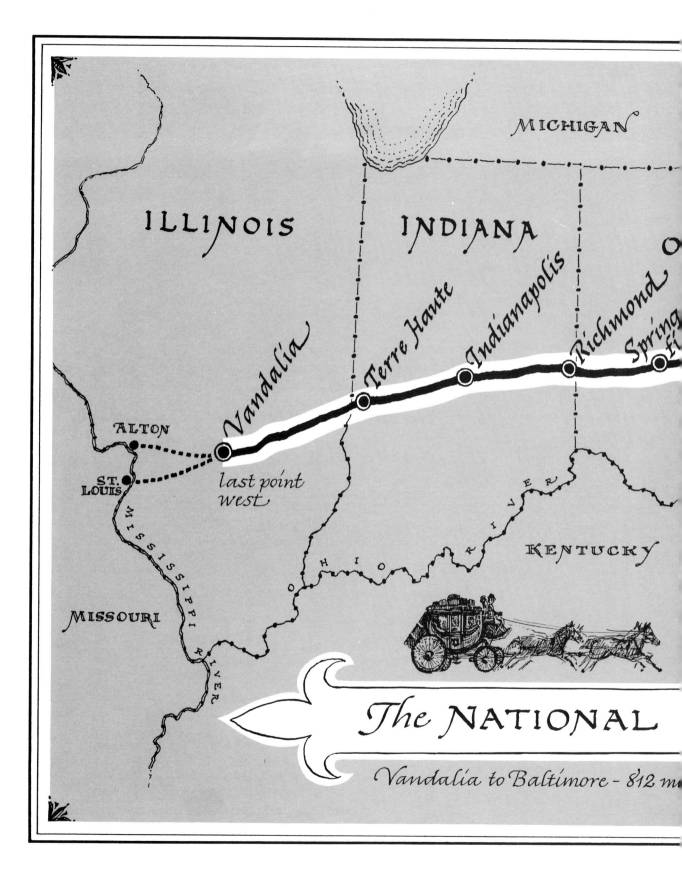

MICHIGAN

ILLINOIS

INDIANA

Vandalia

Terre Haute

Indianapolis

Richmond

O

Spring- f...

ALTON

ST. LOUIS

last point west

MISSISSIPPI RIVER

MISSOURI

OHIO RIVER

KENTUCKY

The NATIONAL

Vandalia to Baltimore - 812 m...

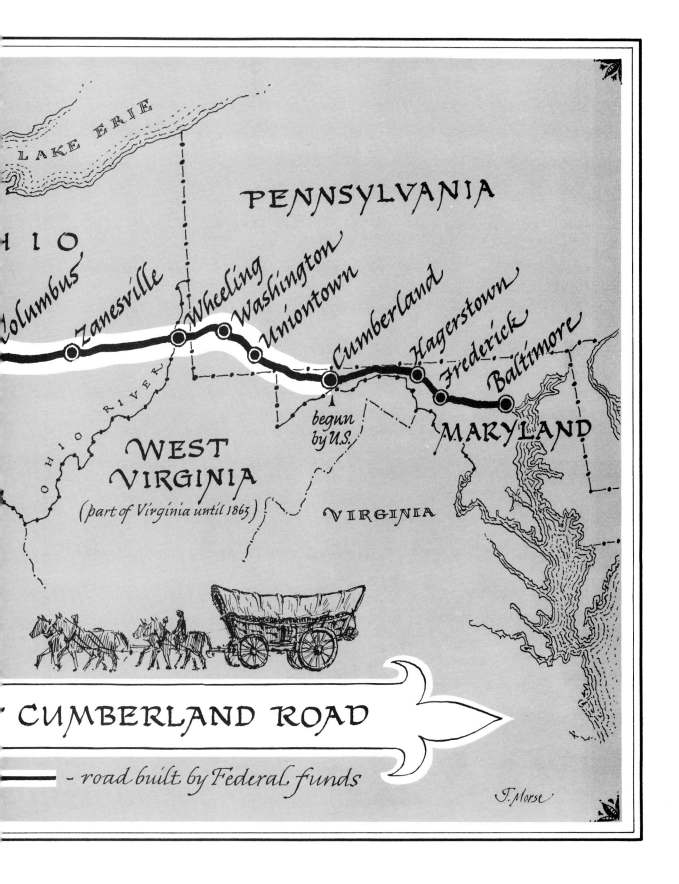

LAKE ERIE

PENNSYLVANIA

OHIO

Columbus Zanesville Wheeling Washington Uniontown Cumberland Hagerstown Frederick Baltimore

OHIO RIVER

begun
by U.S.

WEST
VIRGINIA

(part of Virginia until 1863)

VIRGINIA

MARYLAND

CUMBERLAND ROAD

———— - road built by Federal funds

J. Morse

NINTH CONGRESS OF THE UNITED STATES;

AT THE First Session.

Begun and held at the city of Washington, in the territory of Columbia, on Monday, the second of December, one thousand eight hundred and five.

AN ACT *[to regulate the laying out and making a road from Cumberland, in the state of Maryland, to the state of Ohio.]*

Be it enacted by the Senate and House of Representatives of the United States of America, in Congress assembled, *That the President of the United States be, and he is hereby authorised to appoint, by and with the advice and consent of the Senate, three discreet and disinterested citizens of the United States, to lay out a road from Cumberland, or a point on the northern bank of the river ...*

March 29, 1806

Approved

Th: Jefferson

[Signed] Speaker of the House of Representatives.

[Signed] President of the Senate, pro tempore.

Sam. A. Otis, Secretary.

Thomas Jefferson

Albert Gallatin

I A Great National Highway

The road which forms the subject of this volume, is the only highway of its kind ever wholly constructed by the government of the United States. When Congress first met after the achievement of Independence and the adoption of the Federal Constitution, the lack of good roads was much commented upon by our statesmen and citizens generally, and various schemes were suggested to meet the manifest want. But, it was not until the year 1806, when Jefferson was President, that the proposition for a National Road took practical shape.

Tradition, cheerfully acquiesced in by popular thought, attributes to Henry Clay the conception of the National Road, but this seems to be error. The Hon. Andrew Stewart, in a speech delivered in Congress, January

President Jefferson selected for his Treasury Secretary the very able Albert Gallatin, who, with intuitive vision and sound fiscal reasoning produced the plan that finally won Congressional approval and the National Road was born. Gallatin remained at his treasury post for 13 years and prudently watched expenditures for the Road.

27th, 1829, asserted that "Mr. Gallatin was the very first man who ever suggested the plan for making the Cumberland Road." As this assertion was allowed to go unchallenged, it must be accepted as true, however strongly and strangely it conflicts with the popular belief before stated. The reader will bear in mind that the National Road and the Cumberland Road are one and the same. The road as constructed by authority of Congress, begins at the city of Cumberland, in the State of Maryland, and this is the origin of the name Cumberland Road. All the acts of Congress and of the legislatures of the States through which the road passes, and they are numerous, refer to it as the Cumberland Road. The connecting link between Cumberland and the city of Baltimore is a road much older than the Cumberland Road, constructed and owned by associations of individuals, and the two together constitute the National Road.

While it appears from the authority quoted that Henry Clay was not the planner of the National Road, he was undoubtedly its ablest

11

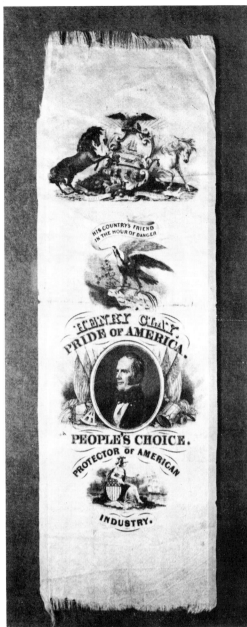

HIS COUNTRYS FRIEND
IN THE HOUR OF DANGER

HENRY CLAY.
PRIDE OF AMERICA.

PEOPLE'S CHOICE.

PROTECTOR OF AMERICAN

INDUSTRY.

Henry Clay became the Old Pike's most indefatigable advocate during the 4 decades of congressional debate over appropriations for the National Road. Though enormously popular along the Pike, Clay was unsuccessful in his campaigns for the presidency in 1824, 1832 and 1844. Pictured (ABOVE) is a ribbon from one of his campaigns.

---

* Benjamin Freeman kept a tavern on the old Braddock Road, a short distance south of Mt. Washington. Locating his house on Laurel Hill, was an error of Mr. Clay, but of little consequence, and readily made under the circumstances.

and most conspicuous champion. In Mallory's Life of Clay it is stated that "he advocated the policy of carrying forward the construction of the Cumberland Road as rapidly as possible," and with what earnestness, continues his biographer, "we may learn from his own language, declaring that he had to *beg, entreat* and *supplicate* Congress, session after session, to grant the necessary appropriations to complete the road." Mr. Clay said, "I have myself toiled until my powers have been exhausted and prostrated to prevail on you to make the grant." No wonder Mr. Clay was a popular favorite along the whole line of the road. At a public dinner tendered him by the mechanics of Wheeling, he spoke of "the great interest the road had awakened in his breast, and expressed an ardent desire that it might be prosecuted to a speedy completion." Among other things he said that "a few years since he and his family had employed the whole or greater part of a day in traveling the distance of about nine miles from Uniontown to Freeman's,* on Laurel Hill, which now, since the construction of the road over the mountains, could be accomplished, together with seventy more in the same time," and that "the road was so important to the maintenance of our Union that he would not consent to give it up to the keeping of the several States through which it passed."

From the time it was thrown open to the public, in the year 1818, until the coming of railroads west of the Allegheny mountains, in 1852, the National Road was the one great highway, over which passed the bulk of trade and travel, and the mails between the East and the West. Its numerous and stately stone bridges with handsomely turned arches, its iron mile posts and its old iron gates, attest the skill of the workmen engaged on its construction, and to this day remain enduring monuments of its grandeur and solidity, all save the imposing iron gates, which have disappeared by process of conversion prompted by some utilitarian idea, savoring in

Traffic on the National Road, according to eyewitnesses was from dawn to dark, a never-ending procession which often sorely taxed maintenance workers. Scene (ABOVE) depicts congestion at bridge over Wills Creek near Cumberland, Maryland.

no little measure of sacrilege. Many of the most illustrious statesmen and heroes of the early period of our national existence passed over the National Road from their homes to the capital and back, at the opening and closing of the sessions of Congress. Jackson, Harrison, Clay, Sam Houston, Polk, Taylor, Crittenden, Shelby, Allen, Scott, Butler, the eccentric Davy Crockett, and many of their contemporaries in public service, were familiar figures in the eyes of the dwellers by the roadside. The writer of these pages frequently saw these distinguished men on their passage over the road, and remembers with no little pride the incident of shaking hands with General Jackson, as he sat in his carriage on the wagon-yard of an old tavern.

As many as twenty-four horse coaches have been counted in line at one time on the road, and large, broad-wheeled wagons, covered with white canvas stretched over bows, laden with merchandise and drawn by six Conestoga horses, were visible all the day long at every point, and many times until late in the evening, besides innumerable caravans of horses, mules, cattle, hogs, and sheep. It looked more like the leading avenue of a great city than a road through rural districts.

The road had a peculiar nomenclature, familiar to the tens of thousands who traveled over it on its palmy days. The names, for example, applied to particular localities on the line, are of striking import, and blend harmoniously with the unique history of the road. With these names omitted, the road would be robbed of much that adds interest to its history. Among the best remembered of these are, The Shades of Death, The Narrows, Piney Grove, Big Crossings, Negro Mountain, Keyser's Ridge, Woodcock Hill, Chalk Hill, Big Savage, Little Savage, Snake Hill, Laurel Hill, The Turkey's Nest, Egg Nog Hill, Coon Island and Wheeling Hill. Rich memories cluster around every one of these names, and

13

Old Hickory traveled the Pike frequently and rivaled Henry Clay as the favorite personality of the Road. Scene (ABOVE) depicts Jackson as the recipient of a complimentary address. Poster (RIGHT) expresses sentiments in the vernacular concurrent with Jackson's presidential campaign.

old wagoners and stage drivers delight to linger over the scenes they bring to mind.

As the phrase "Pike Boys" is frequently used in this volume, it is considered pertinent to give its origin. When first used, it was confined in its application to boys—sons of wagoners, stage drivers, tavern keepers, farmers, and in fact the sons of persons of

14

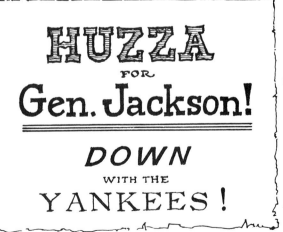

HUZZA
FOR
Gen. Jackson!
DOWN
WITH THE
YANKEES !

every occupation who lived on or adjacent to the road, in the same sense that the boys of a town are called "town boys." Its meaning and import, however, expanded in course of time, until it embraced, as it now does, all persons in any manner and at any time identified with the road, whether by residence or occupation, and without "regard to age, race, color or previous condition of servitude," as the statute puts it, for be it remembered that negro slaves were frequently seen on the National Road. The writer has seen them driven over the road arranged in couples and fastened to a long, thick rope or cable, like horses. This may seem incredible to a majority of persons now living along the road, but it is true, and was a very common sight in the early history of the road and evoked no expression of surprise, or words of censure. Such was the temper of the times. There were negro wagoners on the road, but negro stage drivers were unknown. Stage driving was quite a lofty calling, and the acme of many a young man's ambition. The work was light and the whirl exciting and exhilarating. Wagoners, white and black, stopped overnight at the same taverns, but never sat down together at the same table. A separate table was invariably provided for the colored wagoners, a custom in thorough accord with the public sentiment of the time, and seemingly agreeable to the colored wagoners themselves. Country life in the olden time was enlivened by numerous corn huskings, balls, spelling matches, school exhibitions and frolics of all kinds. Young men and boys along the road, were in the habit of attending these gatherings, going as far as three miles and more in the back country, to reach them, some on foot and others on horseback. A young man would think nothing of getting a girl up behind him on a horse, and hieing away after nightfall, four and five miles to a country dance, and many of the girls of the period considered it but pleasant recreation to walk two or three miles with their lovers, to a spelling match or a revival meeting. A feeling

Dances were a popular form of entertainment along the Pike. The lad (ABOVE) attired in his festive best, sparkles with the youthful exuberance that often whirled him, along with his companions, into the small hours of the morning.

of jealousy always existed between the young men and boys, living along and near the road, and those in the back country, and the occasions before mentioned furnished opportunities from time to time for this feeling to break out, as it often did, in quarrels and fights. The country boys would get together in anticipation of an approaching gathering at some school house, and organize for offense or defense, as the exigencies might require, always calling their rivals and imaginary enemies, "Pike Boys," and this was the origin of that familiar phrase.

The National Road is not in a literal sense a turnpike. A turnpike, in the original meaning of the word, is a road upon which pikes were placed to turn travelers thereon through gates, to prevent them from evading the payment of toll. Pikes were not used, or needed on the National Road. It was always kept in good condition, and travelers thereon, as a rule,

15

16

paid the required toll without complaining. At distances of fifteen miles, on the average, houses were erected for toll collectors to dwell in, and strong iron gates, hung to massive iron posts, were established to enforce the payment of toll in cases of necessity. These toll houses were of uniform size, angular and round, west of the mountains constructed of brick, and through the mountains, of stone, except the one six miles west of Cumberland, which is of brick. They are all standing on their old sites at this date (1893), except the one that stood near Mt. Washington, and the one that stood near the eastern base of Big Savage Mountain. At the last mentioned point, the old iron gate posts are still standing, firmly rooted in their original foundations, and plastered all over with advertisements of Frostburg's business houses, but the old house and the old gates have gone out of sight forever.

It is curious to note how the word turnpike has been perverted from its literal meaning by popular usage. The common idea is that a turnpike is a road made of stone, and that the use of stone is that alone which makes it a turnpike. The common phrase, "piking a road," conveys the idea of putting stones on it, whereas in fact, there is no connection between a stone and a pike, and a road might be a turnpike without a single stone upon it.

In the early work on the road, there was a requirement that stone for the lower stratum or bed should be broken so that the pieces would pass through a seven-inch ring, and for the upper stratum, which was six inches in thickness, would pass through a three-inch ring. Old contractors provided rings of these dimensions, respectively, and enforced a strict compliance with the regulation mentioned. Subsequently the rings fell into disuse, and were ultimately abandoned, but the stones

Droves and drovers (OPPOSITE) were frequently seen on the National Road and though their patronage was welcomed by tavern keepers, they were seldom regarded favorably by stage drivers or residents along the way.

PUBLIC ROADS ADMINISTRATION

Stone used on the National Road was broken by hand. For breaking smaller rock, worker sat (ABOVE) moving backward with rock in a line before him. Pay, based on a linear measure of the rock broken, averaged about one dollar a day. On a section of the original road bed (BELOW) near Uniontown, Pennsylvania, exposed rock suggests appearance of the early Pike surface.

R. DUFF GREEN

17

Built for the farm, the Conestoga wagon with modifications (ABOVE) served the new republic as a vehicle of overland commerce. Then as eastern railroads rendered it obsolete, the Conestoga was again modified and emerged as the prairie schooner carrying pioneers in endless waves across our continent. After the West was won and the young nation it served had become a world power, the Conestoga wagon lived out its last useful days where it had originated a century and a half before, on the farm.

spread over the surface of the road were always broken to small pieces. The hammer of the stone breaker was a very simple contrivance. It was of iron, round as an apple, weighing probably one pound, with a hole through the center for the insertion of a handle. The handle was of hickory wood, slender in the middle, with a thick end for the grasp of the hand. There was also a larger hammer, with a longer and stouter handle, used for breaking stones thrown into holes. In using this hammer the breaker stood on his feet, and in using the smaller one, sat on the stone pile, moving his position as his work advanced. In hot weather the stone breaker, in many instances, used a ready-made, movable bower, to ward off the scorching rays of the sun.

The average result of a stone breaker in a single day was eight perches, and the price paid was twelve and a half cents per perch.

Tradition has it that Robert S. McDowell, Fayette county, Pennsylvania, was the speediest stone breaker on the road. In the year 1848, when Colonel Hopkins was commissioner, Robert S. McDowell broke in one day sixteen perches and two feet. This was done on a bet, and in a contest with Capt. Elias Gilmore. A string of stones one rod in length made two perches, under the gauge in use, and McDowell's string measured eight rods and two feet. Captain Gilmore, who was one of the most vigorous men on the road, gave up the contest about the middle of the afternoon, and yielded the palm to McDowell.

The road was completed from Cumberland to Uniontown at a cost, including all expenses of survey and location, salaries, bridges, and some repairs, of $9,745 per mile. The average cost of the entire road to Wheeling was nearly $13,000 per mile, showing the Eastern division much less costly than the Western.

Down to the year 1834, as has been seen, the road was under the control and supervision of the War Department of the General Government. Brig. Gen. Gratiot was the chief officer in immediate charge. The town of Gratiot on the line of the road in Muskingum County, Ohio, was named in his honor. Captains Delafield, McKee, Bliss, Bartlett, Hartzell, Williams, Colquit and Cass, and Lieuts. Mansfield, Vance and Pickell, all graduates of West Point, were more or less identified with the construction, management and repairs of the road. These army officers were all well known to the people along the National Road.

The old tavern keepers of the National Road were a remarkable body of men. In many instances they were free holders, men well posted in current affairs, and influential in their respective neighborhoods. They were honorable in their dealings, and believed that every man's word should be as good as his bond. As caterers they made no display. They had no bills of fare, printed on gilt edged paper, or fine linen, and it is doubtful if any one of them ever heard the modern word *Menu,* yet spreads of their generous boards would almost kindle exhilaration in the heart of a misanthrope.

The beer of the present day was unknown, or if known, unused on the National Road during the era of its prosperity. Ale was used in limited quantities, but was not a favorite drink. Whisky was the leading beverage, and it was plentiful and cheap.

The National Road had its contingent of quaint characters, eccentric men, philosophers in one sense, and loafers in another. They were indigenous to the road, could not live away from it, and enjoyed the precarious subsistence they obtained on it. The lodestone that attracted them and attached them to the road, probably above all other influences, was the pure whisky.

There was a striking similarity in the habits, manners and pursuits of the old inhabitants of the towns along the National Road, notably between Baltimore and Wheeling. The road was a bond that drew them together and united them as neighbors. Frederick, Hagerstown, Cumberland, Uniontown, Brownsville, Washington and Wheeling derived their main support from the road, and their chief distinction from their location on its line.

Before the road was completed beyond the western boundary of the State of Indiana, the steam railway had become the chief agency of transportation and travel, and our grand old national highway was practically lost amid the primitive prairies of Illinois.

SEARIGHT—OLD PIKE

Congressman T.M.T. McKennan

Of numerous speeches on the National Road excerpted in Searight's text, the following, by T.M.T. McKennan before Congress June 6, 1832, perhaps best eulogizes the Road, its purpose and scope of accomplishment.

This road, Mr. Speaker (the National Road), is a magnificent one—magnificent in extent; it

19

traverses seven different States of this Union, and its whole distance will cover an extent of near eight hundred miles. It is, sir, a splendid monument of national wealth and national greatness, and of the deep interest felt by the government in the wealth and prosperity and happiness of the people.

It is not, sir, like the stupendous monuments of other countries and of other times, which have been erected merely for the purpose of show and of gratifying the pride of some despotic monarch; but this and all similar national improvements are works of utility; they tend to cement the bond of union; they bring together the distant parts of this exalted republic; they diffuse wealth and happiness among a free people, and will be a source of never failing prosperity to millions yet unborn.

It is, sir, a great commercial, military, mail,

James Monroe (BELOW) as Madison's Secretary of State was quite familiar with problems concerning the National Road. In 1822, as President, the vexing question of expanding Federal authority over public works forced Monroe to veto legislation designed to make the National Road a self-sufficient tollroad.

James Madison (ABOVE) as Secretary of State under Jefferson, was a party to the National Road legislation of 1806, but actual construction did not begin until 1811 when he was President. Doubts about the constitutionality of a National Road were for a time dispelled by "Mr. Madison's War" of 1812. As the British blockade of U. S. ports crippled coastal supply routes, the nation was forcefully brought to realize how extremely primitive her arteries of inland commerce were. In the aftermath of war came a vigorous era of road and canal construction and a renewed effort to complete the National Road.

20

national work. To give the House, or those of its members who are unacquainted with the fact, some idea of the immense commercial advantages which the eastern as well as the western country has derived from the construction of this road, let me call their attention to the amount of merchandise transported to the Ohio River in a single year after its completion.

In the year 1822, shortly after the completion of the road, a single house in the town of Wheeling unloaded 1,081 wagons, averaging about 3,500 pounds each, and paid for the carriage of the goods $90,000. At that time there were five other commission houses in the same place, and estimating that each of them received two-thirds the amount of goods consigned to the other, there must have been nearly 5,000 wagons unloaded, and nearly $400,000 paid as the cost of transportation. But, further, it is estimated that at least every tenth wagon passed through that place into the interior of Ohio, Indiana, etc., which would considerably swell the amount. These wagons take their return loads and carry to the eastern markets all the various articles of production and manufacture of the West—their flour, whisky, hemp, tobacco, bacon, and wool. Since this estimate was made, the town of Wheeling is greatly enlarged; its population has nearly doubled; the number of its commercial establishments has greatly increased; and the demand for merchandise in the West has increased with the wealth and improvement and prosperity of the country.

But, further, sir, before the completion of this road, from four to six weeks were usually occupied in the transportation of goods from Baltimore to the Ohio River, and the price varied from six to ten dollars per hundred. Now they can be carried in less than half the time and at one-half the cost, and arrangements are being made by some enterprising gentlemen of the West to have the speed of transportation still increased, and the price of carriage diminished.

Equally important are the benefits derived by

The National Road, once the shining symbol of public endeavor, by the 1830's had become a blemish on the Federal escutcheon. Seeking an end to the controversy over Federal involvement in public works, Congress proposed a return of the Road to the individual states. Noting the poor condition of the Road, several states declined acceptance until it was rebuilt. To these terms Congress agreed. Lewis Cass (ABOVE) who became Jackson's Secretary of War in 1831, fell heir to the task of restoration and directed his subordinates to effect "...the construction of a road unrivaled in the country." Under state ownership tolls were required for funding Pike maintanance and tollhouses of the quaint design (BELOW) were built about 15 miles apart along the Road in Maryland and Pennsylvania.

the government and the people from the rapid, regular, and safe transportation of the mail on this road. Before its completion, eight or more days were occupied in transporting the mail from Baltimore to Wheeling; it was then carried on horseback, and did not reach the western country by this route more than once a week. Now it is carried in comfortable stages, protected from the inclemency of the weather, in forty-eight hours; and no less than twenty-eight mails weekly and regularly pass and repass each other on this road. To show this fact, and the absolute necessity and importance of keeping the road in a good state of repair, in order to enable the post office department to fulfill the expectations of the public, I will ask the favor of the clerk to read to the House a communication received from the Postmaster General on the subject. (Here the clerk read an extract from a letter of the Postmaster General.) The facilities afforded by such a road in time of war for the transportation of the munitions of war, and the means of defense from one point of the country to another, need scarcely be noticed; they must be palpable and plain to every reflecting mind, and I will not take up the time of the House in detailing them.

As I said before, the road traverses seven different States of this Union, and in its whole extent will cover a distance of near 800 miles. Who, then, can doubt its nationality? Who can question the allegation that it is an immensely important national work?

Most of our Presidents, up to the time of Lincoln, were involved with the National Road. John Quincy Adams (TOP, LEFT) traveled the Road and on several occasions gave speeches at towns along the way, as did James K. Polk (CENTER LEFT). "Old Tippecanoe" Harrison (BOTTOM, LEFT) was almost as well known in appearance as in name. During his presidential campaign, a log cabin on wheels was hauled over a good portion of the Pike in his behalf.

II · Baltimore and the Pike west

The bustling port city of Baltimore became the eastern terminus of the National Road. Scene (ABOVE) shows the harbor as viewed from Federal hill soon after the Civil War. Brick structure (BELOW) was the Rising Sun Tavern destroyed almost a hundred years ago.

The road was justly renowned for the great number and excellence of its inns or taverns. On the mountain division, every mile had its tavern. Here one could be seen perched on some elevated site, near the roadside, and there another, sheltered behind a clump of trees, many of them with inviting seats for idlers, and all with cheerful fronts toward the weary traveler. The sign-boards were elevated upon high and heavy posts, and their golden letters winking in the sun, ogled the wayfarer from the hot road-bed and gave promise of good cheer, while the big trough, overflowing with clear, fresh water, and the ground below it sprinkled with droppings of fragrant peppermint, lent a charm to the scene that was well nigh enchanting.

The great majority of the taverns were called wagon stands, because their patrons were largely made up of wagoners, and each provided with grounds called the wagon-yard,

23

As the Old Pike brought more and more freight-ladened Conestoga wagons lumbering into Baltimore, wharves (ABOVE) and markets (BELOW) became familiar haunts of the Old Pike boys. And oysters from the coast soon proved a profitable return load for these enterprising wagoners.

whereon teams were driven to feed, and rest overnight. The very best of entertainment was furnished at these wagon stands. The taverns whereat stage horses were kept and exchanged, and stage passengers took meals, were called "stage houses," located at intervals of about twelve miles, as nearly as practicable.

The outward appearance of an old tavern of the National Road was no index to the quality of the entertainment it afforded. Many of the least pretentious houses furnished the best meals, and paid the most agreeable attention to guests and patrons. It was not unusual to see the wagon yard attached to a small wooden and apparently decaying tavern crowded with teams and wagons, while the inviting grounds of the imposing brick tavern nearby were without an occupant.

The May Pole tavern in Baltimore was a favorite stopping place for old wagoners. It is located on the southwest corner of Paca and German streets, and still standing, an object of much interest to the old people of the road. In front of it stands a tall, slim, granite column, representative of a pole, and preservative of the ancient name. The May Pole was kept in 1833 by Henry Clark, and in 1836 by James Adams, who remained in charge until his death. His successor was Isaac Willison, a Virginian, and before assuming control of the May Pole, an agent of the Baltimore & Ohio Railroad Company, at Frederick City. George Elliott, subsequently manager for Mrs. Adams, at the Mountain City house in Cumberland, was at one time a clerk in the May Pole tavern.

The "Hand in Hand" tavern on Paca, between Lexington and Saratoga streets, and the "White Swan" on Howard Street, were likewise old wagon stands in Baltimore, well patronized in the early days of the National Road. Thomas Elliott also kept a wagon stand in Baltimore, and enjoyed a fair share of patronage. He was the father of George Elliott, above mentioned. The May Pole,

The General Wayne (ABOVE), a well-patronized old Baltimore tavern, stood until the 1880's. Its massive sign depicted the General standing beside his horse.

however, was the favorite tavern of the old wagoners of the National Road. The "Three Ton" and "Gen. Wayne" taverns had each extensive stabling, and furnished accommodations for droves and drovers. The National Road entered the city of Baltimore by way of West Baltimore street.

The first wagon stand west of Baltimore, fifty years ago, was kept by a man whose name was Hawes. It was seven miles from the city, and wagoners often left it in the morning, drove to Baltimore, unloaded, reloaded, and returned to it in the evening of the same day, and the next morning proceeded on the long journey to their western destination. The Hawes tavern ceased to do business after 1840.

At Ellicott's Mills, ten miles west of Baltimore, there was no wagon stand, but stage houses were located there, where stage teams were kept and exchanged.

One mile west of Ellicott's, Frank Earlocker kept a wagon stand that was largely patronized. He was rather of an economical turn of mind, and old wagoners were wont to say of him that he concealed the whisky bottle behind the counter, against the custom of the road, which was to expose it to full view; and it is said that the miserly Earlocker

25

lost more than he gained by his habit, since it induced wagoners to inquire for a drink, more to worry the landlord than to appease the appetite.

A short distance west of Earlocker's is "Pine Orchard," where a tavern was kept by one Goslin. He was a goslin only in name. Otherwise, he was a square man, and knew how to treat strangers and travelers, especially wagoners, who largely favored him with their patronage. James Dehoff kept a tavern at Pine Orchard as early as 1835. His house was a wagoners' resort, and stood on the south side of the road.

At Poplar Springs, one mile west of New Lisbon, there was a wagon stand kept by Allen Dorsie. Near the old tavern is a large, gushing spring, in the midst of tall poplar trees, and hence the name "Poplar Springs." Allen Dorsie, the old proprietor of the tavern

here, was likewise and for many years superintendent of the Maryland division of the road. He was a very large man, six feet in height, and rounded out in proportion. He was besides a man of admitted integrity and good intellect. He ceased keeping tavern at Poplar Springs in 1842.

The city of Frederick fifty years ago was the largest town on the road between Wheeling and Baltimore. James Dehoof and John Lambert kept old wagon stands in Frederick City. Lambert died about 1840, and was succeeded by John Miller, who kept the house down to the year 1853.

Handsome stone tavern on West Patrick Street in Frederick, Maryland, as it appeared in the early 1900's.

DRAWING, JOS. E. MORSE

Four miles west of Frederick City the old wagoners encountered Cotockton mountain, and here was a fine old tavern kept by Getzendanner, a German. His house was a stone building, on the south side of the road. Getzendanner, true to his native traits, was the owner of the property. Old wagoners unite in saying that the old German kept a good house, barring a little too much garlic in his sausages.

Proceeding westward we come to the village of Middletown, which hoped to become a city, and might have succeeded, had not the steam railway eclipsed the glory of the old pike. At Middletown the stages had relays of horses. Here also there was a wagon stand, kept by Samuel Riddlemoser.

Boonsboro is a small town at the foot of South Mountain in Maryland, and in the palmy days of the National Road was a lively village. Old wagoners and stage drivers spread its fame, but railroad conductors are silent as to its memory. The Slifer Brothers kept tavern in Boonsboro in the olden time. Their house was not a wagon stand.

America's first macadam surfaced road was laid by private funds in 1823 on a stretch of the Old Pike (BELOW) between Baltimore and Cumberland, Maryland. Illustration (ABOVE) demonstrates construction method utilizing graduated sizes of rock to form road bed. The rock was passed through iron rings to check uniformity of size in each succeeding layer. The War Department later specified macadam principle for other portions of the National Road.

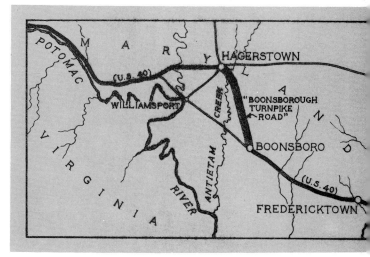

Funkstown appears next in sight. Funkstown, another old village identified with the bygone glories of the old pike. The name of this village brings to mind the once familiar form of John Funk, an old wagoner. John lived at or near Funkstown, and his family may have given the name to the village. Funkstown is located on Little Antietam creek, about seventy miles west of Baltimore. Fifty years ago there was a paper mill and a grist mill at Funkstown. At the east end of Funkstown, Joseph Watts kept a wagon stand, and competed for the custom of the wagoners with William Ashton, who kept a similar tavern at the west end of the town. Ashton will be remembered as the athletic wagoner, who leaped over the top of a road wagon at Petersburg.

After Funkstown, come the classic shades and handsome streets of Hagerstown. Hagerstown was always a prominent point on the road. It ranked with Wheeling, Washington, Brownsville, Uniontown, Cumberland, and Frederick. Hagerstown was a station for the stage lines. It outlived the road, and flourishes as one of the best towns of Maryland. The only old wagon stand in Hagerstown was that of John B. Wrench. But Hagerstown was rather too stylish a place for old wagoners, and Wrench gave up his house there in 1842, and removed to Piney Grove.

Four and a half miles west of Hagerstown, an old wagon stand was kept by David Newcomer. He dealt in horses, in addition to tavern keeping. When offering a horse for sale, his wife was accustomed to say in the hearing of the person proposing to buy: "Now, David, thee must not sell that favorite horse." This, old wagoners say, was a "set-up job" between David and his spouse to gain a good price.

Three miles westward from Newcomer's was the imposing and well-remembered tavern kept by John Miller. There were large rooms in this house, adapted to dancing purposes, and young men and maidens of the vicinity frequently tripped to the notes of the old time music in its spacious halls. The waltz was unknown, and the figures varied from the "hoe down" to the cotillion, closing always with the "Virginia Reel." The old wagoners were invariably invited to participate in these festivities, and engaged in them with a gusto not excelled by the lads and lasses of the surrounding neighborhood.

Gusty Mitchell is a well-remembered character of Clear Spring. He used to steal and drink the wagoner's whisky, and "bum" around their teams in all sorts of ways. One night the wagoners poured turpentine over Gusty and set fire to him, which so frightened him that he never afterward had anything to do with wagoners.

It will be noted that in many instances widows kept the best taverns along the road. There is no record of a widow making a failure as a tavern keeper.

Four miles west of Hancock, Md. is Sideling Hill, so called from the sloping character of the ground upon which the road is laid. The distance from the foot to the summit of Sideling Hill is four miles, and it is the longest hill on the road. In 1837 Jacob Anderson, an old wagoner, was killed on Sideling Hill. His team became frightened on the summit and ran down the western slope, coming in contact with a large tree on the roadside with such force as to break it down, and falling on Anderson, he was instantly killed. The road crosses a stream at Sideling Hill, called Sideling Hill creek. There was a covered bridge over this creek. In 1841 John Moss and Billy George, old wagoners, drove their teams on this bridge, and stopping a while to rest under the shade afforded by the roof, the bridge broke down, precipitating horses, wagons and drivers a distance of fourteen feet to the water, causing considerable damage to the wagons and the goods therein, but strange to say inflicting but slight injuries upon the drivers and teams.

Stone abutments are all that remain of covered bridge over Sideling Hill Creek. The Mason-Dixon Survey map of 1768 identifies this as Sidelong Hill Creek.

III Over the hills from Cumberland

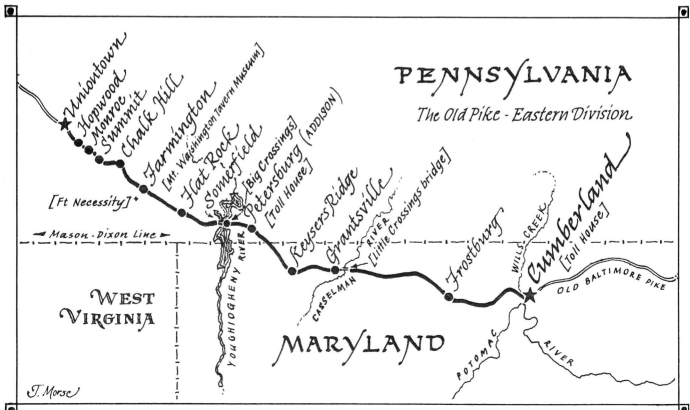

PENNSYLVANIA

The Old Pike - Eastern Division

Uniontown
Hopwood
Monroe
Summit
Chalk Hill
Farmington
[Mt. Washington Tavern Museum]
Flat Rock
Somerfield
[Big Crossings]
Petersburg (ADDISON)
[Toll House]
Keysers Ridge
Grantsville
[Little Crossings bridge]
CASSELMAN RIVER
Frostburg
WILLS CREEK
Cumberland
[Toll House]
OLD BALTIMORE PIKE

[Ft Necessity]

◄ Mason-Dixon Line ►

WEST VIRGINIA

YOUGHIOGHENY RIVER

MARYLAND

POTOMAC RIVER

J. Morse

The city of Cumberland is the initial point of that portion of the National Road which was constructed by authority of Congress, and paid for with funds drawn from the public treasury of the United States.

The preservation of the National Road was considered so vital to the general welfare by everybody living upon its line and adjacent to it, that the deepest interest was manifested in the success of every measure proposed for its benefit. There was no powerful and paid "lobby" around the halls of Congress when the Cumberland Road was the highway of the Republic, as there is at this day, but all measures planned and presented for its preservation and repair, were carefully watched and guarded by such statesmen as Henry Clay, Daniel Sturgeon, Andrew

Baltimore Pike section of the National Road (OPPOSITE) snakes its way into Cumberland from the east. Trolleys and high-wheelers have replaced coaches and conestogas (BELOW) in this 1880's picture of Cumberland. The National House (at left) awaits the coming automobile and "better days."

Stewart, T.M.T. McKennan, Lewis Steenrod, W. T. Hamilton, and Henry W. Beeson. The following from a Cumberland paper published in that place sixty years ago shows the popular feeling in behalf of the road at that date:

"The citizens of the town on the 21st of May, 1832, in demonstration of their great joy growing out of the appropriation made by the National Government for the repair of the Cumberland Road, made arrangements for the celebration of that event. In pursuance of that arrangement, Samuel Slicer illuminated his large and splendid hotel, which patriotic example was followed by James Black. In addition to the illumination, Mr. Bunting (our famous 'old Red'), agent of L. W. Stockton, ordered out a coach, drawn by four large gray stallions, driven by George Shuck. The stage was beautifully illuminated, which presented to the generous citizens of this place a novelty calculated to impress upon the minds of all who witnessed it the great benefits they anticipated by having the road repaired. There were also seated upon the top of the vehicle several gentlemen who played on various

31

instruments, which contributed very much to the amusement of the citizens and gave a zest to everything that inspired delight or created feelings of patriotism. They started from the front of Mr. Slicer's hotel, and as they moved on slowly the band played 'Hail Columbia,' 'Freemason's March,' 'Bonaparte Crossing the Rhine,' 'Washington's March,' together with a

This stone bridge over Wills Creek was built in the 1830's when a portion of the Old Pike was relocated through "The Narrows" west of Cumberland.

new tune composed by Mr. Mobley, of this place, and named by the gentlemen on the stage, 'The Lady We Love Best,' and many others, as they passed through the principal streets of the town. On their return they played 'Home, Sweet Home,' to the admiration of all who heard it.''

In 1835 James Black kept the leading tavern in Cumberland. It was a stage house. In 1836 John and Emory Edwards, of Boonsboro, leased the Black House, and conducted it as a tavern for many years thereafter. At the date last mentioned there were two wagon stands in Cumberland. One of them was kept by Thomas Plumer. Plumer had teams on the road. The other was kept by George Mattingly. Frederic Shipley kept a tavern in Cumberland previous to the year 1840. It was located on Baltimore Street, near the site of the station first established by the Baltimore & Ohio Railroad Company. This house was subsequently conducted by George W. Gump, and after him, in 1857, by David Mahaney. One Kaig, of Bedford county, Pennsylvania, succeeded Mahaney in the control of this house. It was called "The American," and entertained wagoners and the traveling public at large. In 1844 and later, the widow Adams kept a wagon stand in Cumberland, on the site of the present rolling mill. The house was a large brick structure, and known in its day as the "Mountain City House." Lewis Smith kept "The Blue Springs House" on Mechanics street in 1843, and for a period of three years thereafter.

The road, when first laid out, passed over Wills Mountain. In 1834 this location was changed for a better grade, up the valleys of Wills creek and Braddock's Run. To make this change it was necessary to first obtain the consent of the State of Maryland, which was granted by an act of her Legislature in 1832. The old Plumer tavern stood at the eastern end of the old location, and the old Mattingly tavern at the same end of the new location. George Evans kept a tavern, also, near the eastern end of the original location.

FIRST TOLL GATE HOUSE
ON THE
OLD NATIONAL (CUMBERLAND) ROAD.
ERECTED ABOUT 1833 AFTER THIS
PORTION OF THE ROAD WAS TURNED
OVER TO THE STATE OF MARYLAND
BY THE UNITED STATES GOVERNMENT.
THERE WAS ONE OTHER TOLL GATE
IN MARYLAND ON THIS ROAD.
STATE ROADS COMMISSION

When the Federal Government returned ownership of the National Road to the individual states through which it passed, the Pike became a tollroad. Pictured here is the first tollhouse on the Road west of Cumberland (LEFT) as it appeared in the late 1870's, gate opened to a freight wagon heading west. Now restored (BELOW), it stands beside U. S. Route 40 displaying toll rates of a vanished era (BELOW LEFT).

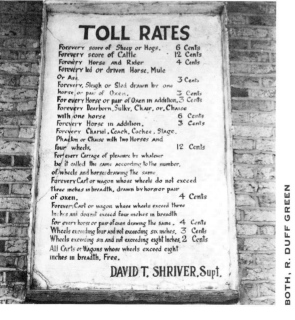

TOLL RATES

For every score of Sheep or Hogs. 6 Cents
For every score of Cattle 12 Cents
For every Horse and Rider 4 Cents
For every led or driven Horse, Mule
Or Ass. 3 Cents
For every Sleigh or Sled drawn by one
horse, or pair of Oxen. 3 Cents
For every Horse or pair of Oxen in addition, 3 Cents
For every Dearborn, Sulky, Chair, or Chaise
with one horse 6 Cents
For every Horse in addition. 3 Cents
For every Chariot, Coach, Cochee, Stage,
Phaeton or Chaise with two Horses and
four wheels, 12 Cents
For every Carriage of pleasure by whatever
be it called the same according to the number,
of wheels and horses drawing the same
For every Cart or wagon whose wheels do not exceed
three inches in breadth, drawn by horse or pair
of oxen. 4 Cents
For every Cart or wagon whose wheels exceed three
inches and does not exceed four inches in breadth
for every horse or pair of oxen drawing the same. 4 Cents
Wheels exceeding four and not exceeding six inches. 3 Cents
Wheels exceeding six and not exceeding eight inches, 2 Cents
All Carts or Wagons whose wheels exceed eight
inches in breadth. Free.

DAVID T. SHRIVER, Supt.

Six miles west from Cumberland there was an old tavern known as the "Six Mile House." It belonged to the Bruces, an old and wealthy family of Alleghany county, Maryland, and many years ago was destroyed by fire.

Eight miles west from Cumberland Aden Clary kept a house. It was a large and commodious brick building on the south side of the road, and is still standing. There was not a more popular house on the road than Aden Clary's.

This 1807 structure (ABOVE) in Clarysville, a hospital during the Civil War, now houses a restaurant. Note buggy sheltered on porch. Adjacent stone bridge (BELOW) dates to 1843.

Frostburg is next reached. This was always a prominent point on the road. It did not derive its name, as many suppose, from the crisp atmosphere in which it was located, but from the original owner of the land on which it stands, whose name was Frost. Frostburg was the first stage station west of Cumberland. The leading taverns of Frostburg in the palmy days of the road were the "Franklin House" and the "Highland Hall House." The Franklin House was kept for many years by Thomas Beall, the father of the Bealls of Uniontown. It was headquarters of the Good Intent stage line. The Highland Hall House was conducted at different times by George W. Claybaugh, George Evans, Samuel Cessna and Thomas Porter. It was the headquarters of the Stockton line of coaches.

About one mile west of Frostburg, and at the foot of Big Savage mountain, is Sand Springs, so called from the gurgling water in the sand at that point. In 1836 the widow Ward kept a wagon stand tavern at Sand Springs. On the night of October 3, 1836, snow fell to the depth of a foot at Sand Springs, breaking down the timber all through the surrounding mountains. Mrs. Ward's wagon yard was crowded with teams and wagons that night, and the snow was so deep the next day that the wagoners deemed it inexpedient to turn out, and remained at Mrs. Ward's until the following morning. Philip Spiker, the old blacksmith at Sand Springs, it is said could shoe more horses in a given time than any other blacksmith on the road. He had a rival, however, in A. Brice Devan, of Dunbar, who, in the palmy days of the road, carried on a shop in Hopwood, and shod horses for old wagoners all night long on many occasions.

A short distance west of Sand Springs, on the side of Big Savage mountain, an old wagon stand was kept by one Cheney. In Cheney's time at this house, Henry Clay Rush, who was an old wagoner, says that metallic mugs were used for drinking purposes, instead of glasses. He further states

The blacksmith was undoubtedly an unsung hero of the National Road, often working on through the night shoeing horses and fitting iron rims to wagon wheels. Print is from a drawing by Edwin Forbes, an artist of Civil War fame.

that the mugs were clean, and probably used through deference to the pure whisky of that day.

Two miles west from Cheney's, and at the foot of Little Savage mountain, Thomas Beall kept a tavern as early as 1830. Thomas Johnson succeeded Thomas Beall in the management of this house. He was a good fiddler and a good dancer. He owned a negro named Dennis, who was also a good dancer,

and night after night in the cheerful barroom of the old tavern, Dennis performed the "double shuffle," responsive to lively music furnished by his old master.

Little Savage mountain has an elevation of two thousand four hundred and eighty feet above the Atlantic, being one hundred feet lower than Big Savage.

Three miles further westward, and at the eastern approach to the Shades of Death, John Recknor kept an old wagon stand, well known, and in its day well patronized. Recknor kept this house as early as 1830, and ended his days in it. It was a log and frame structure on the north side of the road, with a commodious wagon yard attached. The thick

35

The Casselman River Bridge at Little Crossings, when built in 1814 was considered the largest single span stone arch bridge in the nation. As Pike travel declined the bridge deteriorated (LEFT) until automobile traffic brought about its first restoration in 1911. Now restored and preserved (RIGHT) the bridge has been designated a National Historic Landmark.

branches of the pine trees growing on Shade Hill, hung over this old house, imparting to it a romantic, as well as an attractive perspective.

Piney Grove comes next, so called from the numerous pine trees growing in the locality in the olden time. At an early day Joshua Johnson, a wealthy man of Frederick City, owned fifteen thousand acres of land, embracing Piney Grove and the Shades of Death, which he held for many years for speculative purposes. The pine trees were cut down many years ago, sawed up and shipped to market.

Two miles west of Piney Grove is the celebrated old Tomlinson tavern at Little Meadows. This is an old stand; as old as the National Road. Here the lines of the National and the old Braddock roads coincide. James K. Polk dined at the Tomlinson house in the spring of 1845, on his way to Washington to be inaugurated President. Huddleson was keeping house at that time. The occasion brought together a large concourse of mountain people, who were addressed by the President-elect.

Little Crossings is a name given to the locality from the circumstance that here the road crosses the Casselman River, and the prefix "little" is used because the Casselman is a smaller stream than the Youghiogheny, which is crossed a few miles further westward, and called the Big Crossings.

A tavern was established there by Alexander Carlisle, who entertained the traveling public in a satisfactory manner. His house was a large frame structure, on the south side of the road, subsequently kept by John and Samuel McCurdy, and later, at different times, by David Mahaney. Little Crossings beckoned the weary traveler to rest and refreshment, and until business ceased on the line, that locality presented many and rare attractions, as all old pike boys are ready to verify.

Next after leaving the Little Crossings on the westward march, comes Grantsville, a romantic little mountain village in Garrett,

formerly Alleghany county, Maryland, named long before the hero of Appomattox was known to fame, and therefore not in his honor. In 1833 Samuel Gillis kept a tavern in the east end of Grantsville, on the south side of the road, the same house that in later years was kept by John Slicer. It was a wagon stand in the time of Gillis, and Slicer did not take charge of it until business had ceased on the road. John Lehman kept a tavern in Grantsville in 1836. The Lehman House was subsequently kept by Henry Fuller, and after him by George Smouse. It was a frame building near the center of the village. In 1843 Henry Fuller demolished this old house, and erected a new one in its place. Adam Shultz kept a tavern at the east end of Grantsville back in the forties, and dying in

The Casselman (ABOVE), an Old Pike tavern, has been operated continuously since 1824, predating the old iron mile post out front. Cabin (BELOW), an early Grantsville stage stop, was moved to Little Crossings and restored by Penn-Alps, Inc. A stone arch bridge (RIGHT) west of Grantsville slowly dies through neglect.

ALL, R. DUFF GREEN

Winter storms made travel difficult, at best. This mail coach is slowed to a snail's pace by drifting snow.

charge, was succeeded by his son Perry, who continued it down to the year 1852. The Shultz House was an imposing brick structure, on the south side of the road, and was kept for a while by the veteran David Mahaney, and at one time by Jesse King. Solomon Steiner also kept a tavern in Grantsville during a portion of the prosperous era of the road. Grantsville seems to have been a favorite locality for tavern keepers of German names and antecedents. Steiner's tavern was a brick building, and stood on the opposite side of the road from the old Shultz House.

As early as 1836 Thomas Thistle kept a tavern at the foot of Negro Mountain, two miles west of Grantsville. His house was a long, frame wooden building, on the south side of the road, at times a stage station, and throughout its entire existence a wagon stand. Here the National Road crosses the line of the old Braddock road.

Onward, westward and upward, the crest of Negro Mountain is reached. There are several versions of the origin of the name of this mountain. Probably the one most worthy of acceptance is that in the early collisions between the whites and the Indians, a negro appeared as an ally of the Indians in a conflict

on this mountain, and was among the slain. Negro Mountain is two thousand eight hundred and twenty-five feet above the level of the Atlantic Ocean, and the second highest elevation on the line of the road.

Two miles west from Negro Mountain Keyser's Ridge looms up in view. This was a famous locality in the prosperous days of the road. It is a bald, bleak range, not inaptly described as the backbone of the mountains. It is two thousand eight hundred and forty-three feet above sea level, and the highest point on the road. In the olden time snow drifts often accumulated to the depth of twenty feet on Keyser's Ridge, and stages and wagons were compelled to take to the skirting glades to avoid them. The log cabin boys of Uniontown stopped at Stoddard's the first night out on their memorable trip to Baltimore, in 1840, to attend the great Whig mass meeting of that year in that city. They had with them, on wheels, a regular log cabin, well stored with refreshments of every kind, and the very best; and every mile of their long

39

journey resounded with lusty shouts for "Tippecanoe and Tyler, too." Redding Bunting drove the team that hauled the cabin, and Thomas A. Wiley was with the party as an employe of the Stockton stage line, which furnished four coaches for the transportation of the political pilgrims.

From Baltimore to the point last mentioned all the old road taverns are in Maryland. The road crosses the dividing line between the States of Maryland and Pennsylvania, near the eastern foot of Winding Ridge. The crossing point is marked by a metal slab shaped like the ordinary milepost. Winding Ridge derives its name from the tortuous course of the old Braddock road up the mountain, at that point.

The ancient and picturesque village of Petersburg is the next point reached on the westward march. Petersburg is noted for its healthful location and the beauty of the surrounding scenery. It has always been a popular resort for summer tourists seeking exemption from the stifling heat of crowded cities. The first tavern ever kept in Petersburg

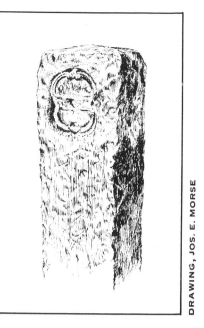

DRAWING, JOS. E. MORSE

A crownstone marker of the Mason-Dixon Line between Maryland and Pennsylvania (ABOVE). Old Pike tollhouse (BELOW) is in Addison, formerly Petersburg, Pennsylvania. This is the only extant stone tollhouse of this design on the Pike. Iron tollgate posts, removed from the tollhouse now mark the entrance to a cemetery (BOTTOM LEFT).

BOTH, R. DUFF GREEN

was by Gabriel Abrams. It was a frame house, on the south side of the road. A frame house on the north erected by Henry Wentling, was conducted by him as a tavern from 1820 to 1829, when he leased it to John Risler.

And now the hills that skirt the Youghiogheny River rise to view, and Somerfield is reached, an ancient little town, which the old metal mileposts on the road persist in calling Smithfield.

At Somerfield the road crosses the Youghiogheny River over a large, handsome and substantial stone bridge, three hundred and seventy-five feet in length, with three symmetrical arches, and appropriately named by old pike boys the Big Crossings. A large dressed stone in the wall of this bridge above the surface of the road, and near the eastern end, bears the inscription: "Kinkead & Evans, builders, July 4th, 1818." The day of the month, the anniversary of Independence, is given because on that day the bridge was finished, and the occasion was celebrated with great eclat. The inhabitants of the mountains for miles around, male and female, old and

The triple-span stone arch bridge (BELOW) at Big Crossings lies hidden on the lake bottom near boat docks (ABOVE). In autumn, when water is released down river, bridge becomes partially visible.

young, with old-fashioned banners and old-fashioned music, turned out in great numbers, inspired by that genuine patriotism which characterized the early period of our country's independence, while yet many of the soldiers of the revolution were living.

The most noted old tavern keeper of

NATIONAL PARK SERVICE

The old Stone Endsley House (TOP) and the Shellbark Tavern (BOTTOM) have now disappeared. The latter was built of logs and later weather-boarded over as were many of the early Pike taverns.

Somerfield was Capt. Thomas Endsley. Somerfield was always a stage station, the second relay east of Uniontown. The Endsley House was the headquarters of Stockton's line. It is a stone building, and stands near the bank of the river at the western end of the town, and was erected in the year 1818 by Kinkead, Beck & Evans, the old bridge builders.

The first old tavern west of the "Big Crossings" is that which for many years was kept by Peter Lenhart, commonly known as "Shellbark." This was a two-story house, originally built with logs, but subsequently weather-boarded and painted red.

The bottom land here along the old pike and stretching eastward to the Youghiogheny River is called "Jockey Hollow," a level piece of road upon which horses were run and cock-fighting practiced. Hence the name Jockey Hollow. Ephriam Vansickle, "Blind Eph," as he was called, kept a tavern many years in an old log house in Jockey Hollow, and did a good business.

The road was frequently in such condition by reason of mud, deep cuts, and other obstacles, that a whole day's progress did not cover a greater distance than three or four miles. To pass through Jockey Hollow it was often found necessary to attach twelve horses to one wagon.

Next we come to Charley Rush's old stand, which was a famous stopping place. He entertained strangers and travelers at his hospitable board, whether they had the means of paying their bills or not, but always preferred that impecunious guests should inform him of their condition before engaging accommodations. On one occasion an Irishman tarried with him overnight, and in the morning, after breakfast, informed him that he had no money to pay his bill. "Why didn't you tell me that last night?" sharply inquired Mr. Rush. "And faith, sir," replied the Irishman, "I'm very sorry to tell you of it this morning." Rush, pleased with his wit, absolved him from his bill, gave him a parting

Sebastian Rush (LEFT) termed "Prince of Landlords" owned and presided over his old tavern, the Rush House (ABOVE) for a number of years. Among items of historic interest currently in the Rush House Collection are: the hotel license of 1858 (TOP RIGHT) and a ledger book of the National Road Stage Company for 1841 (BOTTOM LEFT).

drink, and allowed him to go "Scot free."

We next reach the celebrated house of Sebastian Rush, invariably called "Boss." It is not a wagon stand, but an old stage house. Here stage passengers took meals, which were invariably gotten up in the best style. The house was built in 1837 by Hon. Nathaniel Ewing, who then owned it. Rush moved into it soon after it was finished, as lessee of Judge Ewing, and not long after purchased it, and occupied it uninterruptedly. Here, also, is a store, post office and other improvements, constituting a little village called Farmington, and considered the grand commercial and business center of the mountains. Sebastian Rush was widely known as an influential Republican politician, and had been superintendent of the road by appointment of the Governor. When a young man, and living in a small log house near the tavern stand of his brother, Charles, he was elected constable of his township, and, being too poor to own a

43

R. DUFF GREEN

*Illustrious patrons of the Rush House included Jenny Lind and
Phineas T. Barnum. One of the guest rooms is pictured above
with wagoner's bells displayed over fireplace.*

horse, performed the functions of his office on foot. Previous to 1837 the widow Tantlinger kept tavern in an old wooden house, on the ground now covered by the Rush house.

When Jennie Lind, the world renowned songstress, made her first professional visit to the United States, she returned east from her western tour by way of the National Road, in company with her troupe, and in "chartered" coaches of the Stockton line. P. T. Barnum, the celebrated showman, was the great singer's manager, and was with her on the occasion referred to. The party remained overnight at Boss Rush's tavern, twelve miles east of Uniontown. The people along the road heard of the coming of the distinguished travelers, and a number assembled at the tavern in the evening to get a glimpse of them. William Shaffer drove the coach in which Barnum was seated, and when he halted in front of the tavern one of the curious called up to the driver on the box and inquired: "Which is Barnum?" Shaffer answered gruffly: "I don't know Barnum from the devil." Barnum, meanwhile, had emerged from the coach, and standing by its side overheard the inquiry and the driver's reply,

and stepping up to the inquisitor said to him: "I am Barnum; the driver is right, it is hard to distinguish me from the devil." The party entered the good old tavern and were entertained and lodged in the handsome style for which Boss Rush was greatly and justly distinguished. Fresh trout were served for breakfast, which had been taken the day before in a nearby mountain stream.

Mt. Washington is a point replete with historic interest. Here Washington first measured swords with an enemy, and fought his first battle. It is the site of Fort Necessity, and known in colonial times as the Great Meadows. Gen. Washington subsequently became the owner of this property, and held it until his death. It was no doubt owing to the fact that his first engagement with an armed foe took place on this ground he resolved to buy it. In his last will he directed it to be sold by his executors, together with other real estate he held, and the proceeds divided among parties he named. The tract, when owned by Washington, contained two hundred and thirty-four acres, and he valued it at six dollars an acre. He thus refers to it in a note appended to his will:

This land is valuable on account of its local

44

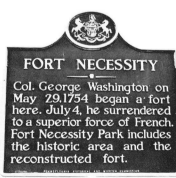

FORT NECESSITY

Col. George Washington on May 29, 1754 began a fort here. July 4, he surrendered to a superior force of French. Fort Necessity Park includes the historic area and the reconstructed fort.

PENNSYLVANIA HISTORICAL AND MUSEUM COMMISSION

In the distant meadow stands a replica of Fort Necessity. Nearby is the Mount Washington tavern.

situation. It affords an exceeding good stand on Braddock's road, from Ft. Cumberland to Pittsburgh, and besides a fertile soil, possesses a large quantity of natural meadow, fit for the scythe. It is distinguished by the appellation of the Great Meadows, where the first action with the French, in 1754, was fought.

This estate passed into the hands of the

45

SEARIGHT—OLD PIKE

The Mount Washington Tavern stands on land once owned by George Washington. Now under jurisdiction of the National Park Service, it serves as a museum. Reminiscent of the Old Pike days are the restored kitchen (BELOW LEFT) and bar (BELOW RIGHT). Of particular interest is the old tin stage horn (RIGHT) almost five feet in length.

LEFT AND ABOVE, R. DUFF GREEN

46

Hon. Nathaniel Ewing, who caused to be erected on the property a large brick house, still standing and one of the most noted old taverns on the road. Judge Ewing subsequently sold and conveyed the property to James Sampey, who went into possession and kept the tavern for many years, and until his death. The first year after Mr. Sampey's death the management of the tavern and farm was placed in charge of Robert Hogsett, who turned over to the representative of the estate the sum of four thousand dollars, as the profits of one year. The Good Intent line of stages stopped at Sampey's, and as showing the extent of the business of the house, Mr. Hogsett mentions that on one morning seventy-two stage passengers took breakfast there.

The next old tavern was at Monroe Springs, on the hillside, a short distance west of one of the old round toll houses. Opposite the house a large water trough was erected, kept full and overflowing from a spring nearby, called "The Monroe Spring," in honor of President Monroe. When McKinney kept this house President Monroe passed along the road, and a public dinner was given him there.

An old stone toll house stood a short distance east of the Monroe Springs, and remained until 1893, when it was torn down. Hiram Seaton was one of the early collectors at this point.

The next old tavern stand was the "Braddock's Run House." Gen. Braddock was buried near this house, a day or two after his disastrous defeat by the French and Indians, at Braddock's Field, near Pittsburgh. The exact spot where he was buried is still pointed out, and can be seen from the road.

General Braddock, mortally wounded in his encounter with the French and Indians, (TOP) was buried under the road by his retreating troops. Burial spot in hollow of old road is still visible (CENTER). Monument marks permanent grave (BOTTOM).

47

When the Federal Government first built the National Road, mile markers of stone were erected. By the 1830's many of the mile stones had disappeared so the familiar iron markers were installed. In the early 1900's only one of the original mile stones could be found (LEFT). This stone stood opposite the Fayette Springs Tavern (RIGHT).

We next reach "Chalk Hill," so called from the circumstance of white clay adhering to the shovels of the workmen engaged in digging the foundation of the road.

Near the top of Laurel Hill on the eastern slope, once lived a noted character named Benjamin Price. His house, a log structure, was built near the roadside, but below its surface, so that the upper story was about on a level with the road. He kept a cake shop, was an acting justice of the peace, and a strict Methodist, and was in the habit of annoying wagoners and hog drovers by fining them for swearing, and they in turn annoyed him by throwing billets of wood and disabled hogs down his chimney.

On the apex of Laurel Hill, large finger boards were erected, indicating distances and routes to the Washington Springs, Dulaney's Cave and Jumonville's Grave. One Molly Calhoun kept a small cake shop at this point, and displayed upon her signboard the following quaint legend:

Out of this rock, runs water clear,
'Tis soon changed into good beer,
Stop, traveler, stop, if you see fit,
And quench your thirst for a fippenybit.

The coin of the road was the big copper cent of United States coinage, the "fippenny bit," Spanish, of the value of six and one-fourth cents, called for brevity a "fip," the "levy," Spanish, of the value of twelve and a half cents, the quarter, the half dollar, and the dollar. The Mexican and Spanish milled dollar were oftener seen than the United States dollar. The silver five-cent piece and the dime of the United States coinage were seen occasionally, but not so much used as the "fip" and the "levy." In times of stringency, the stage companies issued scrip in denominations ranging from five cents to a dollar, which passed readily as money. The scrip was similar to the postal currency of the war period, lacking only in the artistic skill displayed in the engraving of the latter. A hungry traveler could obtain a substantial meal at an old wagon stand tavern for a "levy," and two drinks of whisky for a "fippenny bit." The morning bill of a wagoner with a six-horse team did not exceed one dollar and seventy-five cents, which included grain and hay for the horses, meals for the driver, and all the drinks he saw proper to take.

About a mile down the western slope of Laurel Hill we come to the famous watering trough. Here William Downard lived for many years in a stone house built against the hillside. He did not keep a tavern, for he had no ground for teams to stand upon, and no stabling that was accessible, but he always maintained the big water-trough in good condition *pro bono publico,* and it would be almost impossible for big teams to make the

Coins used on the Road included (BELOW) a fippenny bit (A) or ½ Reale, Spanish, equal to 6¼ cents; the two bits (D) or 2 Reales, Spanish, worth 25 cents. Both were minted in Mexico. U. S. coins are a (C) large copper penny and (B) a silver 50 cent piece.

The watering trough on Laurel Hill as it appeared about 1890. It survived long enough to aid early motorists whose auto radiators boiled over during the climb up the long western slope.

ascent of Laurel Hill, in hot weather without water.

A little over a mile below the big water trough the romantic spot known as the "Turkey's Nest" is reached. The road crosses a small stream here, which, owing to the peculiar formation of the ground, required the erection of a bridge, supported on the south side by an immense stone wall.

We now reach the ancient and celebrated village of Monroe, a name it took in honor of the President hereinbefore mentioned. Approached from the east, the first old tavern and the first house in the place is the "Deford House," in the olden time and by old people called the General Wayne House. It appears that at an early day General Wayne had occasion to pass this way, and tarried overnight with John Deford, who kept tavern in a small log house a short distance in the rear of the present building. Deford at this time was contemplating the erection of a new and more imposing edifice, and applied to his distinguished guest for a plan. It was furnished, and the present stone structure is the outcome of it.

On the hill above Monroe an old two-story brick house, once a well-known and popular tavern stand, was owned and kept by William Morris. He put up an imposing sign, inscribed on the west side with the words, "Welcome from the West," and on the east side the words, "Welcome from the East." This was no false lure, and travelers from the east and west crowded into the old house to enjoy its good cheer.

At the east end of Uniontown the road crosses Redstone creek, over a massive and extensive stone bridge, one of the best and most expensive samples of masonry on the whole line, built by Kinkead, Beck and Evans in 1818.

The bridge in this old photograph is thought to be over Redstone Creek. It is comparable in workmanship to Big Crossings Bridge, built by the same contractors.

SMITHSONIAN INSTITUTION

The Old Pike, now U.S. Route 40, as it rolls into Uniontown from the west. T. B. Searight is interred here, a scant stone's throw away from the road he knew so well.

R. DUFF GREEN

UNIONTOWN
Founded by Henry Beeson, who built a blockhouse on site of the county jail in 1774. Uniontown gained importance with the building of the National Road after 1811.

PENNSYLVANIA HISTORICAL AND MUSEUM COMMISSION

IV Uniontown to Wheeling

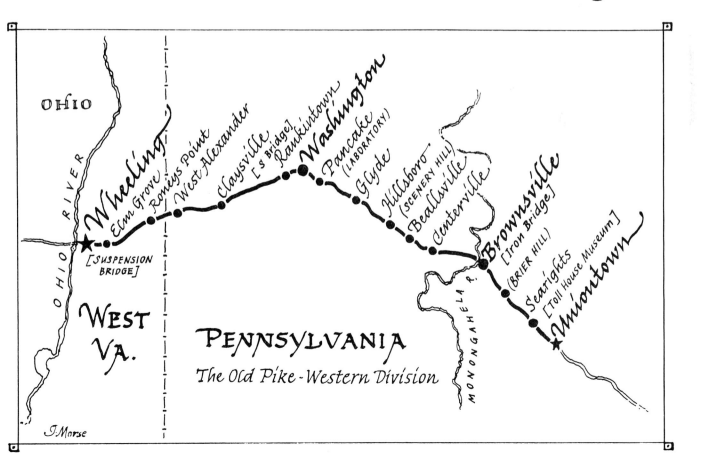

OHIO

OHIO RIVER

Wheeling
[SUSPENSION BRIDGE]
Elm Grove
Roneys Point
West Alexander
Claysville
[S Bridge]
Rankintown
Washington
Pancake
(LABORATORY)
Glyde
Hillsboro
(SCENERY HILL)
Beallsville
Centerville
Brownsville
[Iron Bridge]
(BRIER HILL)
Searights
[Toll House Museum]
Uniontown

WEST VA.

PENNSYLVANIA
The Old Pike - Western Division

MONONGAHELA R.

J. Morse

In 1784, General Ephraim Douglass (LEFT), then living in Uniontown, succinctly stated the plight of most Western Pennsylvania settlers "...Money we have not...How taxes are collected, debts payed or fees discharged, I know not..." Within a decade, a federal tax on whisky, their chief staple of barter, brought about the Whisky Rebellion (BELOW). Use of a large federal force to subdue the dissenters was highly criticized throughout the newly constituted republic. It is interesting to note that in another decade a national road would be planned to pass through this same troubled region.

General Ephraim Douglass, in a letter to General James Irvine, in 1784, describes Uniontown in the following vigorous and graphic style:

My Dear General—... This Uniontown is the most obscure spot on the face of the globe. I have been here seven or eight weeks, without one opportunity of writing to the land of the living, and though considerably south of you, so cold that a person not knowing the latitude, would conclude we were placed near one of the poles. Pray have you had a severe winter below? We have been frozen up here for more than a month past, but a great many of us having been bred in another State, the eating of hominy is as natural to us as the drinking of whisky in the morning. The town and its appurtenances consist of our president and a lovely little family, a courthouse and schoolhouse in one, a mill and consequently a miller, four taverns, three smith shops, five retail stores, two tan yards, one of them only occupied, one saddler's shop, two hatter's shops, one mason, one cake woman (we had two, but one of them having committed a petit larceny is upon banishment), two widows and some reputed maids, to which may be added a distillery... I can say little of the country in general, but that it is very poor in everything but its soil, which is excellent, and that part contiguous to the town is really beautiful, being level and prettily situate, accommodated with good water, and excellent meadow ground. But money we have not, nor any practicable way of making it. How taxes are collected, debts paid, or fees discharged, I know not; and yet the good people appear willing enough to run in debt and go to law..."

Gen. Douglass lived to see Uniontown arise from the mud hole and become a flourishing county seat.

The first tavern in Uniontown was kept by John Collins in 1781. It was a log house on the north side of the main street. Jonathan Rowland, Daniel Culp and Matthew Campbell each kept a tavern in Uniontown as early as 1783. Colin Campbell as early as 1785 kept a tavern in a house that stood on Main street, near the center of the town. Thomas Collins, son of John Collins, before mentioned, kept a tavern as early as 1794 in an old house on the lot, corner of Morgantown and Main street. Thomas Collins commanded a company of soldiers from Uniontown and vicinity in the war of 1812, locally called the "Madison Rowdies."

The Gregg house, situated on the north side of Main street, on the lot now covered by the residence of Dr. J. B. Ewing, was in existence as a tavern as early as 1798, and continued as late as 1865. It was a small house of brick and frame united, but had a large patronage. In early times travelers and other guests at taverns did not desire or expect separate rooms, and hence a small tavern like the Gregg house could accommodate as many persons as the more pretentious hotel of the present day; and at wagon stands the barroom was the only bed chamber for wagoners.

The Swan, Nathaniel Brownfield proprietor, is an old, long frame building at the west end of town, supplemented some years after it commenced business, by a brick addition to the eastern end. Thomas Brownfield, father of Nathaniel, the present proprietor, and grandfather on the maternal side, of the author of this volume, kept this old tavern as early as 1805, and down to the year 1829. When the National Road was opened for business, this house became a wagon stand, and continued such until the last crack of a Battelly White whip was heard on the road.

The McClelland House was one of the best known old taverns on the National Road. This house was the headquarters of the Good Intent line of stages, from the time it was put on the road until it was withdrawn at the end of the road's career as a national highway.

Henry Clay, a staunch proponent and frequent traveler of the National Road, could speak as eloquently in behalf of Old Pike mountain buckwheat cakes as he could the Protective Tariff.

A coach, in which Mr. Clay was proceeding to Washington, was upset on a pile of limestone, in the main street of Uniontown, a few moments after supper at the McClelland house. Sam Sibley was the driver of that coach, and had his nose broken by the accident. Mr. Clay was unhurt, and upon being extricated from the grounded coach, facetiously remarked that: "This is mixing the Clay of Kentucky with the limestone of Pennsylvania."

It is said that Joe Williams, a wit, musician, comedian, lawyer, and in his riper years Chief Justice of the Territorial Court of Iowa, once straddled a big black hog in a drove, and rode it through the main street of Uniontown, playing a clarinet.

The tavern keepers on the "old road," as it is called, were as earnestly opposed to the

53

The Swan Tavern (ABOVE) opened in 1805. In Pike days, known as the Brownfield House, it became a wagon stand. The watering trough and pump were once a welcome sight to travelers.

going east and west, I got four night's bills from the same set of wagoners." "Now," concluded Slack (since the completion of the National Road), with indignation, "the wagoners whiff by without stopping."

The old road referred to was the Braddock road, which from the summit of Laurel Hill, turned northwardly, as before stated, to Gists (Mt. Braddock), Stewart's Crossing (Connellsville), Braddock's Field and Fort Pitt (Pittsburgh).

An old road between Uniontown and Brownsville was laid out in 1774 by viewers appointed by the court of Westmoreland county, Pennsylvania, before Fayette county was established, upon a petition signed mainly by inhabitants of Brownsville and vicinity, who complained that "they had to carry their corn twenty miles to the mill of Henry Beeson at Uniontown." The distance of twenty miles complained of was by way of the old road known as "Burd's," from the mouth of Redstone creek to Gists, where it intersected Braddock's road. The road between Uniontown and Brownsville, above mentioned, was carried east of Uniontown, to intersect the Braddock road, which it did, near Slack's tavern. The line of the National Road closely follows that of the old road between Uniontown and Brownsville. Marks of the old road are visible to this day.

Searights is the old halfway house between Uniontown and Brownsville, a large stone building on the north side of the road, at the crossing of the great drovers' road of other days leading from the Flats of Grave Creek, Virginia, to Bedford, Pennsylvania. In the olden time, in addition to the ordinary travel on the road, sleighing and other parties from Uniontown and Brownsville were accustomed to go to this old tavern for a night's dancing, and the attending festivities. This is also the battleground of the memorable "Gray Meeting" in 1828, where the opposing hosts between Jackson and Adams went into an open field and measured strength by "counting off," the Jacksonians

building of the National Road, as those on the latter were to the building of the railroad, and for like reasons. The following anecdote serves as an illustration: John Slack kept a tavern for many years at the summit of Laurel Hill on the old road, in a house near the Washington Springs. Before the National Road was opened said Slack, in a complaining manner, "Wagons coming up Laurel Hill would stick in the mud a mile or so below my house, when the drivers would unhitch, leave their wagons in the mud, and bring their teams to my house and stay with me all night. In the morning they would return to their stranded wagons, dig and haul them out, and get back to my house and stay with me another night. Thus counting the wagons

SEARIGHT'S TOLLHOUSE

Erected by Pennsylvania, 1835, to collect tolls on the old National Road.

Administered by the Pennsylvania Historical and Museum Commission.

Tolls were collected here for about 70 years. Tollkeepers lived in the building, and thus were always 'on duty'. Legend has it that one tollkeeper, an enterprising widow, kept up to ten boarders in this small dwelling. Being miners, they not only worked in shifts but slept in shifts. The building is now restored (TOP and LEFT) and open to the public. Hiram Seaton (BELOW) was a respected toll collector for many years at a similar tollhouse near the Mount Washington Tavern.

The Searight House (ABOVE) before its destruction (BELOW) was an important tavern and meeting house. William Searight (BOTTOM), prominent in Pike history and father of T. B. Searight, was a contractor for the Iron Bridge at Brownsville and later a road commissioner.

outnumbering their adversaries by a decided preponderance, greatly to the mortification of the weaker column. This meeting was called the "Gray meeting," because the tavern there was then kept by John Gray.

Prior to 1840 many of the Democratic county meetings and conventions were held at Searights. Before the era of railroads it was a central point for Uniontown, Connellsville and Brownsville. A large water trough was always maintained at this old tavern, where teams attached to all kinds of wagons, coaches and other vehicles, as well as horses and mules led in droves, were halted for refreshment. At times relays of stage horses for extra occasions were stationed here, and it was always a relay for the line teams moving merchandise. An old signboard was displayed at the front of the house for many years, bearing in large gilt letters the legend SEARIGHTS. The old tavern at Searights was built by Josiah Frost, about the time the National Road was constructed, and in the year 1821 William Searight acquired it.

West of Searights there is an old stone tavern on the north side of the road, known in early days as Johnson's, later as Hatfield's. This house was built in 1817 by Randolph Dearth for Robert Johnson, who kept it as a tavern down to the year 1841. In 1852 William Hatfield, who had previously bought the property, went into the house and kept it as a tavern until the year 1855, when he closed it as a public house, but continued to occupy it as a private residence until his melancholy death. Before engaging in tavern keeping, William Hatfield served many years as a Justice of the Peace and subsequent to 1855 served a term as Associate Judge. He was a blacksmith by trade, and made the old iron gates of the road. He was industrious and honest, and likewise noted for his kindness to his fellow men. It was while engaged in doing a favor for an old neighbor, in the year 1871, that he lost his life. His neighbor, John C. Craft, had purchased a patent pump, and called on Judge Hatfield to assist him in placing it in his well. The Judge, as was his habit, promptly responded, and, going down to the bottom of the well, called to his neighbor, who stood at the surface, to send him down a saw or an ax. The needed tool was placed in a heavy iron-bound tub and started down, but, through neglect, the cable slipped, and the tub was precipitated a great depth upon Judge Hatfield's head, fatally injuring him. He was extricated from his perilous position in an unconscious state, carried home, and lingering only a few hours, died.

One mile west of Hatfield's is the old Peter Colley stand. It is a stone house on the south side of the road. Peter Colley was the father of Abel Colley, and an early settler. He kept a tavern on the old road before the National Road was made. He was a money maker, and owned the land on which his tavern was erected, in fee. He was probably the first man on the National Road who acquired the fame of having a barrel of money. Old pike boys said he kept his money in a barrel. Peter

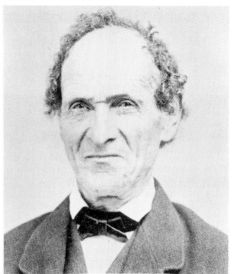

R. DUFF GREEN

William Hatfield (TOP) began his career as a blacksmith and later formed the iron barrier gates for tollhouses along the Pike. Though none of these gates survived, three pairs of iron gateposts remain standing. Hatfield later became owner and proprietor of Stone Tavern (ABOVE). Built in 1817, the tavern is now a private residence.

Colley was well advanced in years when the National Road was made, and did not long enjoy the profits of the new highway. At his death his tavern passed to the hands of his son George, who kept it for many years. The hills on either side of this old house are among the highest on the road.

The next old tavern stand on the westward tramp is Brubaker's, a fine brick building on the north side near Brownsville. Daniel Brubaker purchased this property from David Auld, and went into possession in the year 1826, and from that date until his death was its constant occupant, with the exception of a very brief period that it was occupied and kept as a tavern by Alexander R. Watson. After ascending the long hill out from Brownsville, going east, old wagoners found a pleasant resting place at Brubaker's.

R. DUFF GREEN

The Colley House, built in 1796, was a tavern for many years. A former tenant, Jackey Craft, would "venture out on the road in a sleigh complete with bells when there was no snow on the ground".

Surprise is often expressed that there were so many good taverns in the mountains, remote from fertile fields and needed markets. That they were equal to the best on the road is conceded; and that the old taverns of the National Road have never been surpassed for bounteous entertainment and good cheer, is likewise conceded; in fact, has never been disputed. It may seem a trifling thing to be written down in serious history, that the old taverns of the mountains excelled all others in the matter of serving buckwheat cakes; but it is germane and true. To relieve this statement from the imputation of being a trifling one, it may be added that there were men and women on the line of the National Road who often heard the great statesman, orator and patriot, Henry Clay, praising the good qualities of the buckwheat cakes furnished by the old mountain taverns with as much fervor and more enthusiasm than he ever exhibited in commending his favorite measure, the Protective Tariff. Another memorable feature of the mountain taverns was the immense fires kept constantly burning in the old barrooms during the old-time winters. In many instances the grates were seven feet in length, with corresponding width and depth, and would contain an ordinary wagon load of coal; and when the fires were stirred up in these immense grates, and set to roaring, the jolly old wagoners occupying the barrooms paid little heed to the eagerness of the howling mountain weather. The old landlord of the mountains took special pride in keeping up his barroom fire. He kept a poker from six to eight feet long, and would not allow it to be used by any one but himself. Boss Rush, not inaptly termed "the prince of landlords," was so careful and punctilious about the management of his barroom fire that he kept his big poker under lock and key, so that no one could use it but himself, always using it at the right time, and keeping up a uniform and proper temperature for the comfort of his guests.

The Monongahela River flows in quiet majesty through Brownsville north to Pittsburgh where its junction with the Allegheny River forms the mighty Ohio. An early settlement beyond the Allegheny Mountains, Brownsville once rivaled Pittsburgh as a river gateway to the West. The Bridge (right center) carries U.S. Route 40 from Brownsville (far side of river) into community of West Brownsville.

Brownsville was, for many years, the head of steamboat navigation on the Monongahela River. Here many passengers were transferred from the stage lines to the steamboats **plying** between this point and Pittsburgh. It is shown by official figures that from 1844, the date at which the slack water improvement was completed to Brownsville, to 1852, when through business ceased on the National Road, covering a period of eight years, more than two hundred thousand passengers left the stage lines at Brownsville and took passage on the Monongahela steamers. West-going passengers were "ticketed through" from Cumberland, Baltimore and other points east, to Pittsburgh and other points west, *via* the National Road, and the Monongahela River route. A movement was set on foot as early as the year 1814, looking to the improvement of the navigation of the Monongahela River, by means of locks and dams, followed by later spasmodic efforts, but nothing of a practical nature was accomplished in this direction until 1836, when a company was incorporated to carry forward and complete the work.

There were no wagon stand taverns in Brownsville. Wagoners "put up" at the old

59

Workman House in Brownsville (BELOW) predating the Pike by two decades, played host to many prominent Pike travelers, among them Andrew Jackson. Forewarned of his approach, crowds often gathered to await the arrival of Jackson's coach (RIGHT) hoping to be favored with an address.

SEARIGHT—OLD PIKE

Riley and Bar houses in Bridgeport, and at Brubaker's, east of town. The old Workman House, at the upper end of Market street, was a famous stage house. It had the patronage of the Stockton line. James Workman, the old proprietor, will be remembered as a gentleman of ruddy complexion, gray hair, slim, but erect stature, elastic step and curt speech. He presided at this house for many years, and had a wide reputation for serving good meals. This old house was built by John McClure Hezlop in 1797, who first kept it as a tavern. James Beckley afterwards kept it, and after his decease, it was continued as a tavern by his widow. James Workman took charge of it in 1843.

George E. Hogg, for many years a leading and wealthy citizen of Brownsville, is authority for the following amusing story concerning James Workman. On an occasion of one of General Jackson's frequent trips over the National Road, the citizens of Brownsville resolved to give him a public reception. All the usual arrangements for such an event were made, including a dinner at Workman's tavern. The hero, upon reaching town, was taken to the Presbyterian church to listen to a reception speech and receive the greetings of the people. Soon after the audience had settled down Mr. Workman entered the building, and forcing himself down the main aisle, and to a front pew occupied by General Jackson, accosted him thus: "General Jackson, I have been commissioned by the committee of arrangements to provide your dinner, and have come to inquire if there is any particular article of diet you prefer above another, that I may have the pleasure of gratifying your taste." The old General gravely responded, "Ham and eggs." This seemed rather confusing to the old landlord, who, supposing the General was joking, repeated his inquiry, when the same response came a second time and in an emphatic tone, "HAM AND EGGS." The old landlord then hastily

The growing iron industry of Western Pennsylvania fulfilled many Pike requirements such as the mile posts and toll gates. One outstanding example is the bridge over Dunlap's creek. The Nation's first iron bridge, this single span structure was completed in 1839 (ABOVE) at an approximate cost of $40,000. Subsequent growth of Brownsville has all but engulfed the old bridge. As it appeared about 1910 (CENTER) and in 1971 (BOTTOM).

withdrew, hurried home, and commanded his cook to prepare ham and eggs for General Jackson's dinner.

The road crosses Dunlap's creek over a handsome iron bridge. The stone work, a fine specimen of heavy masonry, was let by contract to William Searight, who pushed it forward and completed it with his characteristic energy. David Chipps, an expert stone mason, was a boss workman on this bridge, and the late Gen. William W. Williams,

61

who in the prime of his life was an excellent mason, also worked on its walls and abutments. The work was done under authority of the War Department of the general government.

After crossing the iron bridge the traveler is in the ancient borough of Bridgeport. Here Jack Arnold kept a tavern at a very early period. He was succeeded by John Riley, who for many years kept a wagon stand. Riley was a staunch citizen, and participated in the public affairs of his town. His tavern was near the market house, and was a popular resort in the olden time. Isaac Kimber, Robert Patterson and John Neelan kept taverns in Bridgeport before the National Road was made. The present Bar House is on the site of the old Kimber House. The Bar House was owned by Ephraim H. Bar, who conducted it as a tavern for many years. It was a wagon stand, and had a good trade. Robert Carter, old wagoner before mentioned, was one of

the men who for a time successfully conducted the Bar House.

It was but a short distance from the iron bridge to the long wooden bridge over the Monongahela River. This bridge, although a link of the National Road, was not built by the government. It was a private enterprise, and was erected in 1833. In 1810 an act was passed by the Legislature of Pennsylvania, authorizing the Governor to incorporate a company to build and operate a bridge at this point; but for some cause the company was not organized, and in 1830 a company was incorporated by the Legislature. Ephraim L. Blaine, father of the brilliant and popular statesman, was an incorporator under the provisions of the act of 1830, and the company authorized by that act promptly organized, and completed the bridge at the date above mentioned.

After crossing the river bridge at Brownsville, going west, the traveler reaches

Built in 1833 with private funds, the wooden covered bridge at Brownsville (BELOW) carried National Road traffic over the Monongahela River for about a century. Bridge as it appeared on a postcard of 1910.

James G. Blaine, prominent statesman and presidential nominee was born in West Brownsville during the 'Palmy days' of the Old Pike.

who catered to the wants of the traveling public at this old tavern was Vincen. Owens, who had been a faithful soldier in Washington's army in the war of the Revolution. The property belonged to the old Krepps family of the vicinity, and the old tavern stood at the northwest landing of the old Krepps ferry. The Krepps ferry was operated in connection with the management of this old tavern, and the ferry was continued down to the year 1845.

About two and one-half miles west of Krepps' Ferry an ancient hamlet called by old pike boys Malden is reached. Here on the north side of the road stands an old stone tavern, which in the palmy days of the road was a popular stopping point. It belonged originally to the old Krepps family, of Brownsville, and was designed and erected for a tavern. It was evidently the belief of the old owners that a town would grow up on this site, as they caused a stone in the front wall of the old tavern, near the top, to be dressed and inscribed in cut letters with the name Kreppsville. This name, however, was not adopted by the public, but the place was, and continues to be known as Malden.

the soil of Washington county, and plants his feet in the ancient village of West Brownsville. From the hill tops on the road, as far west as Hillsboro, glimpses are had of the receding mountains. West Brownsville has the great distinction of being the birthplace of James G. Blaine, the foremost and most popular of all American statesmen of the present day. It is related in Crumrine's history of Washington county, that the land upon which West Brownsville stands was originally owned by Indian Peter. This Indian Peter, at a very early day, lived on lands in the vicinity of Uniontown, and gave name to Peter's street, the oldest street of that town.

Near the foot of the river hill, on the river side, an old stone house was kept as a tavern when the road was first opened, and for a number of years thereafter. The first man

Malden Tavern typifies architecture of stone taverns prevalent along this section of the Pike.

63

The next point west, distant about three miles, is Centreville. Moving onward towards Centreville the traveler passes the old farms and residences of Jonathan Knight, the famous civil engineer of other days. Centreville was laid out in 1821, soon after the road was completed, and with special reference to its completion, and the

Tollhouse near Beallsville (TOP) has now vanished from the Pike. The National Hotel of Beallsville (ABOVE), though still standing, no longer caters to travelers. Many Pike taverns took the name 'National' to gain patronage of the National Road Stage Company coaches.

anticipated prosperity to ensue by reason thereof. It is equidistant between Uniontown and Washington. The leading wagon stand in Centreville was on the hill at the west end of town, a brick house, on the south side of the road. The wagon yard was in the rear. Zephania Riggle kept this house at an early day, and was succeeded in 1845 by Peter Colley, a nephew of Abel Colley.

Proceeding to Beallsville the traveler passes one of the old toll house sites. David Mitchell, the old collector at the gate near Beallsville, is remembered as a straightforward, honest and intelligent citizen. Beallsville, like Centreville as a town, was the outgrowth of the National Road. It was laid out in 1821, and incorporated as a borough in 1852. Jonathan Knight, the engineer, surveyed the site of the town and made the plat. The National Road forms the main street of this town, as it does that of Centreville. The first old tavern reached in Beallsville, going west, was on the north side, at the east end of the town. This house was first kept by Andrew Keys, and after him by Thomas Keys. This was previous to 1840. The old Keys tavern had a commodious wagon yard attached, and entertained many old wagoners.

About the center of the town of Beallsville, Wm. Greenfield kept a famous old tavern, and he was in many other respects a famous old man. The traveler could always get a good cup of coffee at Greenfield's, a rare thing in a tavern and utterly unknown in a hotel. In addition to keeping tavern, William Greenfield was a banker, and established the "Beallsville Savings Bank." His bank was in his tavern, and his safe was his pocket. He issued notes of small denominations, which were handsomely printed and engraved, and they acquired some credit, and a limited circulation. The pressure of redemption, however, was more than the old banker-tavern keeper could withstand, and he was forced to close business as a banker, but continued his tavern successfully.

Three miles west from Beallsville the traveler reaches the village of Hillsboro. This little town is another outgrowth of the National Road, and as at Beallsville and Centreville, the road forms its main street. The grade from Beallsville to Hillsboro is for the most part ascending, the hill going out west from Beallsville being one of the longest on the road, and Hillsboro is situated on a lofty eminence overlooking a wide range of hills, and many fertile slopes and valleys. On the summit above Hillsboro, the traveler coming east, gets the first glimpses of Laurel Hill, thirty miles distant in the mountains.

Crumrine's history of Washington county, informs us that Hillsboro was laid out in the year 1819, a date coincident with the completion of the road, and contains the following notice of the first public sale of lots:

> The public is informed that a town has been laid off, to be called Hillsboro, adjoining Hill's stone tavern, about equal distance from Washington to Brownsville, and that lots will be sold on the premises on Monday, the 19th day of August, at public auction. Sale to commence at 10 o'clock A.M.
>
> July 19, 1819
>
> Stephen Hill
> Thomas McGiffin
> Proprietors

Hill's stone tavern was in existence as early as 1794. In the early history of the National Road, and for a number of years, it was the leading tavern of Hillsboro, kept by Thomas Hill, who was not a son, but a near relative, probably a nephew, of Stephen Hill, the old proprietor.

The first line of passenger coaches put on the road between Brownsville and Wheeling was owned, organized and operated by Stephen Hill and Simms and Pemberton. This was in 1818, and a continuation of the early line from Cumberland to Brownsville.

In the year 1827 James Beck kept a tavern in Hillsboro. He was a member of the old bridge builders firm of Kinkead, Beck & Evans. It was a stage house, but did a general business. This house was kept at different

The Century Inn at Scenery Hill (ABOVE) has served travelers for almost two centuries. A recent renovation revealed this fine old fireplace (BELOW) and many of the utensils displayed around it.

BOTH, R. DUFF GREEN

NOTICE
Is Hereby Given,

THAT the subscriber will attend at his office in Brownsville, in the state of Pennsylvania, on the second Monday in June next, for the purpose of receiving proposals, in writing, for constructing the whole or any part of the

United States' Road

Between Union-town and Washington, in the state of Pennsylvania. A description of the location of the road has been deposited at Union town, Brownsville and Washington. Proposals must embrace the entire expense of completing the road in the same manner that the road has been made between Cumberland and Union-town, with the addition of four feet width.* Contractors are to furnish the materials, and finish the work they respectively undertake, before the first day of October, 1820; but in all cases where the owners of the land upon which the road is located, have granted to the Superintendent the right of taking materials, such grant shall enure to the benefit of the Contractor. The proposals will state the price of the work, payable in drafts upon the bank of Steubenville, and also payable at the Treasury of the United States; or they may state the price, one half payable at the Treasury, and the remainder at Steubenville. In neither case will the drafts of the Superintendent be paid in the commercial cities to the east of the city of Washington.

*This addition is not to affect the width of the pavement, nor the cuttings; but to increase the width of all the filling; when but one side road is made by filling, two feet will only be required.

DAVID SHRIVER,
Superintendent of the U. S. Road, east of Washington, Pennsylvania.

May 19, 1819.

PRINTED BY JOSEPH SMITH, CUMBERLAND, (Md.)

Poster advertising for construction bids is a good example of confusion regarding completion dates of the Pike. The Road was continually under construction and rebuilding during its entire existence, as obvious to the traveler today as it was 150 years ago.

times by John Noble and William Robinson. Noble and Robinson were both old stage drivers. "Billy" Robinson was one of the best known and most popular men of the road. He hauled many an old-time statesman safely in his nimble coach, and afterward dined him sumptuously in his bountiful tavern.

Westward from Hillsboro the road encounters many long and steep hills, which could have been avoided by making side cuts and occupying the valleys, and this is true, but any other location would have lengthened the line and increased the cost of construction

66

and maintenance. David Shriver, of Cumberland, was the chief engineer in charge of the location, and instructed by the Government to make the line as straight as practicable, within the limit of a five degree elevation.

There was a popular theory when the line was located, that a road over hills was not as fatiguing to horses as a road with a uniform grade. It was argued that a horse is provided with two sets of muscles, one of which is used in going up and the other in going down a hill, and the conclusion was that horses were relieved and rested by a change from an up to a down grade.

The iron mileposts, so familiar to the traveler on the road, were turned out in foundries of Connellsville and Brownsville. Major James Francis had the contract for making and delivering those between Cumberland and Brownsville. His foundry was at Connellsville, Pennsylvania. Those between Brownsville and Wheeling were made at Snowden's old foundry, in Brownsville, John Snowden, contractor. They were hauled along the road for distribution in wagons drawn by six horse teams.

R. DUFF GREEN

Many of the iron mile markers placed along the Pike in the 1830's not only survive but remain as helpful guides. The marker pictured here stands adjacent to the Washington-Jefferson College campus.

The twin ribbons of Interstate Route 70 stretch gracefully into Washington, Pennsylvania from the west near path of the Old Pike. When railroads reduced Road traffic, Old Pike boys began drilling for the recently discovered liquid gold (oil derrick, left).

A town invested with more than ordinary interest is Pancake. Sometimes called Martinsburg, and in later years, known as Laboratory, Pancake was the original, and remains the popular name. It is almost within eyesight of Washington. The first tavern here was kept by George Pancake, and hence the name given the place.

Washington became a point on the National Road by force of a provision in the act of Assembly of Pennsylvania, approved April 9th, 1807, before recited. In a retrospective view that seems to have been a wise provision. Washington, it is true, is older than the road, but without the road it would be difficult to conjecture what the history of the town would have been from 1818 down to 1852. That the road had much to do in promoting the growth and prosperity of the town, there

can be no question, and it must also be conceded that the town contributed in good round measure to the life and prosperity of the road.

The "Cross Keys" was a popular tavern of the olden time. It stood on the southeast corner of Main and Wheeling streets. It was opened in 1801 by James McCamant, who kept it until his death, which occurred in 1813. Tradition has it that he died from the effects of a bite by a mad wolf. His widow continued keeping that house as late as 1831. In the year last named she caused to be inserted in a town paper a notice that she furnished dinner and horse feed for twenty-five cents, and boarding and lodging for jurors and others attending court for two dollars a week.

James Wilson hung out the first tavern sign

67

The campus of Washington and Jefferson College in downtown Washington, Pennsylvania, adjoins the National Road. Alumni of this long established College include James G. Blaine and Thomas B. Searight.

in Washington. His house was a log structure, and stood at the northwest corner of Main and Beau streets. He opened up business in 1781, and was licensed by the court to dispense the ardent at "Catfish Camp." The old Supreme Judges stopped at Wilson's tavern when they went to Washington to hold the courts of Oyer and Terminer.

John Kirk kept a tavern about the beginning of the 19th century in a house that stood on Wheeling street, west of Main. This house was painted red and penciled to imitate brick.

The Mansion House was a leading tavern in Washington from the time it commenced business until it was destroyed by fire, which occurred after the National Road ceased to be a great thoroughfare. It was located on the northeast corner of Main and Chestnut streets. The Mansion House had a large country trade, as well as that derived from the

National Road. The old barroom was of immense size, and the old proprietor, John N. Dagg, was one of the largest men on the road. He was not fat, but tall, and widely proportioned. He provided for his country guests a large upright boot jack, with side bars, which acted as levers, designed to steady the toe in the operation of drawing off a boot. Half cut, cheap leather slippers were also provided, and upon pulling their boots, guests put on these slippers, and in the mornings, piles of boots, nicely polished, were placed in a corner of the barroom, to await the return of their owners from the slumbers of the night. It was not an uncommon thing to see scores of country people sitting about in the big barroom after supper, talking over the events of the day, all wearing the slippers referred to, preparatory to going to rest for the night, at the early bedtime of that happy period. James K. Polk, wife and suite, stopped at the Mansion House on the inaugural trip in 1845.

In 1844 and subsequent to that date, Alpheus Murphy, a wagonmaker, lived and operated a shop near the old Rankin tavern. He gained a local notoriety for proclaiming in a loud voice in season and out of season, his sentiments on current topics, and especially political issues. He was a man of great physical strength, and a skillful workman. He had no scruples against taking an occasional glass of the pure whisky that abounded on the road in his day, and was a frequent visitor to Washington. Prompted possibly by the influence of the active element mentioned, he was accustomed to ascend the cupola of the Washington courthouse and from the balustrade near its summit give vent to his feelings, mainly of a Democratic tendency, in stentorian tones that startled the whole community.

The "Globe Inn" was one of the most famous old taverns in Washington. It was located on the west side of Main street, at the corner of Strawberry alley. This house was opened as a tavern in 1797, and in the next year passed to the hands of David Morris, and was kept by him, continuously, until his death in 1834. General LaFayette was entertained at this house in 1825, and it was a favorite stopping place of Henry Clay, and many other statesmen and heroes of the olden time. This old tavern was a frame building, and remained standing until 1891.

Several miles west from Washington the celebrated "S Bridge" is passed. This bridge takes its name from its shape, which resembles the letter "S." It is a large stone bridge over a branch of Buffalo creek. Near this bridge a road leads to Taylorstown, celebrated for its oil developments. There was a post office here called "S Bridge." In early times there was a tavern at the eastern end of "S Bridge" and another at its western end. These old taverns accommodated the public in their day, but ceased to entertain strangers and travelers previous to 1840.

This fine double arch stone bridge is known today as "S Bridge". A post office was once located here with that official designation. An engineer's report of 1844 cited the bridge as "fast deteriorating", but fifty years later (BELOW) the bridge still carried its burden of traffic. Now bypassed by Route 40 (BOTTOM) and minus part of one end, the bridge still stands.

SEARIGHT—OLD PIKE

R. DUFF GREEN

It is stated in Crumrine's history of Washington county, that John Purviance was the first tavern keeper in Claysville, and that he was the founder of the town. "When it became certain," says Crumrine, "that the National Road would pass through the place, Purviance caused the following notice to be inserted in the Washington *Reporter:*

The subscriber having laid off a number of building lots in the new town of Claysville, will offer the same at public sale on the premises, on Thursday, the 8th day of March, next. Claysville is distant ten miles from Washington, westward, and about eighteen east of Wheeling, and six from W. Alexander. The great NATIONAL ROAD from Cumberland to Wheeling as located by Col. Williams and confirmed by the President, and now rapidly progressing towards its completion, passes directly through the town.

Washington, April 21, 1817.

John Purviance

It goes without saying that this town was named in honor of Henry Clay, the unrivaled champion of the road. As at other towns, the road forms the main street of Claysville. In 1821 James Sargent kept a tavern in Claysville, at the sign of the Black Horse. It was a brick building, occupied formerly by John Porter. Bazil Brown kept a tavern in Claysville as early as 1836, and probably before that date. Some time during the forties, Dan Rice, after his circus stranded, was exhibiting a "learned pig" to the people of Claysville, in Bazil Brown's tavern. David Bell, John Walker, James Kelley, Stephen Conkling and John McIlree were all old tavern keepers at Claysville, and kept stage houses.

Beyond Claysville stood another old round toll house, the last one on the road in Pennsylvania. Here William McCleary collected the tolls for many years.

Crumrine's history of Washington county

Crumbling shell (BELOW), photographed about 1930, once housed toll collector at last tollgate west on the Old Pike in Pennsylvania. The Americanized term "piker" possibly came from "shun-piker" meaning a person who used back roads or farm roads to avoid payment of a toll.

OGLEBAY MANSION MUSEUM, WHEELING

states that West Alexander was first laid out in 1796 by Robert Humphreys, that most of the lots were subsequently acquired by Charles D. Hass, who in the year 1817 sold them by public outcry; that the National Road at the last mentioned date was in process of construction, and had been actually opened for travel from Cumberland to the Big Crossings, and it was believed that all the towns upon its route would become places of prosperity and importance. The town of West Alexander was destroyed by fire on May 4, 1831, but slowly recovered from the disaster, and in the succeeding twenty years became a thriving village, by reason of the prosperity of the great thoroughfare on which it was located.

West Alexander is also noted as a rival of the celebrated Gretna Green, of Scotland, by reason of the many clandestine marriages which have taken place there. It is estimated that from 1835 to 1885, the date of the enactment of the Pennsylvania marriage license law, over five thousand eloping couples were married in West Alexander.

Two miles further west a large frame tavern

Mrs. Sarah Beck, a tavernkeeper, eventually followed the Old Pike into Illinois. Residing under her tavern roof in Springfield, a member of the state legislature rejoiced over the birth of son, Robert Todd Lincoln.

The text that accompanies this 1834 woodcut of Scotland's Gretna Green (ABOVE) informs the reader that the marriage ceremony was customarily performed by a blacksmith.

on the north side of the road was kept by Mrs. Sarah Beck as early as 1832. It was a station for the Stockton line of coaches. Mrs. Beck was the widow of James Beck, of the old bridge building firm of Kinkead, Beck & Evans. Her son, William G. Beck, was the hero of the exciting race between two coaches from Cumberland to Piney Grove. She kept tavern at various points, and finally about the year 1847 bade a last adieu to the scenes of the road, amid which she had been reared, and emigrated to the then far west. Leasing a house in Springfield, Illinois, she resumed the business of tavern keeping. While a member of the Illinois Legislature, Abraham Lincoln was a boarder in Mrs. Beck's house, and Robert T. Lincoln was born under her roof.

Roney's Point is a stage station ten miles from Wheeling. The original owner of the land here was Roney, and its peculiar

71

conformation, a high ridge ending in a point on the south side of the road, gave it the name of Roney's Point. On the north side of the road, at Roney's Point, a large stone tavern was kept by one Ninian Bell, prior to the year 1828. He was succeeded by James Beck and Mrs. Sarah Beck.

Further west, Triadelphia is reached, a small village, and like many others, the outgrowth of the National Road. Here John D. Foster kept a tavern at an early day, and very old pike boys say it was a good one. His daughter, Mary, became the wife of C. S. Maltby, a celebrated oyster dealer of Baltimore.

In what is now the community of Elm Grove stood a large monument. This monument was erected by Moses Shepherd and Lydia, his wife, under an inspiration of personal admiration of the great statesman, Henry Clay, and with a further view of commemorating his distinguished public services in behalf of the road. John Acry, of Claysville, and Alexander Ramsey, of Washington, two old and well remembered

72

Lydia Boggs Shepherd and her husband, Colonel Moses Shepherd (RIGHT) were prominently (and sometimes controversially) identified with the National Road. Colonel Shepherd erected a stone mansion (BELOW) in 1798. After legislation was enacted for construction of the National Road Shepherd, through the influence of Henry Clay, brought Pike to Wheeling and secured a contract for all bridges in the area. In gratitude to Clay, Shepherd built monument (OPPOSITE, TOP) in his honor. Though the statue was later destroyed, Shepherd's mansion is still referred to as Monument Place. One of Shepherd's bridges (OPPOSITE, BOTTOM) altered and enlarged, bears crush of present day traffic.

stone-cutters, worked on this monument.

On a picturesque eminence, near the monument, overlooking Big Wheeling Creek, stands the ancient and historic Shepherd mansion, a stone building erected in 1798, and now known as "Monument Place," the delightful and hospitable home of Maj. Alonzo Loring. In the olden time, when the National Road was the bustling highway of the Republic, the handsome and luxurious stage coaches of the period frequently bore Henry Clay and other eminent men of his day to the Shepherd mansion where they reveled in Old Virginia hospitality.

Photographs taken in the late 1800's testify to the continued use of the Pike in West Virginia. An old frame tollhouse at Leatherwood (ABOVE) still housed tenants; the large stone "S" bridge (BELOW) at Elm Grove carried traffic over Wheeling Creek and the railroad; Walter's Tavern (RIGHT) stood prominently at junction of the National Road and the Bethany Pike; and railroad crossed Old Pike blissfully at Elm Grove Train Depot (ABOVE, RIGHT).

ALL, OGLEBAY MANSION MUSEUM, WHEELING

View of Wheeling from a print made about 1850 (ABOVE). Stagecoach in left foreground labors up Wheeling Hill to follow the snake-like path of the Old Pike heading east among the mountains. Tollhouse on Wheeling Hill (BELOW) photographed about 1890 is minus toll gate pole.

And now, after a long journey of two hundred and sixty miles, the city of Wheeling is reached. Wheeling was the western terminus of the road, in contemplation of the Act of Congress of March 29, 1806. John McCortney kept the most noted wagon stand in Wheeling. He was likewise a commission merchant, which further identified him with old wagoners, enabling him to furnish them with back loads. His tavern was located on Main Street, running back east of Fourteenth to alley B, parallel with, and between Main and Market, with ample grounds surrounding it for wagons and teams to stand on. These grounds were so extensive that they accommodated the old time circus, in

75

The mighty Ohio was a formidable obstacle to speed-conscious east-west traffic. Ferries (LEFT) were for many years the only means of crossing the river. A covered toll bridge (BELOW LEFT) in the 1830's connected Bridgeport, Ohio (left) with Wheeling Island (right) Not until 1849 was the Ohio completely bridged. Photograph (BELOW) shows double dwelling house built about 1837 for toll collectors of bridge

East tower of Wheeling Suspension bridge (ABOVE) with support cables 'flying' over present day traffic suggests the exciting spectacle this awesome structure must have presented to mid-19th century travelers. First opened in 1849, during the twilight years of the Old Pike, this bridge was the engineering marvel of its day. Now a national landmark, it carries traffic to Wheeling Island.

addition to wagons and teams of the road, and two distinct circuses have been known to exhibit on them at the same time. They were not of the "triple ring" order, but of the Dan Rice design.

Capt. Frederic Beymer kept a tavern in Wheeling as early as the year 1802, at the sign of the Wagon, and took boarders at two piasters a week. The town council of Wheeling met in Capt. Beymer's tavern in 1806. Beymer's old Landing was at the foot of Ninth street, where the National Road approached the Ohio River.

The mysterious disappearance of a man by the name of Cooper from the Mosier House about 1840, produced a local sensation, followed by an accusation of foul play and a charge of murder. Cooper, in company with a friend and neighbor by the name of Long, put up together one evening at the Mosier House, and on the next morning Cooper was missing. The two had come in from Ohio, and were going to Washington county, Pennsylvania, where they were born and raised, to visit relatives and old friends. It appears that Cooper rose early and took an outgoing coach back to Ohio without notifying his traveling companion or anyone else. A dead body was found in the river and identified as that of Cooper; and Long, after reaching his destination, was arrested for murder and lodged in the Washington jail. The Virginia authorities made no requisition for him, and he was finally discharged, and settled in

This remarkable view of Wheeling is an enlarged segment of an 1852 tintype occasioned by floodwaters of the Ohio River inundating Wheeling Island (top). Of particular interest is the stagecoach yard in foreground. Five coaches may be counted in the yard while tongues of four more extend from shed at right. In street at left hostlers change horses of coach standing at curb.

Wheeling suspension bridge became a navigational hazard for highstacked steamboats. But hinged stacks neatly solved problem for packet (LEFT).

large and profitable. Old wagoners hauled his "tobies" over the road in large quantities, as they did subsequently the Wheeling "tobies," which were, and continued to be, a favorite brand. Many habitual smokers prefer a Washington or a Wheeling "toby" to an alleged fine, high priced cigar, and the writer of these lines is one of them.

Michigan. A few years afterward, Cooper was discovered in Indianapolis, sound and well.

The Forsythes of Wheeling, James H. and his son Leonard, were prominently identified with the destinies of the National Road. The commission house of James H. Forsythe, the senior member of this old firm, was noted for his energy and clear-headedness. He could converse with any number of persons, and indite a letter at the same time, without being in any wise confused.

The origin of Pennsylvania tobies is worth recording, and pertinent to the history of the old wagoners. The author is indebted to J. V. Thompson, esq., president of the First National Bank of Uniontown, for the following clipping from a Philadelphia paper concerning the "toby:"

> It appears that in the old days the drivers of the Conestoga wagons, so common years ago on our National Road, used to buy very cheap cigars. To meet this demand a small cigar manufacturer in Washington, Pennsylvania, whose name is lost to fame, started in to make a cheap 'roll-up' for them at four for a cent. They became very popular with the drivers, and were at first called Conestoga cigars; since, by usage, corrupted into 'stogies' and 'tobies.'

It is probable that the manufacturer referred to in the above was George Black, as that gentleman made "tobies" in Washington at an early day, and continued in the business for many years, and until he became quite wealthy. In his later days his trade was very

Wheeling Stogies, a smoke of almost world renown today, are as humble in origin as the old Conestoga wagoners who, by popularizing them, gave them their name. Though changes have occurred in price (originally four for a cent) and taste (greatly improved), the Stogie still retains its long, thin shape and in some instances even its box label (ABOVE).

79

Jonathan Knight, Commissioner for locating the United States Road from Zanesville, to the seat of Government of Missouri.

To Olcott White   D^r

1825
Aug. 8th To Stationary, to wit,

12 Blank field note Books feint lined	$2.40
2 Quires best writing paper at 37½ cts	.75
12 Sheets common D^o at	.12½
2 Quires Letter paper at 25 cts	.50
1 Wafer Box & wafers	37½
100 Quills best quality at 2 cts	2.00
3 Bolts tape	37½
1 Ball Red Ferreting	37½
½ doz. black lead pencils at 12½ cts	75
1 Ball Twine	12½
1 Whet Stone	37½
1 Vial Red Ink	18¾
2 Ink Stands	37½
1 Blank Book	1.50
	$ 10.21¼

Rec^d of said Commissioner the above sum of Ten Dollars and twenty one and a fourth cents in full —

$10.21¼   (Duplicate.   Olcott White

I certify that the above articles were necessary

Knight
Comm^r

ⅴ Westward into the plains

Thomas B. Searight gives little information about the National Road west of Wheeling for reasons which he partially explains on the following page. In other portions of the text, Searight reiterates nostalgically his conviction that the Old Pike of the Great Era ran only to Wheeling, Virginia. Historically there are points in Searights' favor but, in simple truth, he was prejudiced by a love for his native Pennsylvania soil and the persons, places and events most intimately related to his own experience.

The National Road was originally projected to Jefferson City, the capital of Missouri (RIGHT). But political strife and the westward push of the railroads brought Road construction to a standstill in central Illinois. As a consequence Vandalia became the last point west. National Road document (OPPOSITE) reveals an interesting partial inventory of items used in Road planner's field office. Photograph (ABOVE) depicts Bridgeport, Ohio beyond Wheeling.

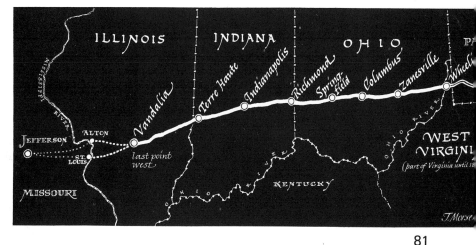

The writer found more difficulty in obtaining information concerning this portion of the road than any other. In fact, he admits his failure to obtain the necessary data for producing an accurate history of it. He wrote to all the postmasters on the Ohio line east of Columbus, for information concerning the road, and no response came, except in one instance, and that was a letter which reached a wrong destination.

It happened that the postmaster who received this letter was a native of Brownsville, Fayette county, Pennsylvania, a member of the old Sloan family of that place, but he was so far away from the road that he could furnish no information concerning it. He, at least, was courteous, a trait for which he is indebted, probably, to the circumstance of his nativity. A self-important postmaster, especially of a little town, like the political carpet-bagger, has no respect for ancient landmarks.

It is estimated that two-fifths of the trade and travel of the road were diverted at Brownsville, and fell into the channel furnished at that point by the slack water improvement of the Monongahela River, and a like proportion descended the Ohio from Wheeling, and the remaining fifth continued on the road to Columbus, Ohio, and points further west. The travel west of Wheeling was chiefly local, and the road presented scarcely a tithe of the thrift, push, whirl and excitement which characterized it, east of that point; and there was a corresponding lack of incident, accident and anecdote on the extreme western division. The distance from Wheeling to Columbus is one hundred and twenty-nine miles, and the road enters the capital of Ohio by way of High street. Before the era of railroads Columbus derived its chief business from the National Road.

Gen. N. P. Talmadge, of whom further mention is made hereafter, owned and

A National Road 'S' bridge near Blaine, Ohio, visually suggests the reason for their demise in the automobile era. Although navigable by slower moving coaches and wagons, 'S' bridges became death traps for cars traveling at increased speeds.

operated a line of coaches also between Wheeling and Columbus, and made things lively along the road. He called his line the "Good Intent."

John Weaver transferred his old line of coaches called the "Peoples," from the eastern to the Ohio portion of the road. There was considerable competition between these old lines, but not comparable to that of the old lines east of Wheeling. The stage stations between Wheeling and Columbus were: St. Clairsville, Morristown, Fairview, Washington, Cambridge, Concord, Zanesville, Gratiot, named in honor of Brig. Gen. Gratiot, Jackson, Etna and Reynoldsburg.

A short distance west of Wheeling the town of St. Clairsville comes in view, one of the oldest towns of Ohio, the seat of justice for Belmont county, and named in honor of the illustrious old Westmoreland county, Pennsylvania, soldier and patriot, Gen. Arthur St. Clair.

In St. Clairsville, James Smith kept the stage office, and bowed in genuine old pike style to the coming and going passengers. One mile west of St. Clairsville, an old German, or Swede, bearing the non-musical name of Neiswanger, or something like it, kept a tavern, and, according to tradition, a good one. His house was a fine brick building, on the north side of the road. One mile further west, one Hoover entertained the traveling public, and beyond him, one Chamberlin presided over a good old tavern.

The village of Sloysville is next reached, which, of course, had its tavern, as all villages have, and probably more than one; but the

Page from an 1836 gazetteer and reference guide to the U. S. (RIGHT) gives principal stage stops in Ohio including the National Road and an interesting conjecture about where the road will terminate. The Valley View Inn (RIGHT, ABOVE) as it appeared in the 1890's. Built in 1806, the frame structure stood on the Pike near Bridgeport, Ohio.

The national road from Cumberland into the west, is completed to the vicinity of Columbus. It is laid out from Columbus through Indianapolis and Terre Haute, in Indiana, to Vandalia, in Illinois, and will terminate at St. Louis. There is nowhere in our country a finer road than the part of it which is finished from Wheeling to Columbus. It is now of great advantage to Ohio, and will be far more so when the whole line is completed.

PRINCIPAL STAGE ROUTES.

1. From Cleaveland to Cincinnati.

	Miles	Miles
To Strongsville, ...	15	
Brunswick, ...	7	22
Medina, ...	7	29
Guilford, ...	6	35
Jackson, ...	6	41
Wooster, ...	12	53
Loudonville, ...	20	73
Mount Vernon, ..	21	94
Sunbury, ...	23	117
Genoa, ...	5	122
Blendon, ...	7	129
COLUMBUS,...	10	139
Cincinnati,....	113	252

2. From Wheeling, Va., to Cincinnati, via Zanesville and Columbus.

	Miles	Miles
To St. Clairsville,	9	
Morristown,.....	9	18
Fairview, ...	10	28
Middleburn, ...	8	36
Washington, ...	6	42
Cambridge, ...	8	50
Norwich, ...	12	62
Zanesville, ...	12	74
Irville, ...	11	85
Hanover, ...	7	92
Newark, ...	8	100
Granville, ...	8	108
COLUMBUS,...	28	136
Franklinton, ...	1	137
Lawrenceville, ...	22	159
Springfield, ...	20	179
Yellow Springs, .	7	186
Xenia, ...	10	196
Waynesville, ...	14	210
Lebanon, ...	10	220
Sharonville, ...	15	235
Reading, ...	4	239
Cincinnati, ...	10	249

3. From Wheeling to Maysville, Ken.

	Miles	Miles
To Zanesville,...	74	
Somerset, ...	18	92
Rushville, ...	8	100
Lancaster, ...	10	110
Tarlton, ...	15	125
Kingston, ...	8	133
Chillicothe.		
Bainbridge, ...	10	143
Sinking Spring,..	18	161
West Union, ...	16	177
Maysville, Ken..	23	200
	18	218

4. From Wheeling to Cincinnati, via Chillicothe.

	Miles	Miles
To Zanesville, as in No. 3, ...	74	
Chillicothe, as in No. 3,	69	143
Cincinnati, as in No. 24,	93	236

5. From Wheeling to Cincinnati, via Circleville and Lebanon.

	Miles	Miles
To Zanesville, as in No. 2, ...	74	
Cincinnati, as in No. 12,	161	235

6. From Sandusky City to Cincinnati, via Dayton.

	Miles	Miles
Lower Sandusky,.	28	
Fort Seneca, ...	9	37
Oakley, ...	6	43
Tymochtee, ...	12	55
Upper Sandusky,	9	64
Grand, ...	10	74
Hardin, ...	16	90
Bellefontaine, ...	20	110
West Liberty, ...	10	120
Urbanna, ...	10	130
Springfield, ...	13	143
Fairfield, ...	13	156
Dayton, ...	10	166
Alexandersville, ..	7	173
Miamisburg, ...	3	176
Franklin, ...	7	183
Middletown, ...	6	189
Hamilton,.......	13	202
Carthage,.......	15	217
Cincinnati,.....	6	223

7. From Ashtabula to Wheeling, Va.

	Miles	Miles
To Jefferson, ...	9	
Austinburg, ...	6	15
Morgan, ...	3	18
Orwell,........	11	29
Bloomfield,.....	5	34
Bristolville, ...	4	38
Warren, ...	11	49
Canfield, ...	16	65
Columbiana,....	11	76
New Lisbon, ...	10	86
Wellsville, ...	12	98
Knoxville, ...	8	106
Steubenville, ...	13	119
Wellsburg, ...	8	127
Wheeling, ...	16	143

8. From Sandusky City to Cincinnati, via Springfield and Yellow Springs.

	Miles	Miles
To Springfield, as in No. 2, ...	143	
From Springfield to Cincinnati, via Yellow Springs, as in No. 2,....	70	213

9. From Zanesville to Cleaveland.

	Miles	Miles
To Dresden, ...	14	
Roscoe, ...	14	28
Coshocton, ...	1	29
Newcomerstown,	17	46
Gnaddenhutten,..	11	57
New Philadelphia,	10	67
Zoar,.........	10	77
Sandyville, ...	4	81
Canton, ...	13	94
Greentown, ...	10	104
Union, ...	4	108
Middleburg,.....	8	116
Talmadge, ...	3	119
Northampton, ...	6	125
Stow, ...	3	128

83

old wagoner who furnished most of the data for this chapter could not recall the names of the old proprietors thereof.

Moving on westwardly, the next point reached is Morristown, the second stage west of Wheeling. This town was at its best when the National Road was the leading avenue of trade and travel. John Bynum and John Lippincott were the old tavern keepers of Morristown.

Samuel Smith kept the old tavern at Elizabethtown. West of Elizabethtown, one Crayton kept a tavern, and beyond him Widow Drake. The widows never surrender.

The village of Washington is next reached. Here Simon Beymer kept at the sign of the "Black Bear" and Peter Colley, formerly of Centerville, kept a tavern in Washington as late as 1854.

Cambridge comes next on the line. This is the capital of Guernsey county, one of the liveliest towns on the road, and surviving its decline, remains prosperous. The old tavern keepers in Cambridge were William Ferguson, Wyatt Hutchinson, Bazil Brown, Mr. Needam, Mr. Pollard, Joseph Bute, Elijah Grimes, John Cook, James B. Moore, Captain Hersing, John Tingle and George Metcalf. The latter kept one of the stage houses.

A writer in a Guernsey county paper gives the following lively description of scenes on the road in that locality:

"Isaac Gleaves was one of the old tavern keepers in Fairview. His house was the stage office, where a halt was made for exchange of horses, and to discharge and take on passengers. The stage offices were places of public resort, and around the barrooms gathered the topers and loafers, by day and by night.

Isaac Gleaves had a famous recipe for the cure of the ague, which for its queer compound he was often required to give, not so much for the ingredients; they were very

Stone walls of this 1828 'S' bridge, (BELOW) west of Hendrysburg, Ohio give the deceptive appearance of fortifications.

The three span stone arch bridge (ABOVE) which stood near St. Clairsville, Ohio, is quite similar to bridge over the Youghiogheny River at Big Crossings, Pennsylvania.

simple; but for the first preparation for the compound. This was to boil down a quart of water to a pint. And to the inquiry, "What is the water boiled down for, Uncle Isaac?" he would reply, "to make it stronger."

Major William Bradshaw was the soul of wit and humor, and gave out many expressions that have become noted. His toast in honor of the Fairview guards, a military company that had been parading "with plumes and banners gay," just after the close of the Mexican war—"Soldiers in peace, civilians in war."

Zanesville is next reached. Zanesville is the county seat of Muskingum county. It is situated on the Muskingum river, fifty-nine miles east from Columbus. Mr. Leslie kept a tavern in Zanesville in the olden time, and entertained the public in a highly satisfactory manner. His house was a brick building on the north side of the street and road, and at the west end of the town. When Leslie kept tavern in Zanesville, the town contained a population of about 7,000. It survived the decline of the road, and grew rapidly in population and wealth.

The largest town on the line of the road west of Columbus, in the State of Ohio, is Springfield, the capital of Clark county. The distance between Columbus and Springfield is forty-five miles. Springfield enjoyed for a number of years the advantages of the road, and felt a pride in being on its line, but its growth and development, the result of other agencies, have thrown a mantle of oblivion over the time when the rattle of the stage coach and the rumble of road wagons furnished the chief excitement of her streets.

The road penetrated Indiana and the boundary line of Wayne county, in that State. The length of the line through Indiana is one hundred and forty-nine and one-fourth miles, and the sum of $513,099 was expended on it for bridges and masonry. Work was begun at Indianapolis and prosecuted east and west from that point, in obedience to an act of Congress given in the chapter on Appropriations. The road was completed through Wayne county in 1827. It was not macadamized or graveled, and in the year 1850 was absorbed by the Wayne County Turnpike Company, under a charter granted by State authority. The length of this pike is twenty-two miles.

Prior to the construction of the National Road in Indiana, Robert Morrisson, the founder of the Morrisson Library, of Richmond, and one of the leading citizens of that place, was mainly instrumental in causing

85

Dr. The United States in account current with Jonathan Knight, Commissioner &c. Cr.

1825.		Dolls	Cts	1825.		Dolls	Cts
To amount of expenditures as per accompanying vouchers and abstract		1177	81¾	By Draft No 371 on the Branch Bank of the U.S. at Pittsburg		2850	00
To my commission for disbursing the above amount at 2½ per cent		29	44¼				
To my services as Commissioner, rendered between the date of my commission the 29th of march & the date of my Report on the route between Zanesville & Columbus the 22d of December 1825 (deducting 66 days for my services east of Zanesville) 171 days at 6$ per day		1026	00				
To office rent		25	00				
		2258	29		By balance due the U.S. $	591	71
To Balance		591	71		Errors excepted		
	$	2850	00		$	2850	00

Document (ABOVE) relates to expenditures by National Road commissioner Jonathan Knight. A civil engineer and former state legislator, Knight was long identified with the National Road. Three known Pike towns: Beallsville, Centerville and Hillsboro, Pennsylvania, were laid out by Knight. Later the railroads would utilize his knowledge and abilities in crossing the Alleghenys and heading west.

a gravel road to be made from Richmond to Dayton, Ohio, which was known as the "Richmond and Short Line Pike." The engineers of the National Road adopted the line of Morrisson's road in Indiana, with the exception of one mile from a point near Clawson's tavern to the Ohio State line.

The rate of toll was two cents a mile for horse and buggy and one-half cent per mile for each additional horse, one cent for a horse and rider per mile, and one-half cent for a led horse.

The toll houses were small frame structures and the gates simply heavy poles to raise and let down after the manner of the beam that lowered and lifted up "the old oaken bucket that hung in the well."

The city of Richmond is the first large town on the line of the road within the borders of the State of Indiana, and the road forms its Main street. It is four miles from the Ohio line, and the county seat of Wayne county.

The first tavern of the road in Richmond was kept by Charles W. Starr. It was a regular old pike tavern, with extensive stabling and drove yards attached, occupying one-fourth of a square on the northeast corner of Eighth, formerly Fifth street. The building was of brick, known in later years as the Tremont Hotel.

A short distance below Starr's, and between Sixth and Seventh streets, stood Sloan's brick stage house, and its proprietor, Daniel D. Sloan, was at one time postmaster of Richmond. This tavern was headquarters for two stage lines, one running to Indianapolis and the other to Cincinnati. The Cincinnati line had opposition, and by cutting rates the fare was reduced by the competition and during its continuance, from five dollars to fifty cents for the round trip, distance seventy miles direct.

It is related in the latest history of Indiana, that Jeremiah Cox, one of the earliest settlers in Richmond, regarded with disfavor the scheme of building up the town; and is said to have remarked, that he would rather see a buck's tail than a tavern sign.

At the west end of Richmond the road crosses Whitewater River over a handsome and expensive bridge. This bridge has seven arches, and is a combination truss and arch design, capable of sustaining an immense weight. On the west side timbers and wool sacks were sunk into a quicksand upon which to rest the foundations of the abutment.

There was a tavern between gate No. 7 and gate No. 8, which was near the Center township line and East Clear creek. West of this point there is a curve in the road caused by the refusal of Thomas Croft to remove his house, which was on the surveyed line. He was offered $500 to remove his house and declined to take it. The road was then of necessity made around his house, and so near it as to loosen its foundations, and it toppled and fell down, causing him to lose his house, and the sum offered him as damages besides.

At the seventh milestone, a little beyond West Clear Creek bridge, stood the shop of Jeremy Mansur, who manufactured the first axes made in the county of Wayne. When Martin Van Buren made his trip through Indiana, many persons denounced him as an enemy of the road, and some one in Richmond, to inflict chastisement upon the distinguished statesman for his supposed unfriendliness, sawed a double-tree of the coach in which he was traveling nearly through, and it broke near Mansur's ax-shop, causing Mr. Van Buren to walk to the top of a hill through thick mud. The author of this mishap to Mr. Van Buren subsequently boasted that he had put a mud polish on

At Richmond, Indiana, the National Road passed over the Whitewater River via bridge (BELOW). Bridge abutments made excellent advertising billboards for land merchants of the 1890's.

SEARIGHT—OLD PIKE

87

A stagecoach mishap occasioned by an irate citizen of a differing political persuasion gave Martin Van Buren's boots an Indiana mud polish.

Gentleman Martin's boots to give him a realizing sense of the importance of good roads.

Centerville boasts of having been a nursery of great men. Here Oliver P. Morton, when a young man, worked as a hatter, and Gen. A. E. Burnside pursued the humble trade of a tailor. Gen. Lew Wallace and Gen. Noble went to school in Centerville, and possibly the germs of Ben Hur had their origin in this rural village.

The road forms the main street of Dublin and is called Cumberland street, by reason of this fact. The first tavern established in Dublin was by Samuel Schoolfield, an old Virginian, pleasantly remembered on account of his staunch patriotism. He displayed on his signboard the motto: "Our country, right or wrong."

The railroad absorbed all passenger and freight traffic in the year 1852, after which date and to the close of the civil war, outside of home travel, the main vehicles on the Indiana division were "Prairie Schooners," or semi-circular bedded, white-covered emigrant wagons, used by parties moving from Virginia and the Carolinas to Illinois.

Indianapolis as before stated is on the line of the road, but her proportions as a city are the outgrowth of other agencies. In the early days of Indiana's capital the National Road was her only commercial artery, and her pioneer citizens regarded it as a great advantage to their aspiring town. The railway era dawned so soon after the road was located through Indianapolis that but few memories cluster about its history in that locality like those east of the Ohio River.

The last and only remaining large town of Indiana on the road is Terre Haute, a city like Indianapolis that has outgrown the memories of the road, and is probably little mindful of the time when her early inhabitants deemed it a matter of high importance to be located on its line. Though remote from the active centres of the historic road, Terre Haute is more or less associated with its stirring scenes and former prestige.

Any one familiar with the National Road in its prosperous era, whose business or other engagements required a divergence from it, invariably returned to it with a sense of security and a feeling of rest and relief. This feeling was universal and profound.

Before the road was completed beyond the western boundary of the State of Indiana, the steam railway had become the chief agency of transportation and travel, and our grand old national highway was practically lost amid the primitive prairies of Illinois, so that whereas its splendor was favored by the rising, it was dispelled beneath the Setting Sun.

Approximately 800 miles from its point of origin the National Road died of old age at Vandalia, Illinois. Pictured during the 1920's (RIGHT) a Madonna of the Trails monument erected by the NSDAR stands in front of the former State Capitol in Vandalia.

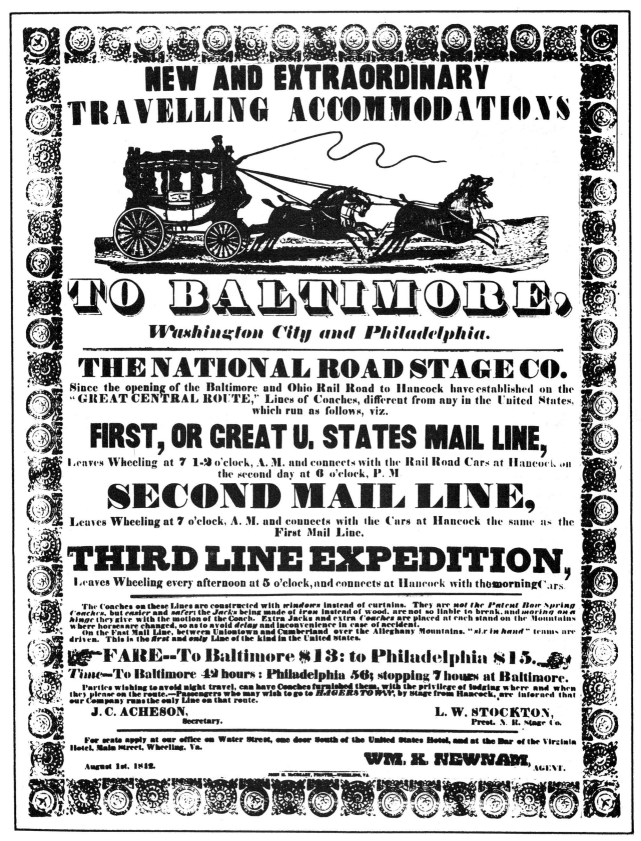

NEW AND EXTRAORDINARY
TRAVELLING ACCOMMODATIONS

TO BALTIMORE,
Washington City and Philadelphia.

THE NATIONAL ROAD STAGE CO.

Since the opening of the Baltimore and Ohio Rail Road to Hancock have established on the "GREAT CENTRAL ROUTE," Lines of Coaches, different from any in the United States, which run as follows, viz.

FIRST, OR GREAT U. STATES MAIL LINE,

Leaves Wheeling at 7 1-2 o'clock, A. M. and connects with the Rail Road Cars at Hancock on the second day at 6 o'clock, P. M.

SECOND MAIL LINE,

Leaves Wheeling at 7 o'clock, A. M. and connects with the Cars at Hancock the same as the First Mail Line.

THIRD LINE EXPEDITION,

Leaves Wheeling every afternoon at 5 o'clock, and connects at Hancock with the morning Cars.

The Coaches on these Lines are constructed with *windows* instead of curtains. They are *not the Patent Bow Spring Coaches*, but *easier* and *safer*; the *Jacks* being made of *iron* instead of wood, are not so liable to break, and *moving on a hinge* they give with the motion of the Coach. Extra Jacks and extra *Coaches* are placed at each stand on the Mountains where horses are changed, so as to avoid *delay* and inconvenience in case of accident.

On the Fast Mail Line, between Uniontown and Cumberland over the Alleghany Mountains. "*six in hand*" teams are driven. This is the *first* and *only* Line of the kind in the United States.

☞ FARE--To Baltimore $13: to Philadelphia $15. ☜

Time—To Baltimore 42 hours : Philadelphia 56; stopping 7 hours at Baltimore.

Parties wishing to avoid night travel, can have Coaches furnished them, with the privilege of lodging where and when they please on the route.—Passengers who may wish to go to *HAGERSTOWN*, by Stage from Hancock, are informed that our Company runs the only Line on that route.

J. C. ACHESON,
Secretary.

L. W. STOCKTON,
Prest. N. R. Stage Co.

For seats apply at our office on Water Street, one door South of the United States Hotel, and at the Bar of the Virginia Hotel, Main Street, Wheeling, Va.

August 1st, 1842.

JOHN B. McCREARY, PRINTER—WHEELING, VA.

WM. K. NEWNAM, AGENT.

VI Coaching in the Palmy Days

Chariots of the Appian Way, drawn by the fastest horses of ancient Italy, formed a dismal cortege in comparison with the sprightly procession of stage coaches on the old American highway. The grandeur of the old mail coach is riveted forever in the memory of the pike boy. To see it ascending a long hill, increasing speed, when nearing the summit, then moving rapidly over the intervening level to the top of the next hill, and dashing down it, a driver like the stately Redding Bunting wielding the whip and

A suggestion of the glamour and excitement of coaching is reflected by an 1842 poster (OPPOSITE) of Lucius Stockton's National Road Stage Company. Stockton and his stage drivers became legendary along route of the Old Pike. Scene (ABOVE) by an English artist symbolizes role stagecoaches played in reducing isolation of the ever expanding frontier.

handling the reins, revealed a scene that will never be forgotten.

Excitement followed in the wake of the coaches all along the road. Their arrival in the towns was the leading event of each day, and they were so regular in transit that farmers along the road knew the exact hour by their coming, without the aid of watch or clock. They ran night and day alike. Relays of fresh horses were placed at intervals of twelve miles, as nearly as practicable. Ordinarily a driver had charge of one team only, which he drove and cared for. Mail drivers, however, in many instances, drove three or four teams and more, which were cared for by grooms at the stations. Teams were changed almost in the twinkling of an eye. The coach was driven rapidly to the station, where a fresh team stood ready harnessed and waiting on the roadside. The moment the team came to a

91

halt the driver threw down the reins, and almost instantly the incoming team was detached, the fresh one attached, the reins thrown back to the driver, who did not leave his seat, and away again went the coach at full speed, the usual group of loafers, meanwhile, looking on and enjoying the exciting scene. The horses used were showy and superb, the admiration of all who beheld them. Mr. Stockton had a strain called the "Murat," and another known as the "Winflower," which have become extinct, but many expert horsemen contend that they have not, in later days, been surpassed for nerve, beauty or speed. A peculiar affliction came upon many of the "wheel horses," expressed by the phrase "sprung in the knees." It is said to have been produced by the efforts of the horses in "holding back," while descending the long and steep hills.

Coaches were all named after the manner of steamboats, and more recently, sleeping cars on the leading railroads. The name of every State of the Union was utilized for this purpose, and the realms of fancy were likewise explored. The coach named for Pennsylvania bore the legend Keystone State; Ohio was honored under the name Buckeye State, New Hampshire, the Granite State, Massachusetts, the Bay State, and so on. Among the fancy names employed, the old pike boy will readily recall the following: Fashion, Palmetto, Central Route, Jewess, Beauty, Pathfinder, Samaritan, Highlander, Ivanhoe, Herald, Industry, National, Republic, Protection, Brilliant, Atlas, Sultana,

In drawing (BELOW) a stagecoach with unusually small wheels stops at the Central House, a popular tavern on the Pike between Baltimore and Cumberland, Maryland.

Clarendon, Chancellor, Moravian, Miantonoma, Loch Lomond.

Warriors, statesmen and old stagers were remembered and honored in the names following: Washington, Lafayette, General Wayne, General St. Clair, General Jackson, General Harrison, Rough and Ready, meaning General Taylor, General Worth, General Cass, Colonel Benton, Madison, Monroe, Henry Clay, The President, James K. Polk, Purviance, Daniel Moore, L. W. Stockton, General Moorehead, David Shriver, William H. Stelle, James C. Acheson, Columbus, Pocahontas, Santa Anna.

Countries and cities were honored in the names that follow: Yucatan, Green Bay, Oronoco, Tampico, Bangor, Mexico, Buena Vista, New Orleans, Erie, Lexington, Vicksburg, Natchez, Trenton, San Francisco, Mobile, Troy, Wyandott, Idaho, Ashland, Westmoreland, Allegany, Raritan, Youghiogheny, Guatemala, Panama, Hungarian, Montgomery, Paoli, Tuscaloosa. One coach took in a hemisphere, and was called America. Another was named Queen

The Stagecoach and Conestoga wagon share a common ancestor, the baggage or freight wagon. Passengers, first hauled at freight rates, soon proved to be equally profitable. Early companies used crude wagons (BELOW) and provided fresh horses at stages along the route. Stagecoaches (ABOVE) began appearing late in the 18th Century.

As the National Road progressed through remote areas of Ohio, Illinois and Indiana, log villages sprang up virtually overnight. Woodcut of the 1830's (ABOVE) depicts excitement generated by arrival of a stagecoach.

Victoria, while another rendered homage to dear old Ireland, by bearing the legend, Erin Go Bragh.

When Harrison, Polk and Taylor passed over the road to the capital, to be installed in the presidential office, a splendid new coach was provided for each occasion, called the President, in which the President-elect and his immediate family were conveyed.

There was one mail coach that was especially imposing. On its gilded sides appeared the picture of a post boy, with flying horse and horn, and beneath it in gilt letters this awe inspiring inscription:

He comes, the herald of a noisy world,
News from all nations lumbering at his back.

No boy who beheld that old coach will ever forget it. The coaches were all handsomely and artistically painted and ornamented, lined inside with soft silk plush. There were three seats furnished with luxurious cushions, and three persons could sit comfortably on each, so that nine passengers made a full load as far as the interior was concerned. A seat by the side of the driver was more coveted in fair weather than a seat within. During the prosperous era of the road it was not uncommon to see as many as fifteen coaches in continuous procession, and both ways, east and west, there would be thirty each day.

The first mail coaches were arranged to carry but three passengers, in addition to the mail pouches, upon a model furnished by the post office department. Drivers and residents along the road called the passenger compartment of the early mail coach a "monkey box." This was at the front end of the vehicle, and rested on springs, and the mail pouches were placed behind it, on a lower plane, and in a long, tight, wooden box or bed, resting on the axles of the wagon, without springs. It made a loud noise when passing over the road, was altogether a curious contrivance, and after a short term of usage was abandoned, and the ordinary passenger coach substituted in its stead. Mr. Stockton established a coach factory in Uniontown, where many of the coaches of his line were made, and as necessity from time to time

94

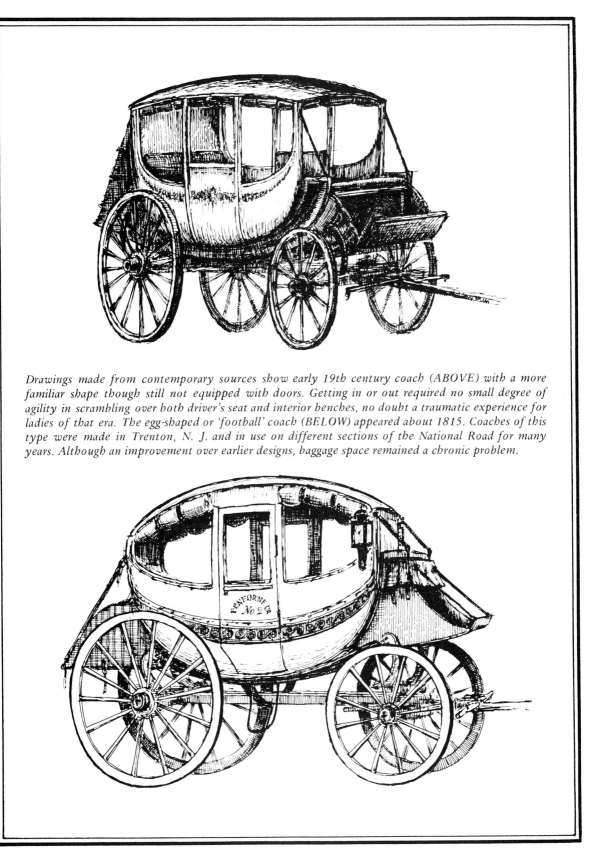

Drawings made from contemporary sources show early 19th century coach (ABOVE) with a more familiar shape though still not equipped with doors. Getting in or out required no small degree of agility in scrambling over both driver's seat and interior benches, no doubt a traumatic experience for ladies of that era. The egg-shaped or 'football' coach (BELOW) appeared about 1815. Coaches of this type were made in Trenton, N. J. and in use on different sections of the National Road for many years. Although an improvement over earlier designs, baggage space remained a chronic problem.

Denis Diderot, in his A Diderot Pictorial Encyclopedia of Trades and Industry *protrayed the interior of an 18th century French farrier's shop (ABOVE) who specialized in forming horseshoes. The American blacksmith, unlike his counterpart above, turned his hand to many tasks. But Yankee ingenuity was hard at work perfecting machines that would change the role of smiths almost the world over. By 1843 one factory alone in Troy, New York (also famous for its coaches) was producing 50 tons of horseshoes per day which sold at the low rate of 5 cents per pound.*

existed, repaired. Blacksmith shops were also set up in connection with this factory, where the stage horses of the Stockton line were shod. It was called the "stage yard," and located on Morgantown street. Many mechanics in different lines of work were employed in the "stage yard."

At an early day there was a coach factory at or near the Little Crossings, where many of the first passenger coaches used on the road were made. They were without through braces, or springs of any kind. Their bodies were long, and the inside seats for passengers placed crosswise. They had but one door, and that was in the front, so that passengers on entering were compelled to climb over the front seats to reach those in the rear.

The first coach of the Troy pattern was placed on the road in the year 1829 by James Reeside, and tradition has it that he won this coach with a bet on Gen. Jackson's election to the presidency. Mr. Reeside was desirous that Gen. Jackson should be the first person to ride in this coach, and accordingly tendered it to the President-elect when on his way to Washington, who true to his habit of refusing gifts, declined the proffered compliment as to himself, but consented that his family might occupy the coach. Charley Howell was the driver, and his team was one of the finest on the road. Many coaches were brought out on the road afterward from the

Troy and Concord factories. These coaches cost between five and six hundred dollars each.

One feature of the old stage lines that left a lasting mark on memory's tablet was the "Postilion." A groom with two horses was stationed at the foot of many of the long hills, and added to the ordinary team of four horses to aid in making the ascent. The summit gained, the extra horses were quickly detached and returned to await and aid the next coming coach, and this was the "Postilion." Nathan Hutton is a well remembered old postilion. He was a tall, spare man, and lived in a small log house on the roadside, a short distance west of the old Johnson tavern, and four and a half miles east of Brownsville. At the foot of the hill below his house, he reinforced the coaches with his postilion both ways, east and west, up Colley's hill, going west, and the equally long hill, coming east from the point. When he wanted a man or horse to be faithful to duty he exhorted him to "stand by his 'tarnal

Stagecoaches of Troy, New York, were early rivals of the Concord Coach on the National Road and may have pioneered features later attributed to the Concord. Coach (BELOW) with rear outside seat, fits general description of Troy pattern. Postilion (ABOVE) waits with extra team to aid coach over mountain grade.

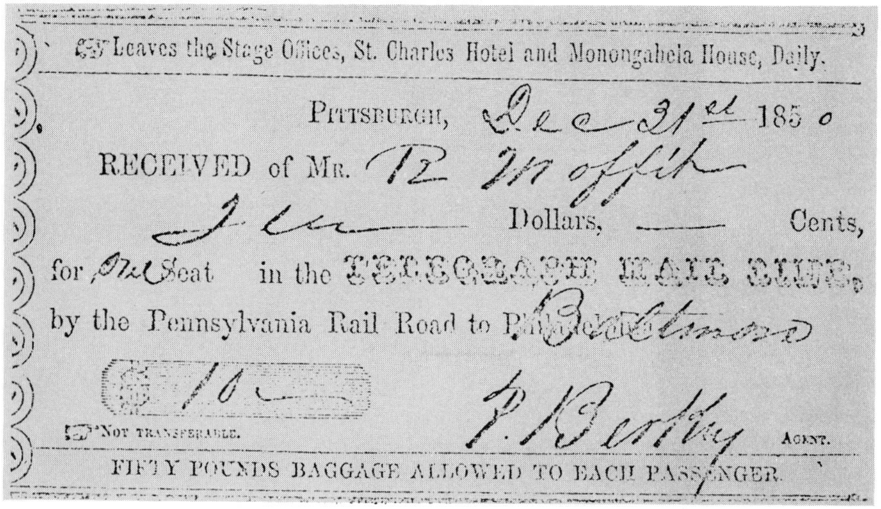

Leaves the Stage Offices, St. Charles Hotel and Monongahela House, Daily.

PITTSBURGH, *Dec 31st* 185 0

RECEIVED of MR. *R Moffit*

J on Dollars, _____ Cents,

for *One Seat* in the TELEGRAPH MAIL LINE,

by the Pennsylvania Rail Road to Philadelphia *Baltimore*

$16

NOT TRANSFERABLE.

P Berkly AGENT.

FIFTY POUNDS BAGGAGE ALLOWED TO EACH PASSENGER.

In 1849, President-elect Zachary Taylor traveled by coach over the Old Pike on his trip to Washington. A winter storm which enveloped his entourage captivated the General with its beauty and as the party approached Cumberland, Taylor halted his coach on a high bluff and stepped out for a better view of the arctic panorama. Under similar circumstances, it is highly doubtful that the stage driver (OPPOSITE) shared Taylor's esthetic appreciation of the raging elements. Stagecoach ticket (LEFT) indicates the fate of most eastern stage lines as railroad companies multiplied.

integrity." The old postilion bade adieu to the scenes of earth long ago, and nothing is left to indicate the spot where his lowly dwelling stood except a few perishing quince bushes.

Scharts' history of Western Maryland gives the following account of President Taylor's ride over the mountain division of the road, when on his way to Washington to be inaugurated:

President Taylor and his party were, in 1849, conveyed over the road under the marshalship of that most indefatigable Whig, Thomas Shriver, who, with some other Cumberlanders, proceeded to the Ohio river and met the presidential party. Among the party were statesmen, politicians, and office-hunters, notably Col. Bullet, a brilliant editor from New Orleans, who was to occupy a relation to President Taylor something like that of Henry J. Raymond to Lincoln. The road was a perfect glare of ice, and everything above ground was literally plated with sleeted frost. The scenery was beautiful; to native mountaineers too common to be of much interest, but to a Southerner like Gen. Taylor, who had never seen the like, it was a phenomenon. In going down a spur of Meadow Mountain, the presidential coach, with the others, danced and waltzed on the polished road, first on one side and then on the other, with every sign of an immediate capsize, but the coaches were manned with the most expert of the whole corps of drivers. Shriver was in the rear, and in the greatest trepidation for the safety of the President. He seemed to feel himself responsible for the security of the head of the Nation. Down each hill and mountain his bare head could be seen protruding through the window of his coach to discover if the President's coach was still upon wheels. The iron gray head of the General could almost with the same frequency be seen outside of his window, not to see after anybody's safety, but to look upon what seemed to him an arctic panorama. After a ride of many miles the last long slope was passed and everything was safe. At twilight the Narrows were reached, two miles west of Cumberland, one of the boldest and most sublime views on the Atlantic slope. Gen. Taylor assumed authority and ordered a halt, and out he got in the storm and snow and looked at the giddy heights on either side of Wills creek, until he had taken in the grandeur of the scenery. He had beheld nothing like it before, even in his campaigns in Northern Mexico. The President-elect was tendered a reception on his arrival at Cumberland, and the next morning he and his party left on the cars for Washington.

The ubiquitous Concord, built in Concord, New Hampshire carried passengers and mail for almost a century. One early Concord feature was the flattened roof which solved baggage problems and later provided space for additional passengers. A small restored Concord (ABOVE) of Civil War vintage photographed before its unfortunate destruction by fire. Heavy Concord built by Abbot and Downing (BELOW) displays the classic profile of world renown.

100

STAGECOACH COMPANIES, LINES, PROPRIETORS AND DRIVERS

The most conspicuous of all the old stage proprietors of the National Road was Lucius Witham Stockton. James Reeside was probably an older stage man, and may have owned and operated more stage lines; but Mr. Stockton was longer and more prominently identified with the business on the National Road. He was born at Flemington, New Jersey, September 1, 1799. He was a son of Lucius Stockton, and a grandson of the Rev. Philip Stockton, known in his day and among his countrymen as "The Revolutionary Preacher," who was a brother of Richard Stockton, a signer of the Declaration of Independence from the colony of New Jersey. L. W. Stockton appeared in Uniontown as a stage proprietor previous to the year 1824, the exact date not ascertainable.

It is related as an incident in the early career of Mr. Stockton that he had a race with a horse and buggy against a locomotive, between the Relay House and Baltimore, in which he came out ahead. The horse he drove on that occasion was a favorite gray. He had a pair of "Winflower" mares, which he drove frequently from Uniontown to Wheeling between breakfast and teatime, tarrying two or three hours at midday in Washington. At the watering places he ordered a little whisky to be added to the water given these spirited and fleet animals, and they became so accustomed to it that, it is said, they refused to drink unless the water contained the stimulating element. He would also drive from Uniontown to Cumberland in a day, stopping at the stations to transact business, and from Cumberland to Hagerstown, sixty-six miles, was an ordinary day's drive for him. His private carriage was a long open vehicle which he called "The Flying Dutchman." Hanson Willison, who has a vivid recollection of Mr. Stockton and his lively trips over the road, says that the names of his sorrel mares (the "Winflowers") were "Bet" and "Sal," and

Lucius Stockton, for 20 years the colorful captain of many stage lines on and in the vicinity of the National Road, fed his own matched team of horses water flavored with whiskey.

that they once ran off. On that occasion Mr. Stockton was accompanied by his wife and a sister. Miss Stockton was much alarmed, and pulling the coat-tail of her brother cried out piteously, "Hold on, brother William, hold on, or we'll all be killed!" But Mr. Stockton heeded not the cries of his sister, and having no fear of horses, soon regained control of the runaways without sustaining loss or injury.

In 1834 or 1835, Mr. Stockton transferred a number of stage teams and drivers, from the Baltimore and Washington City road, to the National Road. Two of these teams ran in and out from Somerfield. One called "the Kangaroo team" was driven by John Mills. They were large, dark bays, and much

101

Stagecoach travel, although far less plagued by the horrible accidents of early railroading, was not without its perils and the safe return of a loved one was a joyous occasion as protrayed by song front (ABOVE) for a Stephen Foster melody. Major Donaldson (BELOW) was assigned task of erasing a president, in name only, from one of Stockton's elaborately decorated coaches.

admired by lovers of fine horses. Mills knew how to handle them. He was a superb driver. Another of these "transferred" teams was driven by William Bishop. The horses in this team were light bays, all "bob-tails," and notwithstanding there was but one good eye in the whole team, and all were "sprung in the knees," it is asserted by many old pike boys that this unique and "blemished" team was the fastest on the road. It was brought out from the Baltimore and Washington road by Charles Howell, who drove it a short time before it was turned over to William Bishop. Bishop was a capital reinsman.

Mr. Stockton had one of his coaches named John Tyler, in honor of the vice-president of the first Harrison administration. When Tyler, by the death of Harrison, succeeded to the presidency, and vetoed the United States bank bill, Mr. Stockton was very much angered thereat, and going into the stage yard, soon after the veto was announced, accosted a Maj. Donaldson thus: "Donaldson, can't you erase that name (pointing to the Tyler coach) and substitute another? I won't have one of my coaches named for a traitor." "Certainly I can," replied Donaldson, "what shall the new name be?" "Call it Gen. Harrison," said Stockton. "All right," said Donaldson, and the change was made. Maj. Donaldson was a Democrat, and much amused by the incident.

Mr. Stockton died at Uniontown on April 25, 1844, at "Ben Lomond," the name he gave his residence.

James Kinkead, Jacob Sides and Abraham Russell put on the first line of passenger coaches west of Cumberland, and as early as 1818 John and Andrew Shaffer, Garrett Clark, Aaron Wyatt, Morris Mauler, John Farrell, Quill and Nathan Smith, and Peter Null, were drivers on this line. The Smiths and Null drove in and out from Uniontown. One of the Smiths subsequently became the agent of a stage line in Ohio. James Kinkead, above mentioned, was the senior member of the firm of Kinkead, Beck and Evans, who built most of the large stone bridges on the line of the road. This early line of stages was owned and operated in sections. Kinkead owned the line from Brownsville to Somerfield; Sides, from Somerfield to the Little Crossings, and thence to Cumberland Russell was the proprietor. Kinkead sold his section to George Dawson, of Brownsville, and Alpheus Beall, of Cumberland, bought out Russell's interest. This line was subsequently purchased by, and merged in, the National Road Stage Company, the principal and most active member of which was Lucius W. Stockton. The other members of this company were Daniel Moore, of Washington, Pennsylvania, Richard Stokes and Moore N. Falls, of Baltimore, and Dr. Howard Kennedy, of Hagerstown, Maryland. After the death of Mr. Stockton, in 1844, Dr. Kennedy and Mr. Acheson were the active members of the firm. John W. Weaver put a line of stages on the road at an early day, known as the People's Line. After a short run it was withdrawn from the road east of Wheeling, and transferred to the Ohio division. Previous to 1840, James Reeside put on a line which Mr. Stockton nicknamed the "June Bug," for the reason, as he alleged, it would not survive the coming of the June bugs. Mr. Stockton subsequently bought out this line and consolidated it with his own. There was a line of stages on the road called the "Good Intent," which came to stay, and did stay until driven off by the irresistible force of the Steam King. This line was owned by Shriver, Steele & Company, and was equal in vim, vigor and general equipment to the Stockton line. The headquarters of the Good Intent line at Uniontown was the McClelland house. There passengers took their meals, and the horses were kept in the stables appurtenant. The "old line" (Stockton's) had its headquarters at the National house, on Morgantown street, now the private residence of that worthy and well known citizen, Thomas Batton. This little *bon mot* is one among a thousand, illustrative of the spirit of the competition between these rival lines. There was one Peter Burdine, a driver on the Good Intent line, noted for his dashing qualities, who was accustomed to give vent to his fidelity to his employers, and his confidence in himself in these words:

> If you take a seat in Stockton's line,
> You are sure to be passed by Pete Burdine.

And this became a popular ditty all along the road.

On authority of Hanson Willison, the old stage driver of Cumberland, the first line of stages put on the road east of Cumberland, in opposition to the Stockton line, was owned, from Frederick to Hagerstown, by Hutchinson and Wirt; from Hagerstown to Piney Plains, by William F. Steele; from Piney Plains to Cumberland, by Thomas Shriver.

SEARIGHT—OLD PIKE

A coach of the Good Intent Line (ABOVE) may be the product of area craftsmen. Searight lists four towns along the Old Pike where coaches were manufactured.

103

James 'Land Admiral' Reeside (LEFT), prominent stage line entrepreneur and his friend Col. Richard M. Johnson (RIGHT), vice president under Martin Van Buren wore vests and neckties of scarlet which matched the interior of Reeside's coaches.

James Reeside was born near Paisley, Renfrew, Scotland, and was brought, when an infant, to Baltimore county, Md., in 1789, where he was raised. His parents being in humble circumstances, toil was his first estate. Poor in book learning and in earthly goods, he possessed genius, energy, executive ability, and an ambition that fitted him to be a leader of men. Before the war of 1812 he was a wagoner, hauling merchandise from Baltimore and Philadelphia to Pittsburgh and west to Zanesville and Columbus, Ohio. His promptness and sagacity soon enabled him to own his own teams, which were employed in hauling artillery to Canada. Commissioned a forage master under General Winfield Scott, at Lundy's Lane, his Scottish blood prompted him to seize a musket, as a volunteer, from which hard-fought battle he carried honorable scars. On his return he settled at Hagerstown, Md., where, in 1816, he married Mary, the daughter of John Weis, a soldier of the Revolutionary War. Abandoning wagoning, he ran a stage line, in 1816 to 1818, from Hagerstown *via* Greencastle and Mercersburg to McConnellstown, there connecting with the stage line then in operation from Chambersburg to Pittsburgh by Bedford, Somerset and Mt. Pleasant. In 1818, in connection with Stockton & Stokes, of Baltimore; Joseph Boyd, of Hagerstown; Kincaid, Beck & Evans, of Uniontown; George Dawson, of Brownsville; Stephen Hill, of Hillsboro; and Simms & Pemberton, of

Wheeling, he put on the first regular stage line, carrying the mail, between Baltimore and Wheeling, before the construction of the turnpikes between Hagerstown and Cumberland. This division of the route being from Hancock to Frostburg, he removed to Cumberland, where, in conjunction with his stage line, he kept the "McKinley Tavern," at the corner of Baltimore and Mechanics streets, afterward kept by Jacob Fechtig, James Stoddard, John Edwards, and others, and now known as the "Elberon." In 1820 he quit tavern keeping, and confined himself to mail contracting and the stage business. In 1827 John McLean, Postmaster General, afterward one of the Justices of the Supreme Court of the United States, prevailed on him to take the mail contract between Philadelphia and New York, and he moved from Cumberland to Philadelphia. In the first year he reduced the time for transporting the mail between the two cities from twenty-three to sixteen hours, and soon thereafter to twelve hours. He soon became the owner of most of the lines running out of Philadelphia and New York, and the largest mail contractor in the United States. He employed in this service more than one thousand horses and four hundred men. The wagoner soon became the "Land Admiral," a title given him by the press in recognition of his energy and ability.

The Post Office Department at that time having to rely on its own resources, and under Major W. T. Barry, then Postmaster-General, the service had so increased in thinly settled sections it became deeply in debt. Mr. Reeside raised, on his personal responsibility, large sums of money to relieve it. His efforts were appreciated, and he was the esteemed friend of Andrew Jackson, Henry Clay, and other distinguished men, without regard to politics, although he was a pronounced Democrat. Of massive frame, six feet five inches in height, yet spare in flesh, clear cut features, sparkling, clear blue-gray eyes, fair complexion, with dark, sandy, curly hair, he was a true Highlander in appearance, genial in disposition, with quick and ready wit.

Controversies arising between Amos Kendall, the successor of Barry, and all the old mail contractors, their pay was suspended upon frivolous grounds, compelling them to bring suits, among the most celebrated of which were those of Reeside and Stockton & Stokes. The latter's case was referred to Virgil Maxy, who found in their favor about $140,000. Mr. Reeside's claim was tried before Justice Baldwin and a jury in 1841, and resulted in a verdict for plaintiff of $196,496.06, which, after seventeen years, was paid, with interest. As soon as his contracts under Kendall expired he quit the mail service, after putting the Philadelphia and New York mail on the Camden & Amboy railroad during the residue of his contract term.

In 1836 he bought the interest of John W. Weaver between Cumberland and Wheeling, then a tri-weekly line; increased it to a daily, then twice daily, and added another tri-weekly line, and named the lines "Good Intent," which was the name he had previously given the fast mail line between Philadelphia and Pittsburgh. In 1839 he sold his entire interest in the National Road lines, and gave his attention to his suit against the United States. His health being impaired, he spent the winter of 1842 in New Orleans. Returning in the ensuing spring, without benefit to his health, he died in Philadelphia on the 3d of September, 1842.

Mr. Reeside attracted attention by reason of the peculiar garb he appeared in. In the winter season he always wore a long drab overcoat and a fur cap. Once in passing along a street in Philadelphia in company with Col. Richard M. Johnson, of Kentucky, Vice-President of the United States, some scarlet cloth was observed in a tailor's window, which prompted Col. Johnson to say: "Reeside, as your coaches are all red, you ought to wear a red vest." Mr. Reeside replied: "I will get one if you will."

"Agreed," said Johnson, and straightway both ordered red vests and red neckties, and from that time as long as they lived continued to wear vests and neckties of scarlet colors. James Reeside aided in an early day to develop the mighty resources of our country, with such agencies as were then available, and his name and good work deserve to be perpetuated in history.

Dr. Howard Kennedy, an owner of stock in the National Road Stage Company, and for a brief period a trustee of the road under the provisions of a Pennsylvania law, enacted in 1848, repealed in 1856, was born in Washington county, Maryland, September 15, 1809. His father was the Hon. Thomas Kennedy, an illustrious citizen, who figured conspicuously in the history of Maryland in the olden time. Dr. Kennedy was a graduate of the Medical University of Baltimore, and a thoroughly educated physician, but the practice of medicine not proving congenial to his tastes, he soon abandoned it and embarked in other pursuits. About the year 1840, or a little before that time, he was appointed a special, confidential agent of the general post office department, in which relation he achieved distinction by detecting numerous mail robberies, and bringing the perpetrators before the courts for trial and punishment. It was through the vigilance of Dr. Kennedy that the mail robberies of the Haldeman brothers, Pete and Abe, and Pate Sides, at Negro Mountain, were discovered, and the offenders apprehended and punished.

The Haldemans and Sides were stage drivers, and their calling through the dismal shades of death and other dark regions in the mountains with big, tempting, mail bags in their charge, no doubt turned their minds to what they considered a speedy, if not altogether a safe method of getting money. Whispers of suspicion growing out of the vigilance of Dr. Kennedy in pushing his investigations, reached the ears of the suspected ones, and they fled to Canada, but not to be thwarted in his purposes, Dr. Kennedy pursued them thither, had them arrested and brought back to Baltimore for trial. Abe Haldeman was acquitted, but Pete and Pate Sides were convicted and sent to the penitentiary. Dr. Kennedy was also the prime mover in bringing to light the noted mail robberies of Dr. John F. Braddee, of Uniontown. as will be seen by the following

As before stated, Dr. Kennedy was one of the owners of the line of coaches known as the National Road Stage Company. This was popularly known as the Stockton line, called "the old line," because it was the oldest on the road. Dr. Kennedy managed all the business of this line relating to the transportation of the mails. He was also one of the original members of the Western Express Company, doing business between Cumberland and Wheeling and Pittsburgh *via* the Monongahela River.

Agents of the stage lines possessed functions somewhat, but not altogether, like those of railroad conductors. Some agents passed constantly over the road, paying bills, providing horses and equipage, and giving general direction to the running of the lines. Others were stationary, attending to local business. These agents were prominent characters of the road, and popularly esteemed as men of high position. One of the earliest agents was Charles Rettig, who subsequently kept the tavern two and one-half miles east of Washington, and referred to in a chapter on taverns and tavern keepers. John Risly, of Frederick, Md., and William Biddle and James Coudy, of Hancock, were old agents of lines east of Cumberland. Redding Bunting, Edward Lane, Theodore Granger and Charles Danforth were agents of the Old Line west of Cumberland, with authority extending to Wheeling. Bunting also kept the National House in Uniontown, and Lane kept the National House in Washington, which were headquarters at those points respectively for their line. Charles Danforth was a leading local agent of the Stockton line at Uniontown.

Stagecoaches operating at night in the mountainous sections of the Old Pike offered highwaymen a temptation hard to resist, so a 'Guardsman' was often sent along on these runs. In scene (ABOVE) men check weapons before entering section of the Pike referred to as "Shades of Death".

The fares on the stage lines were as follows:

From Baltimore to Frederick	$ 2.00
From Frederick to Hagerstown	2.00
From Hagerstown to Cumberland	5.00
From Cumberland to Uniontown	4.00
From Uniontown to Washington	2.25
From Washington to Wheeling	2.00
Through fare	$17.25

A paper was prepared by the agent of the line at the starting point of the coach in the nature of a bill of lading, called the "way bill." This bill was given to the driver, and by him delivered to the landlord at the station immediately upon the arrival of the coach. It contained the name and destination of each passenger, and the several sums paid as fare. It also bore the time of departure from the starting point, and contained blanks for

107

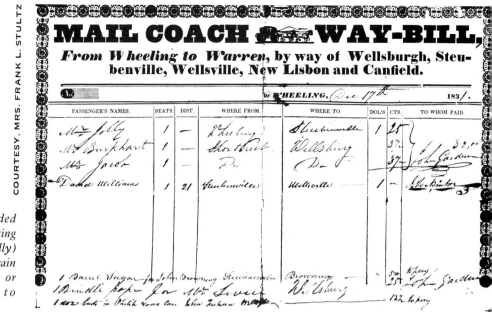

The stagecoach way-bill aided management in tallying revenues and (hopefully) helped coach drivers refrain from pocketing fares or offering transport to non-paying guests.

noting the time of the arrival and departure at every station. The time was noted by an agent of the line, if one were at the station, and in the absence of an agent, the noting was done by the landlord. If a passenger got on at a way station, and this was of daily occurrence, he paid his fare to the landlord or agent, which was duly noted on the way bill, together with the passenger's destination.

Gen. N. P. Talmadge placed on the road what was called the opposition, or Good Intent, line of stages. This was just after the Washingtonian temperance movement. He made temperance speeches along the line, and required his drivers to take the pledge. He stopped at Cambridge and made a speech in the old Presbyterian church, and sang a song, his drivers taking up the chorus. We give in substance, if not in word, a verse:

> Our horses are true and coaches fine,
> No upsets or runaways;
> Nor drunken drivers to swear and curse,
> For its cold water all the days.

In addition to the stage lines hereinbefore mentioned, there was a line known as the "Landlord's Line," put on the road by tavern keepers, prominent among whom were William Willis, Joseph Dilly, and Samuel Luman. There was also a "Pilot Line," and a "Pioneer Line." These lines had but a short run. The railroad managers east of Cumberland favored the older lines, and gave them such advantages in rates that the new lines were compelled to retire from the competition. They sold out their stock to the old companies. James Reeside owned the "Pilot Line," and the "Pioneer Line" was owned by Peters, Moore & Co.

The Good Intent and Stockton lines were taken from the National Road in 1851, and placed on the plank road from Cumberland to West Newton. From the latter point passengers were conveyed by steamboat to Pittsburgh by way of the Youghiogheny river, which was made navigable at that date by a system of locks and dams like that of the Monongahela. Upon the withdrawal of the lines mentioned, a line was put on the National Road by Redding Bunting and Joshua Marshe, and ran as far west as Washington, Pennsylvania. William Hall subsequently purchased the interest of Mr. Marshe in this line, which was kept on the road until about the close of the year 1852, when the era of four-horse coaches ended.

Stage drivers as a class did not rank as high morally as wagoners, but despite this there were among them men of good sense, honest intentions and steady habits. As typical of the better class, the reader who is familiar with the old road will readily recall Redding Bunting, Samuel Luman, Elliott Seaburn, Watty Noble, James Carroll, Aquila and Nat Smith, William Scott, David Gordon, James Burr, William Robinson, John Huhn, David Bell, John Guttery, John Ritter, Joseph Henderson and Peter Null. Others will be instantly recognized as their names shall appear on these pages. It is the sincere belief of all old pike boys that the stage lines of the National Road were never equalled in spirit and dash on any road, in any age or country.

Henry Clay knew many of the old stage drivers personally, and would call them by name when he met them at different points along the road.

Mr. A. J. Endsley, of Somerset, furnishes his juvenile opinion of stages and stage drivers, which was shared in by all the boys of the road, as follows:

"My earliest recollections are intimately associated with coaches, teams and drivers, and like most boys raised in an old stage tavern, I longed to be a man when I could aspire to the greatness and dignity of a professional stage driver. In my boyish eyes no position in life had so many attractions as that of driving a stage team. A Judge, a Congressman, even Henry Clay or President Jackson, did not measure up to the character of John Mills and Charley Howell, in my juvenile fancy."

Mr. Endsley divides the old stage drivers in four classes, as follows: (1) Awkward, slovenly, careless drivers, such as handled the whip and "ribbons" so clumsily, and kept their teams so unseemly together, up hill, down grades and on the level, that it was painful to see them on the box. (2) Cruel men—their cruelty amounting almost to brutality. This class seemed to take a fiendish

Two Concord coaches (BELOW) departing from an Allegheny Mountain Resort Hotel. After stagecoach lines had disappeared Concord coaches were operated by railroad lines and hotels as buses and taxicabs.

delight in whipping, lashing and gashing horses. (3) Careful, easy-going, common, every day kind of drivers—men who never made pretensions to fancy styles. They were such as John Bunting (Old Judy), Jim Reynolds, James Carroll (Flaxey), Blanchard (Hatchet Face), Billy Armor and Josh Boyd. (4) Well dressed drivers, clean and neat in person, and men who regarded sitting down to a meal in shirt sleeves as *contra, bonos mores.* This class manipulated the whip and 'ribbons' scientifically, and sat on the box in a way that showed they were masters of the situation.

John E. Reeside, a son of Commodore James Reeside, the old stage proprietor, who had a general supervision of his father's lines on the National Road, gives three styles of stage driving, as follows, viz: (1) The Flat Rein (English); (2) the Top and Bottom (Pennsylvania); (3) the Side Rein (Eastern).

The compensation paid stage drivers was twelve dollars a month, with boarding and lodging. They took their meals and lodged at the stage houses, except the married men, who lodged in their own dwellings when chance threw them at home.

At Uniontown a number of contiguous frame buildings on Mill and South streets, in the rear of Brownfield's tavern, known as "Hopwood's Row," were occupied almost exclusively by the families of stage drivers.

Daniel Leggett was an old stage driver, well known, and will be long remembered. He once had the distinction of hauling the celebrated Indian chief, Black Hawk, and his *suite.* The party ascended the Ohio river by steamboat, and took stage at Wheeling. Upon entering the coach at that point, Black Hawk showed shyness, fancying it might be a trap set for him by his pale faced enemies, and it required some persuasion by an interpreter, who accompanied his party, to induce him to enter and take a seat. The coach passed over the road without unusual incident until it reached Washington, Pennsylvania. Going down the main street of Washington, from the

Indian Chief Black Hawk (ABOVE) traveling over the Old Pike, became a victim of an overturned coach. Slightly scratched, the chief was nevertheless convinced the accident was a "paleface plot" to assassinate him.

post office, which was in the neighborhood of the court house, the breast strap of one of the wheel horses broke, causing a precipitation of the coach upon the leaders, and the team becoming frightened, dashed down the street at fearful speed. One of the party of Indians was seated by the driver, and thrown off, carrying down with him the driver. The team, thus left without a driver, rushed headlong for the stable of the National House, and at the corner of Main and Maiden streets, the coach upset. It contained nine passengers, eight Indians and one half-breed. The first one to show up from the wreck was Black Hawk, who stood upright in the middle of the street, disclosing a single drop of blood on his forehead, and manifesting much excitement and indignation, as he uttered "Ugh! Ugh! Ugh!" The interpreter had an arm broken,

110

which was the only serious casualty attending the accident. Black Hawk now became almost wholly irreconcilable. The interpretor tried to explain to him the true situation, and to assure him that no harm was aimed at him, but the dusky warrior repelled the approaches of the friendly mediator, and refused to be reconciled. He was now certain that the white men intended to kill him. After a little while the excitement abated, and with it the temper of the unfortunate Indian chieftain. He was persuaded to enter the tavern, and observing that the surroundings were not hostile, threw off his sullenness, and became somewhat sensible of the situation, and apparently reconciled to it. Another coach of the line was provided, and the party proceeded on their journey to parley with the Great Father of the White House.

John Buck was one of the oldest and best stage drivers on the road. He lived in Washington, Pennsylvania, and drove on the old line in the lifetime of Daniel Moore, and was a great favorite of that ancient stage proprietor. When Lafayette visited Washington in 1825, Mr. Moore was active and prominent in arranging for his reception at that place, and assigned John Buck to drive the coach in which the illustrious visitor entered the town. It was a proud day for the old driver, who shared with the hero of the occasion, the plaudits of the people. Buck subsequently became the senior member of the firm of Buck, Lyon & Wolf, contractors, who built most of the locks and dams on the Muskingum river, in the State of Ohio. This old firm was called the "Menagerie Company," on account of the names of its members.

Jack Bailiss was a widely known and popular driver, a married man, and a resident of Washington, Pennsylvania. He was accounted a reckless driver, and delighted in exciting the apprehension of his passengers, often filling them with terror by specimens of what they considered reckless driving. He knew the danger line however, and always

kept within it. He drove the coach from Claysville to Washington, Pennsylvania, in which Gen. Taylor traveled on his way to the Capital to assume the Presidency.

Henry A. Wise, an old driver, is well remembered by the old people of the road on account of the quaintness of his character. He always had plenty of slack in his reins, and as a consequence rarely kept his team straight in the road. It is said that on one occasion, while half asleep on the box, his team turned from the road through an open gap into a field, and commenced eagerly to graze on the growing clover. Wise was tall and spare, and habitually wore a high silk hat.

Jason Eddy was one of the many drivers sent out on the road in an early day from New Jersey by "Commodore" Reeside, as James, the old stage proprietor, was frequently called. Eddy was an expert driver, and it was said of him that "he could turn his team and coach on a silver dollar." He was likewise a good musician, and played well on the bugle. He often entertained his passengers with stirring bugle blasts.

Model (ABOVE) served as three dimensional advertisement in a stagecoach ticket office.

David Bonebraker was a stage driver of good reputation, and a general favorite. While his name would import otherwise, he was a careful driver and never during his whole service did he break a bone of man or beast.

William G. Beck, an old stage driver, has vivid recollections of the road. In a letter he states that in 1846 the Old Line and the Good Intent both carried the mails. There was a "Lock mail" in leather pouches, and a

"Canvas mail," the latter very frequently called "the second mail," carried in alternate months by the respective lines. In December, 1846, he says the Old Line carried the "Lock mail."

The details of an exciting race on the road he furnishes as follows: "A Good Intent coach was driven by Jacob Cronch to the railway station, immediately upon the arrival of the train at Cumberland, loaded up with the 'Canvas mail,' and started off under full speed for the West. The 'Lock mail,' which fell to me, was taken to the post office and overhauled, causing a considerable detention. While waiting in front of the post office for the mail bags, Jacob Shuck and other Good Intent drivers chided me with the fact that the 'Canvas' had such a start that I could not get near it. I made up my mind that if it was in the hides of my two teams I would catch him, and pass him. It was after nightfall, and in crossing a waterway in Cumberland my lamps went out, and what I deemed a calamity turned out in the end to be an advantage. As soon as I crossed the Wills creek bridge, I put my team in a full run and never pulled them up until I reached Rock Hill, seven miles out of Cumberland. At that point, in the winding of the road, I espied the lights on the coach of my rival, while he, by reason of the going out of my lights, was unable to see me, although, on the long stretches, he was constantly watching for a glimpse of me. Much to his surprise I drew up along side of him, and side by side we drove into Frostburg, lashing our tired teams at every jump. The grooms at the Frostburg station had my second team hitched to the coach by the time I was fairly stopped. A friendly driver ran with the way mail to the Frostburg post office, while another re-lit my lamps. I did not leave my seat. The reins over the fresh team were thrown up to me, and I was off again in a full run. The way mail bag was thrown into the front boot as I dashed past the post office. At Sand Spring (foot of Big Savage) I passed the 'Canvas' and held the

Regular stage drivers were usually assigned to one stage of the road and were given one team to work different coaches over that same section. Mail coach drivers like William Beck (ABOVE) would be assigned to one coach working it the length of the route.

lead, trotting my team every inch of the road to Piney Grove, the end of my route, which I reached twenty-two minutes in advance of my competitor. Lem Cross kept the tavern where our line stopped at Piney Grove. I made my route of twenty-two miles with two teams in two hours and ten minutes, fourteen miles of the distance, to the top of Big Savage, being ascending grade.

Redding Bunting was probably more widely known and had more friends than any other old stage driver on the road. His entire service on the road, covering many years, was in connection with the "Old Line." He was a great favorite of Mr. Stockton, the leading proprietor of that line. His commanding appearance is impressed upon the memories of all who knew him. He stood six feet six inches high in his stockings, and straight as an arrow, without any redundant flesh. His complexion was of a reddish hue and his features pronounced and striking. His voice was of the baritone order, deep and sonorous, but he was not loquacious and had a habit of munching. He was endowed with strong common sense, which the pike boys called "horse sense," to emphasize its excellence. He was affable, companionable and convivial. He was a native of Fayette county, Pa., and born in Menallen township. He was not only a stage driver, but a trusted stage agent, stage proprietor, and also a tavern keeper. During the presidency of Mr. Van Buren, it was deemed desirable by the authorities that one of his special messages should be speedily spread before the people. Accordingly arrangements were made by the Stockton line, which had the contract for carrying the mails, to transmit the message of the President with more than ordinary celerity. The Baltimore and Ohio railroad at the time was not in operation west of Frederick City,

Redding Bunting (BELOW) a driver with exceptional talents, carried news of the Mexican War by coach from Cumberland, Maryland to Wheeling, Virginia, a distance of 131 miles in 12 hours.

Maryland. Mr. Bunting, as agent of the company, repaired to that point to receive the coming document and convey it to Wheeling. He sat by the side of the driver the entire distance from Frederick to Wheeling to superintend the mission and urge up the speed. The distance between the points named is two hundred and twenty-two miles, and was covered in twenty-three hours and thirty minutes.

In the year 1846, after the railroad was completed to Cumberland, Redding Bunting rivaled, if he did not surpass, the feat of rapid transit above described. He drove the great mail coach from Cumberland to Wheeling, which carried the message of President Polk, officially proclaiming that war existed between the United States and Mexico. Leaving Cumberland at two o'clock in the morning, he reached Uniontown at eight o'clock of the same morning, breakfasted there with his passengers, at his own house (for he was then the proprietor of the National), and after breakfast, which was soon disposed of, proceeded with his charge, reaching Washington at eleven a.m. and Wheeling at two p.m., covering a distance of one hundred and thirty-one miles in twelve hours. He was not at that time an ordinary driver, but an agent of the line, and took the reins in person for the avowed purpose of making the highest speed attainable.

Joseph Woolley had a brother, William, who was also a well-known stage driver. When the staging days on the road were ended, and the exciting incidents thereof relegated to the domain of history, Joseph and William Woolley sought and obtained employment in the service of the Baltimore and Ohio Railroad company, and both ultimately became competent and trustworthy locomotive engineers.

Samuel Luman was one of the best equipped stage drivers on the road. His experience covers many of the most exciting and interesting events in the road's history. He commenced his career as a stage driver in

113

Samuel Luman, with an amazing display of courage and skill once aborted a desperate attempt to ambush the stagecoach he was driving.

1832. He tells of a collision with highwaymen in the mountains, which was attended by thrilling details. On the 12th of August, 1834, he was on the road between Piney Grove and Frostburg, with a mail and passenger coach going east. After nightfall, and at a point studded by a thick growth of pine trees, he was confronted by a party of foot-pads, five in number, and strange to relate, one a woman, bent on felony. The outlook was alarming. Luman carried no firearms, and there was but one weapon among his passengers, a small, brass pistol, not brought into requisition, as the sequel shows. The assailants had thrown across the road an obstruction like a rude fence, made of logs, stumps and brush. As Luman's trusty leaders approached the obstruction, one of the highwaymen stepped out from his cover and seized a bridle, and the coach was stopped. The assailant ordered Luman to descend from his seat and surrender his charge. This he very politely, but very decidedly declined to do. "What do you want?" queried Luman, with seeming innocence. "We are traders," was the response. "Well," rejoined Luman, coolly, "I have nothing to trade; I am satisfied with my trappings, and not desirous of exchanging them." During this little parley the would-be robber, who held a leader by the bridle, cried out to a partner in crime, who was near at hand, though under cover of darkness, to shoot the driver, and denounced him as a coward for not firing. The party thus addressed then leveled a pistol at Luman and pulled the trigger, but the result was nothing more than a "snap," the night air being damp and the powder failing to explode. These favorable surroundings, no doubt, saved Luman's life. The foot-pads at the heads of the leaders had, in the confusion and excitement of the moment, turned the horses squarely around, so that the leaders faced west, while the wheel horses stood to the east. In this conjuncture the party in charge of the leaders undertook to unhitch them, and to guard against the movements of Luman, wrapped a driving rein tightly around one of his arms. This was Luman's opportunity, and summoning all his resources, he poured a volley of stinging lashes upon his antagonist, smiting him on the face and arm, alternately, and most vigorously. The bandit winced, and soon relinquished his grasp, when, almost in the twinkling of an eye, the team under Luman's skillful hands started up on a full run, leaping the improvised fence, and speeding on, leaving the foot-pads behind to lament their discomfiture. Mr. Luman relates that in crossing the improvised fence, he fairly trembled for the fate of himself and passengers, as the coach was within the ace of capsizing. He also states that the ruffian who seized his leader wore a gown that covered his whole person, tied around the middle of his body with a belt, and that another of his assailants wore a white vest, dark pantaloons, and covered his face with a black mask. The other three kept in the background during the attack, so that he is unable to recall their appearance. Mr. Luman further relates that when the first assault was made on him, he apprized his passengers of the impending danger and besought their assistance, but they crouched in their seats and made no effort to aid him or defend themselves. They were western merchants going east to buy goods, and had among them as much as sixty thousand dollars in cash. When the coach arrived safely at the Highland house, Frostburg, George Evans at that time proprietor thereof, the grateful passengers "took up" a collection for the benefit of their courageous and faithful driver and deliverer, but Luman says the sum proffered was so ludicrously small that he declined to receive it, and ever thereafter regarded that lot of passengers as a "mean set."

David Gordon was sent out from the east by James Reeside, and drove first on the "June Bug Line." Going out west from Claysville soon after he commenced driving, his team ran off with a full load of passengers. Discerning in a moment that the flying team could not be checked by ordinary methods, he pulled it off the road and turned the coach over against a high bank. The passengers were badly frightened, but none were hurt, and attributed their escape from injury to the skillfulness of the driver. After "righting up," the coach but little damaged, proceeded to Roney's Point without further casualty.

Among old stage drivers there was one conspicuous above all others, on account of his immense size. It was Montgomery Demmings, known as "Old Mount." He was six feet and upward in height, and his average weight was four hundred and sixty-five. It was a common remark, in the days of staging on the National Road, that "Old Mount on the front boot of a coach balanced all the trunks that could be put in the rear boot." As he grew old his weight increased, and at his death, upon authority of his widow, was six hundred and fifty pounds. He was born and reared in Allentown, New Jersey, and was sent out on the road in 1836 by James Reeside. His first service was on the "June Bug Line." "Old Mount" relinquished his connection with the passenger coaches, and became a driver on the express line. This line carried small packages of light goods, and oysters, known as fast freight, and the people along the road, by way of derision, called it "The Shake Gut Line." The vehicles of this line were long and strong box-shaped wagons, something like the wagons used for transporting a menagerie. They were drawn by four horses, with relays at established points, driven by check reins or lines, as stage teams were driven. The speed of the express wagons was almost equal to that of the coaches of the stage lines. They made a great noise in their rapid passage over the road, and coming down some of the long hills, could be heard for miles. By the side of the drivers frequently sat one or more way-goers whose necessities impelled them to seek cheap transportation. What proportion of their meager fares went to the driver, and what to the owners of the line, has never been definitely ascertained. "Old Mount" died at McKeesport on March 4, 1855, and thus terminated the career of one whose name was familiarly spoken in every town, tavern and wayside cabin, from Baltimore to Wheeling.

Henry Farwell was an old stage driver. He came to Uniontown in 1839, "the winter of the deep snow." He came on the Oyster Line from Little Crossings, working his way through the snow, which averaged a depth of four feet on the level, and was three days on the way. The oyster boxes were placed on a sled, drawn by six horses, and the Oyster Line made as good time as the stage lines while the deep snow lasted, and passenger coaches, like oyster boxes, were moved on sleds.

Archie McNeil was of the class of merry stage drivers, and enlivened the road with his quaint tricks and humorous jokes. His service as a driver was confined for the most part to the western end of the road, between Brownsville and Wheeling. An unsophisticated youth from the back country, of ungainly form and manners, near the close of the forties, sauntered into Washington, Pennsylvania, to seek employment, with an ambition not uncommon among young men of that period, to become a stage driver. In his wanderings about the town he halted at the National House, then kept by Edward Lane, where he fell in with Archie McNeil, and to him made known the object of his visit. Archie, ever ready to perpetrate a joke, encouraged the aspirations of the young "greenhorn," and questioned him concerning his experience in driving horses and divers other matters and things pertaining to the work he proposed to engage in. Opposite the National House, on the Maiden street front, there was a long wooden shed, into which empty coaches were run for shelter, the tongues thereof protruding toward the street. McNeil proposed to the supplicating youth that he furnish a practical illustration of his talent as a driver, to which he readily assented, and crossing the street to the shed where the coaches were, he was commanded to climb up on the driver's seat, which he promptly did. McNeil then fastened a full set of reins used for driving, to the end of the coach tongue, and handed them up to the young man. He next placed in his hands a driver's whip, and told him to show what he could do. The coach bodies, it will be remembered, were placed on long, wide, and stout leather springs, which caused a gentle rocking when in motion. The weakling, fully equipped as a driver, swayed himself back and forth, cracked the whip first on one side, and then on the other of the tongue, rocked the coach vehemently, manipulated the reins in various forms and with great pomp, and continued exercising himself in this manner for a considerable time, without evincing the slightest consciousness that he was the victim of a joke. A number of persons, the writer

116

of a joke. A number of persons, the writer included, witnessed this ludicrous scene, and heartily enjoyed the fun. Among the spectators was James G. Blaine, then a student at Washington College.

In the year 1835 or 6, Amos Kendall, being Postmaster-General, placed on the road a line of couriers, called the "Pony Express." It was intended to carry light mails with more speed than the general mail was carried by the coaches. The Pony Express was a single horse and a boy rider, with a leather mail pouch thrown over the horse's back, something after the style of the old-fashioned saddlebags. The route for each horse covered a distance of about six miles on the average. The horse was put to his utmost speed, and the rider carried a tin horn which was vigorously blown when approaching a station. William Moore, Thomas Wooley, subsequently stage drivers, William Meredith, Frank Holly and James Neese were among the riders on the Pony Express east of Cumberland, and Sandy Conner, Pate Sides and Thomas A. Wiley, all three afterward stage drivers, and William Conn rode west of Cumberland. Wiley rode from Uniontown to Washington, Pennsylvania, and also between Washington and Wheeling. He went with the log cabin boys from Uniontown to Baltimore in 1840 as a driver of one of the stage teams employed on that occasion.

"The Pony Express" did not remain long on the road, but when it was on, old pike boys say "it kicked up a dust."

Young berrypickers in Winslow Homer's print (OPPOSITE) reflect in wistful silence the lament of many as they watched the old familiar coaches fade into visions of the past.

The picture of the stage coach era herein drawn may be lacking in vigor and perspicuity of style, but it contains no exaggeration. Much more could be written concerning it, and the story would still be incomplete. When the old pike was superseded by the railroad, many of the stage drivers went west and continued their calling on stage lines occupying ground in advance of the approaching railway. Others lingered on the confines of the familiar road, and fell into various pursuits of common life.

We hear no more of the clanging hoof,
And the stage coach, rattling by;
For the steam king rules the traveled world,
And the old pike's left to die.

117

The Conestoga wagon originated about 1750 in a Pennsylvania valley named for the Conestoga Indians. Although built for the farm this sturdy wagon found its way onto the primitive roads of the new republic and for half of a century was a prime mover of American land freight. Seldom identical, each Conestoga was individually constructed for a specific amount of tonnage. A distinguishing characteristic was the bowed bottom which helped stabilize the cargo and strengthened the body. Patriotic in appearance, Conestoga colors were usually white homespun top, blue body and oxblood red undercarriage and wheels. Paint for the wagons often had a buttermilk base. Massive hub of wagon wheel (OPPOSITE).

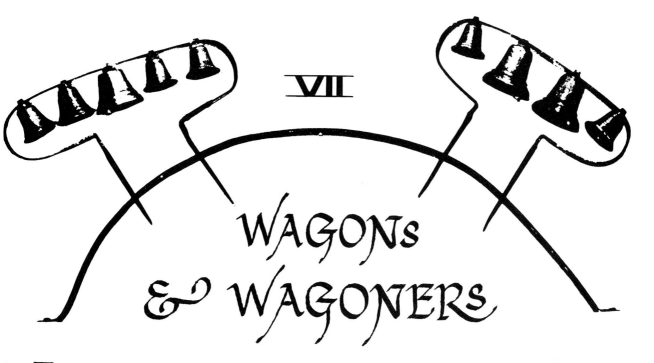

VII

WAGONS & WAGONERS

The first wagons used on the National Road were made with narrow rimmed wheels. It was not long, however, after the opening of the road, until the broad wheeled, or "broad tread wagon," as it was called, was introduced, and came into general use by the "regulars." The "sharpshooters," as a rule, retained the narrow tread, as their wagons were designed mainly for farm service. The width of the broad tread was about four inches, and lighter tolls were exacted at the gates from broad than from narrow tread wagons for the obvious reason that narrow wheels cut deeper into the road than broad wheels.

A gentleman of Wheeling interested in the transportation business at one time, conceived the idea of constructing a wagon that would make so wide a track as to be allowed to pass over the road for a very low rate of toll, if not entirely exempt. His model was a wagon with the rear axle four inches shorter than the front one, so that a track was made of eight inches in width. To this wagon nine horses were attached—three abreast. It passed over the road several times, with Joseph Sopher as driver, attracting much attention, but turning

out a failure as well in the matter of saving toll as in being an impracticable vehicle of transportation.

The bed of the regular road wagon was long and deep, bending upward at the bottom in front and rear. The lower broad side was painted blue, with a movable board inserted above, painted red. The covering was of white

R. DUFF GREEN

Contrary to popular belief, a bell team (ABOVE) was the exception rather than the rule on the Old Pike. But should a bell team wagon break down, it became customary for the wagoner to relinquish his bells to the wagoner who helped him get rolling again. Consequently the expression "being there with bells on" signified arriving safely on time. A wagoner worked his team from three positions: riding, standing on lazy board (both as in illustration above) or walking by front left wheel, keeping team to right side of road. Noting the wagoners' custom, Henry Ford perpetuated this practice by placing auto steering wheel on the left.

canvas stretched over broad wooden bows, so that the old road wagon, probably more as a matter of taste than design, disclosed the tri-colors of the American escutcheon, red, white and blue.

An average load was 6,000 pounds, but loads weighing 10,000 pounds, "a hundred hundred," as all old wagoners boastfully put it, were frequently hauled over the road.

The reader who never saw the endless procession on the old pike, in the days of its glory, may have the impression that the bells used by some of the old wagoners on their teams were like sleigh bells, and in like manner strapped around the horses. But that was not the way of it. The bells of the old wagoners were cone shaped, with an open end, not unlike a small dinner bell, and were attached to a thin iron arch, sprung over the tops of the hames. The motion of the horses caused a quiver in the arch, and the bell teams moved majestically along the road attracting

attention and eliciting admiration. The great majority of wagoners did not use bells.

The men who hauled merchandise over the road were invariably called wagoners, not teamsters, as is the modern word, and they were both, since Webster defines wagoner as one who conducts a wagon, and teamster as one who drives a team. The teams of the old wagoners, consisting, as a rule, of six horses, were very rarely stabled, but rested over night in the wagon yards of the old taverns, no matter how inclement the weather. Blankets were used to protect them in the winter season. Feed troughs were suspended at the rear end of the wagon bed, and carried along in this manner, day after day all the year round. In the evening, when the day's journey was ended, the troughs were taken down and fastened on the tongues of the wagon to which the horses were tied, three on a side, with their heads to the trough. Wagoners carried their beds, rolled up, in the forepart of the wagon, and spread them out in a semi-circle on the bar room floor in front of the big bar room fire upon going to rest. Some of the old bar room grates would hold as much as six bushels of coal, and iron pokers from four to six feet in length, weighing eight and ten pounds, were used for stirring the fires. To get down an icy hill with safety, it was necessary to use an ice cutter, a rough lock, or a clevis, and sometimes all combined, contingent upon the thickness and smoothness of the ice, and the length and steepness of the hill. The ice cutter was of steel or iron, in appearance like a small sled, fitted on the hind wheels, which were first securely locked. The rough lock was a short chain with large, rough links, and the clevis was like that used on an ordinary plow, except that it was larger and stronger. These instruments were essential parts of the wagoners' "outfit." There were two classes of wagoners, the "regular" and the "sharpshooter." The regular was on the road constantly with his team and wagon, and had no other pursuit than hauling goods and merchandise on the road. The sharpshooters were for the most part farmers, who put their farm teams on the road in seasons when freights were high, and took them off when prices of hauling declined; and there was jealousy between the two classes. The regular drove his team about fifteen miles a day on the average, while the sharpshooter could cover twenty miles and more. Line teams were those controlled by an association or company. Many of the regular wagoners became members of these companies and put in their teams. The main object of the combination was to transport goods more rapidly than by the ordinary method. Line teams were stationed along the road, at distances of about fifteen miles, and horses were exchanged after the manner of the stage lines. Many of the old wagoners had bull-dogs tied at the rear of their wagons, and these dogs were often seen pressing with all their strength against the collar about their necks,

Ornate ironwork on wagon toolbox (ABOVE) expressed individuality of smiths and wagoners. Extended lazy board slides under wagon bed when not in use. Iron brake handle is in forward position which applies brake to wheel. Photograph (BELOW) shows hammer-shaped pin which held doubletree to wagon. In case of an upset or accident pin could be quickly pulled to free team from wagon. As a hammer it was also handy for adjustments and repairs often necessary on the road.

121

On the road, wagon's feed box was carried at the rear (ABOVE LEFT). Early Conestogas, with a two-horse, or four-horse team, fed horses from feedbox at rear. When six-horse teams became the working standard, the wagoner, when stopped for the night, placed feed box on wagon tongue (DRAWING ABOVE) and tied horses three to a side for feeding.

as if to aid the horses in moving their load; and this is probably the origin of the common form of boast about a man being equal in strength to "a six-horse team with a cross dog under the wagon."

Gears was the name old wagoners applied to harness. The gears used on the team of the regular wagoner were of immense proportions. The back bands were fifteen and the hip straps ten inches wide, and heavy black housing covered the horses' shoulders down to the bottom of the hames. The traces used were iron chains with short and thick links. It required a strong man to throw these heavy gears on the back of a big horse. Heavy and broad as they were, these gears were not out of proportion to the large fat horses of the old teams, and looked well on their broad and shining backs. The wagoner's saddle was unique. It was made over an ordinary wooden model, covered with thick, black leather, and had long and wide skirts or aprons, cut straight on the edges and ends.

The whip used by old wagoners was apparently five feet long, thick and hard at the butt, and tapering rapidly to the end in a silken cracker. Battley White, of Centerville, Washington county, Pa., made more of these whips than any other man on the road. The interior of his whip was a raw hide. John Morrow, of Petersburg, Somerset county, Pa., also made many whips for the old wagoners. There was another whip, much used by old wagoners, known as the "Loudoun Whip." The inner portion of this whip was an elastic wooden stock, much approved by the wagoners. It was manufactured in the village of Loudoun, Franklin county, Pa., and hence its name. It was used almost exclusively on what was called the "Glade Road," from Philadelphia to Pittsburgh, *via* Chambersburg and Bedford.

Old wagoners, as a class, were robust, hardy, honest and jovial. But one of the long list is remembered as a criminal. His name was Ben Pratt, and he belonged to Philadelphia. He turned out to be a counterfeiter of coin and currency, and suffered the punishment that all counterfeiters deserve. Many old wagoners were fond of fun and frolic, but very few of them were intemperate, although they had the readiest opportunities for unrestrained drinking. Every old tavern had its odd shaped little bar, ornamented in many instances with fancy lattice work, and well stocked with whiskey of the purest distillation, almost as cheap as water. In fact all kinds of liquors were kept at the old taverns of the National Road, except the impure stuff of the present day. The bottles used were of plain glass, each marked in large letters with the name of the liquor it contained, and the old landlord would place these bottles on the narrow counter of the little bar, in the presence of a room filled with wagoners, so that all could have free access to them. None of the old tavern keepers made profit from the sales of liquor. They kept it more for the accommodation of their guests, than for money making purposes. There was probably a tavern on every mile of the road, between Cumberland and Wheeling, and all combined did not realize as much profit from the sales of liquor in a year as is realized by one licensed hotel keeper of Uniontown, at the present day.

Many old wagoners wore a curious garment called a hunting shirt. It was of woolen stuff, after the style of "blue jeans," with a large cape trimmed with red. It was called a hunting shirt because first used by hunters in the mountains.

Some of the old wagoners of the National Road became rich. John Snider was one of these. He drove a six-horse team on the road for twenty years, and died on his farm near Uniontown in December, 1889, much lamented. Few men possessed more of the higher attributes of true manhood than John

National Road traffic included vehicles of every size, shape and description as evidenced by toll rate sign (page 33). Express wagons similar to drawing in Harper's Weekly (ABOVE) rattled over the Pike at speeds equal to the fastest coaches. Calling a spade a spade, one express company was dubbed the Shake Gut Line.

123

Shaping and fitting iron rims to the giant wagon wheels took skill, strength and a good measure of luck. Workmen (ABOVE) illustrate tasks required in applying rim to wheel in 18th Century France. Differing from method above, American smith applied rim to wheel while iron was hot. When iron cooled, shrinkage held rim tightly in place. But occasionally, too much contraction would demolish the wheel.

Snider. The author of this volume gratefully and cheerfully acknowledges his indebtedness to John Snider for many of the facts and incidents it contains.

We have in the story of these old wagoners, examples of the possibilities for achievement, under the inspiring genius of American institutions. Poor boys, starting out in life as wagoners, with wages barely sufficient for their subsistence, pushing on and up with ceaseless vigilance, attaining the dignity of farmers, in all ages the highest type of industrial life, and now each bearing, though meekly, the proud title of "freeholder," which Mr. Blaine said in his celebrated eulogium of Garfield, "has been the patent

and passport of self-respect with the Anglo-Saxon race ever since Horsa and Hengist landed on the shores of England."

Thomas Corwin, the famous Ohio statesman and popular orator of the olden time, was not a stage driver, but he was a wagoner, and one of the rallying cries of his friends, in the campaign that resulted in his election as governor, was: "Hurrah for Tom Corwin, the wagoner boy."

Joseph Lawson was, like his fellow teamster, John Galwix, considered a fancy wagoner. He took pride in his calling, and his team consisted of six stallions, well mated and of gigantic size. The gears he used were the very best of the John Morrow pattern, and his "outfit" attracted attention and evoked words of praise from the throngs that lined the road in that day. There was a regulation tread and an air about the old wagoner, especially of the regular line, that rose almost, if not altogether, to the standard of dignity.

William Ashton, a well-known old wagoner, was an Englishman by birth. He was also an old tavern keeper. He was noted for his mental vivacity, and for his achievements as an athlete. At Petersburg, he once bounded over the top of one of the big road wagons with the aid of a long pole. He kept a tavern at Funkstown, seventy miles west of Baltimore, and was largely patronized by wagoners. While keeping tavern he had two teams on the road in charge of hired drivers. This was as early as 1835. His drivers were Samuel Kelly and William Jones, and they hauled goods from Hagerstown, Maryland (then the terminus of the railroad), to Terre Haute, Indiana, and to Springfield, Illinois, involving a trip of four months duration, and the compensation was six dollars per hundred pounds.

Mr. Barcus states in a letter to the writer of these pages, that the first lot of goods shipped over the Baltimore and Ohio railway, after its completion to Cumberland, destined for Wheeling, was consigned to Shriver and Dixon, commission merchants of Cumberland, and by that firm consigned to Forsythe and Son, of Wheeling. This lot of goods aggregated 6,143 pounds, an average load for a six-horse team, and Mr. Barcus contracted with Shriver and Dixon to haul it through to Wheeling in six days for fifty cents a hundred, which he accomplished. He further states that a delegation of wholesale and retail merchants of Wheeling met him at Steenrod's tavern, east of Wheeling Hill, and escorted him to town, then a place of 4,000 or 5,000

Model of heavy farm wagon (BELOW) shows basic design that endured for many decades. Often used by sharpshooters or part-time wagoners, these wagons, as well as the Conestogas, had removable bodies and special racks could be substituted for haying, hauling timber and other similar chores around the farm.

inhabitants, and in the evening there was public rejoicing over the unprecedented event of goods reaching Wheeling from Baltimore in the short space of seven days.

There was an Ohio man of the name of Lucas, called Gov. Lucas, because a man of like name was an early Governor of Ohio, who was an old wagoner, and his team consisted of but five horses, yet he hauled the biggest loads on the road. He was the owner of the team he drove. In the year 1844, one of his loads weighed twelve thousand pounds—"one hundred and twenty hundred," as the old wagoners termed it, and the biggest load hauled over the road up to that date.

In the year 1842 John Snider hauled a load of butter from Wheeling to Washington, D. C. The owner of this butter was a man by the name of Oyster, a butter dealer of Wheeling. He could have shipped his butter from Cumberland to its destination by rail, as the Baltimore & Ohio road had just then been finished to Cumberland; but his animosity against railroads was so deep-seated that he engaged Snider to haul it all the way through

John Snider (ABOVE), who became a well-to-do wagoner on the Old Pike, recalled spending three days traveling a mud road between Frederick, Maryland and Washington, D. C.

with his big team. On his way to Washington with this load he struck off from the National Road at Frederick City, Maryland. He reached that city on Christmas night and "put up" at Miller's tavern. The guests of that old tavern danced all of that night, and early in the morning of the day after Christmas, Snider "pulled out" on a strange road for the city of Washington with his load of butter. He was three days on a mud road between Frederick and Washington, but, nevertheless, delivered his butter in "good condition" to the consignee. This butter was bought up in small quantities in the vicinity of Wheeling for ten cents per pound, and Snider got two dollars and fifty cents per hundred pounds for hauling it to Washington.

There is not a more familiar name among the old pike boys than that of Morris Mauler. He was an old wagoner, stage driver and tavern keeper. He was born in Uniontown in

A restored Pennsylvania farm wagon (ABOVE) with homespun top, built about 1860, now in the Smithsonian Institution.

the year 1806. The house in which he first beheld the light of day, was a log building on the Skiles corner, kept as a tavern by his father. Before he reached the age of twenty-one he was on the road with a six-horse team and a big wagon, hauling goods from the city of Baltimore to points west. He continued a wagoner for many years, and afterward became a stage driver. He drove on Stockton's line. From stage driving he went to tavern keeping. His first venture as a tavern keeper was at Mt. Washington, when the old tavern stand at that point was owned by the late Hon. Nathaniel Ewing. He subsequently and successively kept the old Probasco house at Jockey Hollow, the old Gaither house, the Yeast house, and a house in Hopwood. He always furnished good entertainment for strangers and travelers, as well as for friends and acquaintances, and as a consequence, was well patronized.

Morris Mauler (BELOW) began his career as wagoner in the 1820's, then became a stagecoach driver and eventually turned to tavern keeping as did a number of the Old Pike boys.

Robert Allison, one of the best known of the old wagoners, was a fighting man. He did not seem to be quarrelsome, yet was often, as by some sort of untoward destiny, involved in pugilistic encounters along the road. In one of these at Fear's tavern, on Keyser's Ridge, he bit off the nose of a stage driver.

Henry Puffenberger, a "regular," given to blustering, but not a vicious man, and Jacob Breakiron, a "sharpshooter" and a fat man, met one day on the road and indulged in a wrangle about the right of way. Strings of fresh broken stone on either side of the road, as was often the case, left but a narrow passage where the meeting occurred, and this led to the difficulty. "Old Puff," as he was called, demanded of Breakiron, with an air of authority, that he should "turn out." Breakiron declined to obey, and showed a determined spirit of resistance. After an exchange of angry words Puffenberger inquired of Breakiron his name, and he answered, "my name is Breakiron." "That," said Puffenberger, "is a hard name," but you look harder than your name." "I am as hard as my name," said Breakiron, "and what is your name?" "Puffenberger," was the reply. "That," said Breakiron, "is a windy name." "Yes," rejoined Puffenberger, "but there is thunder with it." After this explosion of wit the contestants compromised, shook hands, and passed without colliding. Puffenberger was a Maryland man, became a Confederate soldier, and was killed in battle. Breakiron was a farmer of Georges Township, Fayette county, Pennsylvania.

James Murray, an old wagoner, is remembered for his extravagance of speech. One of his sayings was, that "he saw the wind blow so hard on Keyser's Ridge, that it took six men to hold the hair on one man's head."

Neither tradition or kindred evidence was necessary to prove the race status of Westley Strother. He showed up for himself. He was as black as black could be, and a stalwart in size and shape. He was well liked by all the old wagoners, and by every one who knew him.

127

He was mild in manner, and honest in purpose. He had the strongest affection for the road, delighted in its stirring scenes, and when he saw the wagons and the wagoners, one after another, departing from the old highway, he repined and prematurely died at Uniontown.

John Deets was a wagoner on the road as early as 1826, before the invention of the rubber, or at least before its application to wagons on the National Road. The following from his own pen furnishes a graphic account of life on the road in his day:

...The pike boys had some hard times and they had some good times. They were generally very fond of sport, and mostly tried to put up where the landlord was a fiddler, so that they could take a hoe-down. Every one carried his own bed, and after they had all the sport they wanted they put their beds down on the floor in a circle, with their feet to the fire, and slept like a mouse in a mill. And with regard to getting up and down the hills. They had no trouble to get up, but the trouble was in getting down, for they had no rubbers then, and to tight lock would soon wear out their tires. They would cut a small pole about 10 or 11 feet long and tie it to the bed with the lock chain and then bend it against the hind wheel and tie to the feed trough, or the hind part of the wagon bed, just tight enough to let the wheel turn slow. Sometimes one driver would wear out from 15 to 20 poles between Baltimore and Wheeling. Sometimes others would cut down a big tree and tie it to the hind end of the wagon and drop it at the foot of the hill. When there was ice, and there was much of it in winter, they had to use rough locks and cutters, and the wagon would sometimes be straight across the road, if not the hind end foremost. The snow was sometimes so deep that they had to go through fields, and shovel the drifts from the fences, and often had to get sleds to take their loads across Negro Mountain, and on as far as Hopwood. Those of us who had to go through the fields were three days going nine miles. This was in the neighborhood of Frostburg, Md.

128

According to wagoner, John Deets (ABOVE) a large tree would often be tied to the back axle and dragged behind to slow the wagon on steep grades. Ellis B. Woodward (BELOW) was a sharpshooter and made countless trips over the Old Pike hauling freight in his Conestoga wagon.

There were no bridges then across the Monongahela or the Ohio rivers. Wagoners had to ferry across in small flat-boats, and sometimes to lay at the rivers for some days, until the ice would run out or the river freeze over. A small bridge across Dunlap's creek, at Brownsville, broke down with one of the pike boys and did a great deal of damage. Sometimes a barrel of coffee would spring a leak and the coffee would be scattered along the road, and women would gather it up and be glad for such a prize. The writer has scattered some in his time. Some of the old citizens of Uniontown, no doubt, well remember the time, when scores of poor slaves were driven through that place, handcuffed and tied two and two to a rope that was extended some 40 or 50 feet, one on each side. And thousands of droves of hogs were driven through to Baltimore, some from Ohio. Sometimes they would have to lay by two or three days on account of the frozen road, which cut their feet and lamed them. While the writer was wagoning on the old pike, the canal was made from Cumberland to Harper's Ferry. The pike boys were bitterly opposed to railroads and so were the tavern keepers.

Robert Q. Fleming, an old wagoner, hauled whiskey from the old Overholt distillery, near Mt. Pleasant, to Baltimore for many years, and loaded back with merchandise to various points in the west. One of his earliest back loads consisted of oysters for Pittsburgh, *via* Brownsville. The oyster boxes were piled up to the canvas covering, and upon reaching Brownsville he was required to drive down the wharf to the steamboat landing, which was "sidling," and at the time icy. Some of the top boxes fell out and were broken, whereupon the bystanders helped themselves to fresh shell oysters. They were not carried away, but the eager oyster lovers picked them up, racked open the shells on the wagon wheels and gulped down the juicy bivalves on the ground. Fleming was "docked," as they termed the abating of loss.

A great phenomenon occurred on the 13th of November, 1833, often called, the Shooting Stars. That circumstance caused a great deal of excitement. Some became very much alarmed, and it was reported that some went crazy, and thought the world was coming to an end. The writer was at Hopwood that night with his team and wagon. The phenomenon was also seen in Ohio.

One wagoner of the road vividly recalled in his later years the night of the Shooting Stars, November 13, 1833. At that time it was described by the press "...the whole firmament, over all the United States, being then, for hours, in fiery commotion."

*Sidewheeler "Wild Wagoner" (ABOVE) dramatically characterizes
a hauler of freight. How wagoners themselves viewed this visual
comment is a matter for speculation.*

The following letters from Jesse J. Peirsol, a prosperous farmer of Fayette county, Pennsylvania, of vigorous health and unimpaired memory, furnish a graphic description of life on the road in its palmy days:

...I have stayed overnight...when there would be thirty-six horse teams in the wagon yard, one hundred Kentucky mules in an adjacent lot, one thousand hogs in other enclosures, and as many fat cattle from Illinois in adjoining fields. The music made by this large number of hogs, in eating corn on a frosty night, I will never forget. After supper and attention to the teams, the wagoners would gather in the bar room and listen to music on the violin, furnished by one of their fellows, have a "Virginia hoe-down," sing songs, tell anecdotes, and hear the experience of drivers and drovers from all points on the road, and when it was all over, unroll their beds, lay them down on the floor before the bar room fire, side by side, and sleep, with their feet near the fire, as soundly as under the paternal roof.

In September, 1844 or 5, my father came home from Uniontown late at night, and woke me up to tell me that there had been a big break in the Pennsylvania Canal, and that all western freights were coming out over the National Road in wagons. The stage coaches brought out posters, soliciting teams. By sunrise next morning, I was in Brownsville with my team, and loaded up at Cass's warehouse with tobacco, bacon, and wool, and whipped off for Cumberland. I drove to Hopwood the first day and stayed overnight with John Wallace. That night Thomas Snyder, a Virginia wagoner, came into Hopwood with a load of flour from a back country mill. When we got beyond Laurel Hill, Snyder retailed his flour by the barrel to the tavern keepers, and was all sold out when we reached Coonrod's tavern, on Big Savage. I was a mere boy, and Snyder told me to unhitch and feed, but leave the harness on. At midnight we rose, hitched up, Snyder lending me two horses, making me a team of eight, pulled out, and reached Cumberland that night. On leaving Coonrod's the night was dark, and I shall never forget the sounds of crunching stones under the wheels of my wagon, and the streaks of fire rolling out from the horses' feet. In Cumberland, we found the commission houses, and the cars on sidings filled with goods, and men cursing loudly because the latter were not unloaded. Large boxes of valuable goods were likewise on the platform of the station, protected by armed guards. After unloading my own load, I reloaded at McKaig & Maguire's commission house for Brownsville, at one dollar and twenty-five cents a hundred. We reached Brownsville without incident or accident, made a little money, and loaded back again for Cumberland. On my return I found plenty of goods for shipment, and loaded up at Tuttle's house for Wheeling, at two dollars and twenty-five cents a hundred. In coming back, it looked as if the whole earth was on the road; wagons, stages, horses, cattle, hogs, sheep, and turkeys without number. Teams of every description appeared in view, from the massive outfit of Governor Lucas down to the old bates hitched to a chicken coop. The commission merchants, seeing the multitude of wagons, sought to reduce prices, whereupon the old wagoners called a meeting and made a vigorous kick against the proposed reduction. It was the first strike I ever heard of. Nothing worried a sharpshooter more than lying at expense in Cumberland waiting for a load. Two of the "sharps," unwilling to endure the delay caused by the strike, drove their four-horse rigs to a warehouse to load at the reduction. This excited the "regulars," and they massed with horns, tin buckets, oyster-cans and the like, and made a descent upon the "sharps," pelting and guying them unmercifully. An old wagoner named Butler commanded the striking regulars with a pine sword, and marched them back and forth through the streets. Finally the police quelled the disturbance, and the "sharps" loaded up and drove out sixteen miles, to find

their harness cut and their axles sawed off in the morning. In this dilemma an old regular, going down empty for a load, took the contract of the "sharps," and made them promise to never return on the road, a promise they faithfully kept...

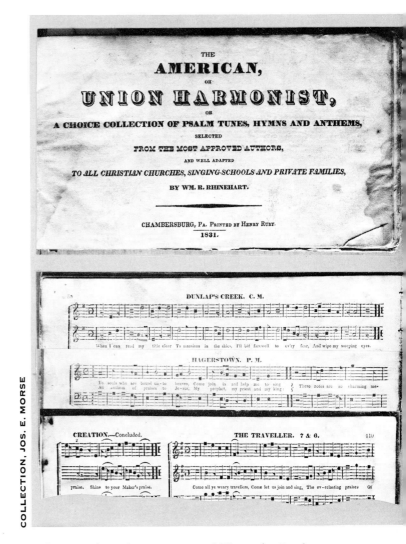

COLLECTION, JOS. E. MORSE

Religion and music were a part of life on the Road. Book (ABOVE) contained several songs collected along its path. One can almost hear the robust voices of wagoners booming out a familiar theme expressed in "The Traveller": "We've had a tedious journey and tiresome it is true, but see how many dangers the Lord has brought us through."

131

WAGONERS OF THE NATIONAL ROAD

Henry Clay Rush (1) and William "Wagoner Billy" Shaw (2) left the road to become tavern keepers. Both men, at different times, presided over the popular Searight tavern.

1   2

A true story of crime and detection on the National Road in which the victim turns sleuth and produces amazing results.

The year 1823 developed one of the most extraordinary examples of grand larceny that ever occurred on the road, and excited the people all along the line from Baltimore to the farthest point west. During the early spring of the year mentioned a merchant whose name was Abraham Boring, doing business in an Ohio town, took passage in a coach of one of the regular stage lines for Baltimore to purchase a stock of fresh goods. At Tomlinson's tavern, west of Cumberland, John Keagy and David Crider, merchants, of Salisbury, Somerset county, Pennsylvania, took seats in the same coach that was conveying Boring, destined also for Baltimore, on a like mission. It required considerable time to reach Baltimore, and passengers in a stage coach became acquainted, one with another. The three merchants not only became personally acquainted with each other, during their long stage ride, but formed strong friendly relations. Reaching Baltimore they stopped together at the same hotel and talked over their business, the quality and quantity of goods required by each forming the leading topic of their conversation. They went out among the wholesale stores of the city and bought the goods they desired, the

stock purchased by Mr. Boring being much larger, finer and more varied than the stock bought by the Somerset county merchants. Upon completing his purchases, Mr. Boring's first thought was to have his goods safely shipped upon the best terms obtainable. Messrs. Keagy and Crider kindly tendered their services to aid him in engaging a trusty wagoner to haul his goods to Ohio, and introduced one Edward Tissue as the right man for that purpose. Tissue was engaged, but one wagon bed would not hold all the goods, and Tissue brought in and introduced another wagoner by the name of Edward Mitchell, who was engaged to haul the remnant that could not be handled by Tissue. Mr. Boring having arranged for the transportation of his goods, said good-bye to his friends Keagy and Crider, and left for his home in Ohio. His goods not arriving when due, he supposed some accident had caused a delay, and that they would be forthcoming as soon as practicable. But days and weeks passed and Mr. Boring began to feel uneasy about the long delay, and wrote the consignors in Baltimore for an explanation. They replied that the goods had been carefully loaded in the wagons of Tissue and Mitchell, according to the agreement, and they knew nothing of their destiny beyond that. Boring then took to the road to find his goods. He went first to Baltimore and learned that Tissue and Mitchell had left the city with the goods in

132

John Kelso (3), was a wagoner turned tavern keeper. John Thompson (4) gave up wagoning to pan for gold as a forty-niner. Moderately successful, he returned to his farm and struck oil.

their wagons, and proceeded westward. He traced them as far as Hagerstown, and at that point lost his clue. He proceeded to Cumberland without tidings of his lost goods. From Cumberland he went on, making inquiry at every tavern and toll gate, until he reached Somerfield, but heard nothing of Tissue or his companion, Mitchell. He put up for the night at a tavern in Somerfield, and while at supper discovered an important clue. The waiting maid at the table wore a tortoise shell comb, resembling very much those in a package he had bought in Baltimore. In polite and delicate terms he inquired of the girl where she obtained so handsome a comb. She replied, "In a store at Salisbury." In an instant Mr. Boring recalled his fellow merchants and recent fellow travelers, Messrs. Keagy and Crider, of Salisbury, but concluding that they had purchased the same quality of combs in Baltimore, went to bed, with a purpose of continuing his researches along the National Road. During the night he changed his purpose, and in the morning returned to Tomlinson's tavern, and thence directly to Salisbury. Reaching Salisbury he entered a store, and to his amazement saw upon the counters and shelves various articles which he recognized as belonging to his stock. Investigation disclosed a remarkable example of criminal conduct. Keagy, Crider, Tissue and Mitchell entered into a conspiracy to steal Boring's goods. The acquaintance formed in the stage coach constituted the initial point of the scheme, and Keagy and Crider found ready confederates in Tissue and Mitchell. There was of course to be a division of the spoils, but in what proportion never was made public. The wagoners to avoid identification changed the color of their wagon beds, and upon reaching Hagerstown diverged from the National Road and took the country by-ways. The goods were placed at first in a large barn in the vicinity of Salisbury, and thence carried in small lots to the store of Keagy & Co. A portion of the goods consisting of fine chinaware, thought to be too expensive for the Salisbury trade, was broken up and buried underground. There was a third owner of the Salisbury store by the name of Markley, who did not accompany his partners on their tour to raise stock. Boring, after thoroughly satisfying himself that he had found his goods, proceeded to Somerset and swore out a warrant against the parties accused. The warrant was placed for execution in the hands of Sheriff Philson of Somerset county. Keagy was first arrested and promptly gave bail for trial, but goaded by the weight of his offense, soon thereafter committed suicide. Tissue fled the jurisdiction and was never apprehended. Crider also fled and located in the wilds of Ohio. Markley essayed to flee, but made a failure of it.

133

When, at last, the Conestoga horse yielded up the palm to the Iron horse, and it became manifest that the glory of the old road was departing, never to return, the old wagoners, many of whom had spent their best days on the road, sang in chorus the following lament:

Now all ye jolly wagoners,
                who have got good wives,
Go home to your farms,
                and there spend your lives.
When your corn is all cribbed,
                and your small grain is good,
You'll have nothing to do
                But curse the railroad.

R. DUFF GREEN

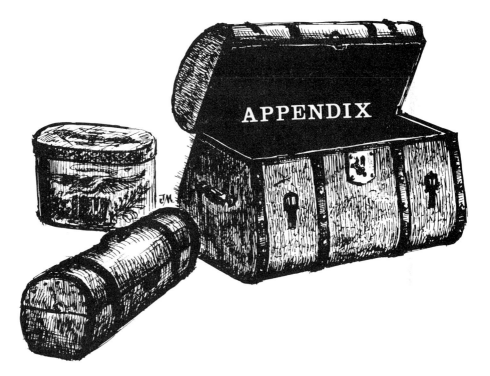

Appropriations by Congress for making, repairing and continuing the National Road. Aggregate of Appropriations, $6,824,919.30

U.S. half dollar, obverse.

1. Act of March 29, 1806, authorizes the President to appoint a commission of three citizens to lay out a road four rods in width " from Cumberland or a point on the northern bank of the river Potomac in the State of Maryland, between Cumberland and the place where the main road leading from Gwinn's to Winchester, in Virginia, crosses the river, * * * to strike the river Ohio at the most convenient place between a point on its eastern bank, opposite to the northern boundary of Steubenville and the mouth of Grave creek, which empties into the said river a little below Wheeling, in Virginia." Provides for obtaining the consent of the States through which the road passes, and appropriates for the expenses, to be paid from the reserve fund under the act of April 30, 1802.....................................$ 30,000 00

2. Act of February 14, 1810, appropriates to be expended under the direction of the President, in making the road between Cumberland and Brownsville, to be paid from fund act of April 30, 1802   60,000 00

3. Act of March 3, 1811, appropriates to be expended under the direction of the President, in making the road between Cumberland and Brownsville, and authorizes the President to permit deviations from a line established by the Commissioners under the original act as may be expedient; *Provided*, that no deviation shall be made from the principal points established on said road between Cumberland and Brownsville, to be paid from fund act of April 30, 1802.........................   50,000 00

4. Act of February 26, 1812, appropriates balance of a former appropriation not used, but carried to surplus fund.................................   3,786 60

5. Act of May 6, 1812, appropriates to be expended under direction of the President, for making the road from Cumberland to Brownsville, to be paid from fund act of April 30, 1802...............   30,000 00

6. Act of March 3, 1813 (General Appropriation Bill), appropriates for making the road from Cumberland to the State of Ohio, to be paid from fund act of April 30, 1802.........................   140,000 00

7. Act of February 14, 1815, appropriates to be expended under the direction of the President, for making the road between Cumberland and Brownsville, to be paid from fund act of April 30, 1802..   100,000 00

8. Act of April 16, 1816 (General Appropriation Bill), appropriates for making the road from Cumberland to the State of Ohio, to be paid from the fund act, April 30, 1802.........................   300,000 00

9. Act of April 14, 1818, appropriates to meet claims due and unpaid.....................................   52,984 60
Demands under existing contracts.............   260,000 00
from money in the treasury not otherwise appropriated.

10. Act of March 3, 1819, appropriates for existing claims and contracts...................... 250,000 00
    Completing road............................ 285,000 00
    To be paid from reserved funds, acts admitting Ohio, Indiana, and Illinois.

11. Act of May 15, 1820, appropriates for laying out the road between Wheeling, Va., and a point on the left bank of the Mississippi river, between St. Louis and the mouth of the Illinois river, road to be eighty feet wide and on a straight line, and authorizes the President to appoint Commissioners. To be paid out of any money in the treasury not otherwise appropriated.............. 10,000 00

12. Act of April 11, 1820, appropriates for completing contract for road from Washington, Pa., to Wheeling, out of any money in the treasury not otherwise appropriated.......................... 141,000 00

13. Act of February 28, 1823, appropriates for repairs between Cumberland and Wheeling, and authorizes the President to appoint a superintendent at a compensation of $3.00 per day. To be paid out of money not otherwise appropriated............. 25,000 00

U.S. copper penny, obverse and reverse.

14. Act of March 3, 1825, appropriates for opening and making a road from the town of Canton, in the State of Ohio, opposite Wheeling, to Zanesville, and for the completion of the surveys of the road, directed to be made by the act of May 15, 1820, and orders its extension to the permanent seat of government of Missouri, and to pass by the seats of government of Ohio, Indiana, and Illinois, said road to commence at Zanesville, Ohio; also authorizes the appointment of a superintendent by the President, at a salary of $1,500 per annum, who shall make all contracts, receive and disburse all moneys, &c.; also authorizes the appointment of one commissioner, who shall have power according to provisions of the act of May 15, 1820; $10,000 of the money appropriated by this act is to be expended in completing the survey mentioned. The whole sum appropriated to be advanced from moneys not otherwise appropriated, and replaced from reserve fund, acts admitting Ohio, Indiana, Illinois, and Missouri........................ 150,000 00

15. Act of March 14, 1826 (General Appropriation Bill), appropriates for balance due superintendent, $3,000; assistant superintendent, $158.90; contractor, $252.13............................ 3,411 03
    from moneys not otherwise appropriated.

16. Act of March 25, 1826 (Military Service), appropriates for continuation of the Cumberland Road during the year 1825................... 110,749 00

17. Act of March 2, 1827 (Military Service), appropriates for construction of road from Canton to Zanesville, and continuing and completing the survey

Spanish one half Reale, obverse and reverse (minted in Mexico).

Spanish 2 Reales or 2 bits, reverse.

from Zanesville to the seat of government of Missouri, to be paid from reserve fund, acts admitting Ohio, Indiana, Illinois, and Missouri........... 170,000 00

For balance due superintendent, from moneys not otherwise appropriated 510 00

18. Act of March 2, 1827, appropriates for repairs between Cumberland and Wheeling, and authorizes the appointment of a superintendent of repairs, at a compensation to be fixed by the President. To be paid from moneys not otherwise appropriated. The language of this act is, "For repairing the public road from Cumberland to Wheeling"..... 30,000 00

19. Act of May 19, 1828, appropriates for the completion of the road to Zanesville, Ohio, to be paid from fund, acts admitting Ohio, Indiana, Illinois, and Missouri.............................. 175.000 00

20. Act of March 2, 1829, appropriates for opening road westwardly, from Zanesville, Ohio, to be paid from fund, acts admitting Ohio, Indiana, Illinois, and Missouri.............................. 100,000 00

21. Act of March 2, 1829, appropriates for opening road eighty feet wide in Indiana, east and west from Indianapolis, and to appoint two superintendents, at $800 each per annum, to be paid from fund, acts admitting Ohio, Indiana, Illinois, and Missouri.............................. 51,600 00

22. Act of March 3, 1829, appropriates for repairing bridges, &c., on road east of Wheeling.......... 100.000 00

23. Act of May 31, 1830 (Internal Improvements), appropriates for opening and grading road west of Zanesville, Ohio, $100,000; for opening and grading road in Indiana, $60,000, commencing at Indianapolis, and progressing with the work to the eastern and western boundaries of said State; for opening, grading, &c., in Illinois, $40,000, to be paid from reserve fund, acts admitting Ohio, Indiana, Illinois, and Missouri; for claims due and remaining unpaid on account of road east of Wheeling, $15.000; to be paid from moneys in the treasury not otherwise appropriated................ 215.000 00

To this act is appended the following note:

"I approve this bill, and ask a reference to my communication to Congress of this date in relation thereto.

"ANDREW JACKSON."*

*The following is the communication referred to by President Jackson:

SPECIAL MESSAGE.

MAY 30, 1830.

To the Senate of the United States :

Gentlemen : I have approved and signed the bill entitled "An act making appropriations for examinations and surveys, and also for certain works of internal improvement," but as the phraseology of the section, which appropriates the sum of eight thousand dollars for the road from Detroit to Chicago, may be construed to authorize the application of the appropriation for the continuance of the road beyond the limits of the territory of Michigan, I desire to be understood as having approved this bill with the understanding that the road, authorized by this section, is not to be extended beyond the limits of the said territory. ANDREW JACKSON,

24. Act of March 2, 1831, appropriates $100,000 for opening, grading, &c., west of Zanesville, Ohio; $950 for repairs during the year 1830; $2,700 for work heretofore done east of Zanesville; $265.85 for arrearages for the survey from Zanesville to the capital of Missouri; and $75,000 for opening, grading, &c., in the State of Indiana, including bridge over White river, near Indianapolis, and progressing to eastern and western boundaries; $66,000 for opening, grading, and bridging in Illinois; to be paid from the fund, acts admitting Ohio, Indiana, Illinois, and Missouri.................   244,915 85

25. Act of July 3, 1832, appropriates $150,000 for repairs east of the Ohio river; $100,000 for continuing the road west of Zanesville; $100,000 for continuing the road in Indiana, including bridge over east and west branch of White river; $70,000 for continuing road in Illinois; to be paid from the fund acts admitting Ohio, Indiana and Illinois,...   420,000 00

26. Act of March 2, 1833, appropriates to carry on certain improvements east of the Ohio river, $125,000; in Ohio, west of Zanesville, $130,000; in Indiana, $100,000; in Illinois, $70,000; in Virginia, $34,440.................................   459,440 00

27. Act of June 24, 1834, appropriates $200,000 for continuing the road in Ohio; $150,000 for continuing the road in Indiana; $100,000 for continuing the road in Illinois, and $300,000 for the entire completion of repairs east of Ohio, to meet provisions of the Acts of Pennsylvania (April 4, 1831), Maryland (Jan. 23, 1832), and Virginia (Feb. 7, 1832), accepting the road surrendered to the States, the United States not thereafter to be subject for any expense for repairs. Places engineer officer of army in control of road through Indiana and Illinois, and in charge of all appropriations. $300,000 to be paid out of any money in the Treasury not otherwise appropriated, balance from acts admitting Ohio, Indiana and Illinois...   750,000 00

*Spanish 8 Reales
or piece of eight,
obverse and reverse.*

28. Act of June 27, 1837, (General Appropriation) for arrearages due contractors....................   1,609 36

29. Act of March 3, 1835, appropriates $200,000 for continuing the road in the State of Ohio; $100,000 for continuing road in the State of Indiana; to be out of fund acts admitting Ohio, Indiana and Illinois, and $346,186.58 for the entire completion of repairs in Maryland, Pennsylvania and Virginia; but before any part of this sum can be expended east of the Ohio river, the road shall be surrendered to and accepted by the States through which it passes, and the United States shall not thereafter be subject to any expense in relation to said road. Out of any money in the Treasury not otherwise appropriated 646,186 58

30. Act of March 3, 1835, (Repair of Roads) appropriates to pay for work heretofore done by Isaiah

Frost on the Cumberland Road, $320; to pay late Superintendent of road a salary, $862.87........   1,182 87

31. Act of July 2, 1836, appropriates for continuing the road in Ohio, $200,000; for continuing road in Indiana, $250,000, including materials for a bridge over the Wabash river; $150,000 for continuing the road in Illinois, provided that the appropriation for Illinois shall be limited to grading and bridging, and shall not be construed as pledging Congress to future appropriations for the purpose of macadamizing the road, and the moneys herein appropriated for said road in Ohio and Indiana must be expended in completing the greatest possible continuous portion of said road in said States so that said finished part thereof may be surrendered to the States respectively; to be paid from acts admitting Ohio, Indiana, Illinois and Missouri   600,000 00

32. Act of March 3, 1837, appropriates $190,000 for continuing the road in Ohio; $100,000 for continuing the road in Indiana; $100,000 for continuing road in Illinois, provided the road in Illinois shall not be stoned or graveled, unless it can be done at a cost not greater than the average cost of stoning and graveling the road in Ohio and Indiana, and provided that in all cases where it can be done the work to be laid off in sections and let to the lowest substantial bidder. Sec. 2 of the act provides that Sec. 2 of act of July 2, 1836, shall not be applicable to expenditures hereafter made on the road, and $7,183.63 is appropriated by this act for repairs east of the Ohio river; to be paid from the acts admitting Ohio, Indiana and Illinois........   397,183 63

33. Act of May 25, 1838, appropriates for continuing the road in Ohio, $150,000; for continuing it in Indiana, including bridges, $150,000; for continuing it in Illinois, $9,000; for the completion of a bridge over Dunlap's creek at Brownsville; to be paid from moneys in the Treasury not otherwise appropriated and subject to provisions and conditions of act of March 3, 1837.................   459,000 00

34. Act of June 17, 1844, (Civil and Diplomatic) appropriates for arrearages on account of survey to Jefferson, Mo................................   1,359 81

Total.............................$6,824,919 33

Note—The appropriation of $3,786 60, made by act of Feb. 26, 1812, is not included in the above total for the reason that it was a balance from a former appropriation.

The act of March 3, 1843, appropriates so much as is necessary to settle certain claims on contract for building bridges over Kaskaskia river and constructing part of Cumberland Road.

The following were the rates of toll fixed by the act of April 11th, 1831, which were subsequently, however changed: For every score of sheep or hogs, six cents; for every score of cattle, twelve cents; for every led or driven horse, three cents; for every horse and rider, four cents; for every sleigh or sled, for each horse or pair of oxen drawing the same, three cents; for every dearborn, sulky, chair or chaise, with one horse, six cents; for every chariot, coach, coachee, stage, wagon, phaeton, chaise, with two horses and four wheels, twelve cents; for either of the carriages last mentioned with four horses, eighteen cents; for every other carriage of pleasure, under whatever name it may go, the like sum, according to the number of wheels and horses drawing the same; for every cart or wagon whose wheels shall exceed two and one-half inches in breadth, and not exceeding four inches, four cents; for every horse or pair of oxen drawing the same, and every other cart or wagon, whose wheels shall exceed four inches, and not exceeding five inches in breadth, three cents; for every horse or pair of oxen drawing the same, and for every other cart or wagon whose wheels shall exceed six inches, and not more than eight inches, two cents; for every horse or pair of oxen drawing the same, all other carts or wagons whose wheels shall exceed eight inches in breadth, shall pass the gates free of tolls, and no tolls shall be collected from any person or persons passing or repassing from one part of his farm to another, or to or from a mill, or to or from any place of public worship, funeral, militia training, elections, or from any student or child going to or from any school or seminary of learning, or from persons and witnesses going to and returning from courts, or from any wagon or carriage laden with the property of the United States, or any canon or military stores belonging to the United States, or to any State. The reader will note that the exemptions provided for by this act are changed by force of the act of May 3, 1850, which authorized the commissioner and the court of quarter sessions to determine who and what shall be exempt from the payment of toll. A large wide board, having the appearance of a mock window, was firmly fixed in the walls of every toll house, displaying in plain letters the rates above given, so that the wayfarer might not err therein.

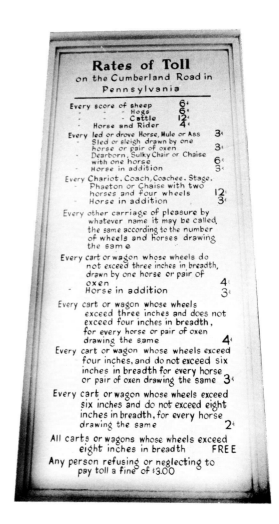

Note—Gate No. 1 was located at the east end of Petersburg, Gate No. 2 was near Mt. Washington, Gate No. 3 was near Searights, Gate No. 4 was near Beallsville, Gate No. 5 was near Washington, and Gate No. 6 near West Alexander.

Origin of the Fund for Making the Road.—Acts for the Admission of Ohio, Indiana, Illinois and Missouri —Report of a Committee of Congress as to the Manner of Applying the Ohio Fund — Distances from Important Eastern Cities to the Ohio River — The Richmond Route Postponed — The Spirit and Perseverance of Pennsylvania — Maryland, "My Maryland," not behind Pennsylvania — Wheeling the Objective Point — Brownsville a Prominent Point — Rivers tend to Union, Mountains to Disunion.

Act of April 30, 1802, for the admission of Ohio, provides that one-twentieth part of the net proceeds of the lands lying within the said State sold by Congress, from and after the 30th of June next, after deducting all expenses incident to the same, shall be applied to laying out and making public roads leading from navigable waters emptying into the Atlantic to the Ohio, to the said State and through the same, such roads to be laid out under the authority of Congress, with the consent of the several States through which the road shall pass.

Act of April 19, 1816, for the admission of Indiana, provides that five per cent. of the net proceeds of lands lying within the said territory, and which shall be sold by Congress from and after the first day of December next, after deducting all expenses incident to the same, shall be reserved for making public roads and canals, of which three-fifths shall be applied to those objects within the said State under the direction of the Legislature thereof, and two-fifths to the making of a road or roads leading to the said State under the direction of Congress.

Act of April 18, 1818, for the admission of Illinois, provides that five per cent. of the net proceeds of the lands lying within the said State, and which shall be sold by Congress from and after the first day of January, 1819, after deducting all expenses incident to the same, shall be reserved for the purposes following, viz: Two-fifths to be disbursed under the direction of Congress in making roads leading to the State, the residue to be appropriated by the Legislature of the State for the encouragement of learning, of which one-sixth part shall be exclusively bestowed on a college or university.

Act of March 6, 1820, admitting Missouri, provides that five per cent. of the net proceeds of the sale of lands lying within the said Territory or State, and which shall be sold by Congress from and after the first day of January next, after deducting all expenses incident to the same, shall be reserved for making public roads and canals, of which three-fifths shall be applied to those objects within the State under the direction of the Legislature thereof, and the other two-fifths in defraying, under the direction of Congress, the expenses to be incurred in making a road or roads, canal or canals, leading to the said State.

No. 195.

NINTH CONGRESS — FIRST SESSION.

CUMBERLAND ROAD.

Communicated to the Senate December 19, 1805.

Mr. Tracy, from the committee to whom was referred the examination of the act entitled, "An act to enable the people of the eastern division of the territory northwest of the river Ohio to form a Constitution and State Government, and for the admission of such State into the Union on an equal footing with the original States, and for other purposes;" and to report the manner in which, in their opinion, the money appropriated by said act ought to be applied, made the following report:

That, upon examination of the act aforesaid, they find "the one-twentieth part, or five per cent., of the net proceeds of the lands lying within the State of Ohio, and sold by Congress from and after the 30th day of June, 1802, is appropriated for the laying out and making public roads leading from the navigable waters emptying into the Atlantic to the river Ohio, to said State, and through the same; such

roads to be laid out under the authority of Congress, with the consent of the several States through which the road shall pass."

They find that by a subsequent law, passed on the 3d day of March, 1803, Congress appropriated three per cent. of the said five per cent. to laying out and making roads *within* the State of Ohio, leaving two per cent. of the appropriation contained in the first mentioned law unexpended, which now remains for "*the laying out and making roads from the navigable waters emptying into the Atlantic to the river Ohio, to said State.*"

They find that the net proceeds of sales of land in the State of Ohio,

From 1st July, 1802, to June 30, 1803, both inclusive, were	$124,400 92
From 1st July, 1803, to June 30, 1804	176,203 35
From 1st July, 1804, to June 30, 1805	266,000 00
From 1st July, 1805, to Sept. 30, 1805	66,000 00

Amounting, in the whole, to $632,604 27

Two per cent. on which sum amounts to $12,652. Twelve thousand six hundred and fifty-two dollars were, therefore, on the 1st day of October last, subject to the uses directed by law, as mentioned in this report; and it will be discerned that the fund is constantly accumulating, and will, probably, by the time regular preparations can be made for its expenditure, amount to eighteen or twenty thousand dollars. The committee have examined, as far as their limited time and the scanty sources of facts within their reach would permit, the various routes which have been contemplated for laying out roads pursuant to the provisions of the act mentioned in this report.

They find that the distance from Philadelphia to Pittsburg is 314 miles by the usual route, and on a straight line about 270.

From Philadelphia to the nearest point on the river Ohio, contiguous to the State of Ohio, which is probably between Steubenville and the mouth of Grave creek, the distance by the usual route is 360 miles, and on a straight line about 308.

From Baltimore to the river Ohio, between the same points, and by the usual route, is 275 miles, and on a straight line 224.

From this city (Washington) to the same points on the river Ohio, the distance is nearly the same as from Baltimore; probably the difference is not a plurality of miles.

From Richmond, in Virginia, to the nearest point on the river Ohio, the distance by the usual route is 377 miles; but new roads are opening which will shorten the distance fifty or sixty miles; 247 miles of the contemplated road, from Richmond northwesterly, will be as good as the roads usually are in that country, but the remaining seventy or eighty miles are bad, for the present, and probably will remain so for a length of time, as there seems to be no existing inducement for the State of Virginia to incur the expense of making that part of the road passable.

From Baltimore to the Monongahela river, where the route from Baltimore to the Ohio river will intersect it, the distance as usually traveled is 218 miles, and on a straight line about 184. From this point, which is at or near Brownsville, boats can pass down, with great facility, to the State of Ohio, during a number of months in every year.

The above distances are not all stated from actual mensuration, but it is believed they are sufficiently correct for the present purpose.

The committee have not examined any routes northward of that leading from Philadelphia to the river Ohio, nor southward of that leading from Richmond, because they suppose the roads to be laid out must strike the river Ohio on some point contiguous to the State of Ohio, in order to satisfy the words of the law making the appropriation; the words are: "Leading from the navigable waters emptying into the Atlantic, to the river Ohio, to the said State, and through the same."

The mercantile intercourse of the citizens of Ohio with those of the Atlantic States is chiefly in Philadelphia and Baltimore; not very extensive in the towns on the Potomac, within the District of Columbia, and still less with Richmond, in Virginia. At present, the greatest portion of their trade is with Philadelphia; but it is believed their trade is rapidly increasing with Baltimore, owing to the difference of distance in favor of Baltimore, and to the advantage of boating down the Monongahela river, from the point where the road strikes it, about 70 miles by water, and 50 by land, above Pittsburg.

The sum appropriated for laying out and making roads is so small that the committee have thought it most expedient to direct an expenditure to one route only. They have therefore endeavored to fix on that which, for the present, will be most accommodating to the citizens of the State of Ohio; leaving to the future benevolence and policy of congress, an extension of their operations on this or other routes, and an increase of the requisite fund, as the discoveries of experience may point out their expediency and necessity. The committee being fully convinced that a wise government can never lose sight of an object so important as that of connecting a numerous and rapidly increasing population, spread upon a fertile and extensive territory, with the Atlantic States, now separated from them by mountains, which, by industry and an expense moderate in comparison with the advantages, can be rendered passable.

The route from Richmond must necessarily approach the State of Ohio in a part thinly inhabited, and which, from the nature of the soil and other circumstances, must remain so, at least for a considerable time; and, from the hilly and rough condition of the country, no roads are or can be conveniently made, leading to the principal population of the State of Ohio.

These considerations have induced the committee to postpone, for the present, any further consideration of that route.

The spirit and perseverance of Pennsylvania are such, in the matter of road making, that no doubt can remain but they will, in a little time, complete a road from Philadelphia to Pittsburg, as good as the nature of the ground will permit. They are so particularly interested to facilitate the intercourse between their trading capital, Philadelphia, not only to Pittsburg, but also to the extensive country within that State, on the western waters, that they will, of course, surmount the difficulties presented by the Allegheny mountain, Chesnut Ridge and Laurel Hill, the three great and almost exclusive impediments which now exist on that route.

The State of Maryland, with no less spirit and perseverance, are engaged in making roads from Baltimore and from the western boundary of the District of Columbia, through Fredericktown, to Williamsport. Were the Government of the United States to direct the expenditure of the fund in contemplation upon either of these routes, for the present, in Pennsylvania or Maryland, it would, probably, so far interfere with the operations of the respective States, as to produce mischief instead of benefit; especially as the sum to be laid out by the United States is too inconsiderable, alone, to effect objects of such magnitude. But as the State of Maryland have no particular interest to extend their road across the mountains (and if they had it would be impracticable, because the State does not extend so far), the committee have thought it expedient to recommend the laying out and making a road from Cumberland, on the northerly bank of the Potomac, and within the State of Maryland, to the river Ohio, at the most convenient place between a point on the easterly bank of said river, opposite to Steubenville, and the mouth of Grave creek, which empties into said river Ohio a little below Wheeling, in Virginia. This route will meet and accommodate the roads leading from Baltimore and the District of Columbia; it will cross the Monongahela river, at or near Brownsville, sometimes called Redstone, where the advantage of boating can be taken; and from the point where it will probably intersect the river Ohio, there are now roads, or they can easily be made over feasible and proper ground, to and through the principal population of the State of Ohio.

Cumberland is situated at the eastern foot of the Allegheny mountains, about eighty miles from Williamsport, by the usual route, which is circuitous, owing to a large bend in the river Potomac, on the bank of which the road now runs, the distance on a straight line is not more than fifty or fifty-five miles, and over tolerable ground for a road, which will probably be opened by the State of Maryland, should the route be established over the mountains, as contemplated by this report.

From Cumberland to the western extremity of Laurel Hill, by the route now travelled, the distance is sixty-six miles, and on a straight line about fifty-five; on this part of the route, the committee suppose the first and very considerable expenditures are specially necessary. From Laurel Hill to the Ohio river, by the usual route, is about seventy miles, and on a straight line fifty-four or five; the road is tolerable, though capable of amelioration.

To carry into effect the principles arising from the foregoing facts, the committee present herewith a bill for the consideration of the Senate. They suppose that to take the proper measures for carrying into effect the section of the law respecting a road or roads to the State of Ohio, is a duty imposed upon Congress by the law itself, and that a sense of duty will always be sufficient to insure the passage of the bill now offered to the Senate. To enlarge upon the highly important considerations of cementing the union of our citizens located on the Western waters with those of the Atlantic States, would be an indelicacy offered to the understandings of the body to whom this report is addressed, as it might seem to distrust them. But from the interesting nature of the subject, the committee are induced to ask the indulgence of a single observation: Politicians have generally agreed that rivers unite the interests and promote the friendship of those who inhabit their banks; while mountains, on the contrary, tend to the disunion and estrangement of those who are separated by their intervention. In the present case, to make the crooked ways straight, and the rough ways smooth will, in effect, remove the intervening mountains, and by facilitating the intercourse of our Western brethren with those on the Atlantic, substantially unite them in interest, which, the committee believe, is the most effectual cement of union applicable to the human race.

All which is most respectfully submitted.

An Act to Regulate the Laying Out and Making a Road from Cumberland, in the State of Maryland, to the State of Ohio.

Be it enacted by the Senate and House of Representatives of the United States of America in Congress assembled, That the President of the United States be, and he is hereby authorized to appoint, by and with the advice and consent of the Senate, three discreet and disinterested citizens of the United States, to lay out a road from Cumberland, or a point on the northern bank of the river Potomac, in the State of Maryland, between Cumberland and the place where the main road leading from Gwynn's to Winchester, in Virginia, crosses the river, to the State of Ohio; whose duty it shall be, as soon as may be, after their appointment, to repair to Cumberland aforesaid, and view the ground, from the points on the river Potomac hereinbefore designated, to the river Ohio; and to lay out in such direction as they shall judge, under all circumstances the most proper, a road from thence to the river Ohio, to strike the same at the most convenient place, between a point on its eastern bank, opposite the northern boundary of Steubenville, in said State of Ohio, and the mouth of Grave creek, which empties into the said river a little below Wheeling, in Virginia.

Sec. 2. *And be it further enacted*, That the aforesaid road shall be laid out four rods in width, and designated on each side by a plain and distinguishable mark on a tree, or by the erection of a stake or monument sufficiently conspicuous, in every quarter of a mile of the distance at least, where the road pursues a straight course so far or farther, and on each side, at every point where an angle occurs in its course.

Sec. 3. *And be it further enacted*, That the commissioners shall, as soon as may be, after they have laid out said road, as aforesaid, present to the President an accurate plan of the same, with its several courses and distances, accompanied by a written report of their proceedings, describing the marks and monuments by which the road is designated, and the face of the country over which it passes, and pointing out the particular parts which they shall judge require the most and immediate attention and amelioration, and the probable expense of making the same passable in the most difficult parts, and through the whole distance; designating the State or States through which said road has been laid out, and the length of the several parts which are laid out on new ground, as well as the length of those parts laid out on the road now traveled. Which report the President is hereby authorized to accept or reject, in the whole or in part. If he accepts, he is hereby further authorized and requested to pursue such measures, as in his opinion shall be proper, to obtain consent for making the road, of the State or States through which the same has been laid out. Which consent being obtained, he is further authorized to take prompt and effectual measures to cause said road to be made through the whole distance, or in any part or parts of the same as he shall judge most conducive to the public good, having reference to the sum appropriated for the purpose.

Sec. 4. *And be it further enacted*, That all parts of the road which the President shall direct to be made, in case the trees are standing, shall be cleared the whole width of four rods; and the road shall be raised in the middle of the carriageway with stone, earth, or gravel and sand, or a combination of some or all of them, leaving or making, as the case may be, a ditch or water course on each side and contiguous to said carriageway, and in no instance shall there be an elevation in said road, when finished, greater than an angle of five degrees with the horizon. But the manner of making said road, in every other particular, is left to the direction of the President.

Sec. 5. *And be it further enacted*, That said Commissioners shall each receive four dollars per day, while employed as aforesaid, in full for their compensation, including all expenses. And they are hereby authorized to employ one surveyor, two chainmen and one marker, for whose faithfulness and accuracy they, the said Commissioners, shall be responsible, to attend them in laying out said road, who shall receive in full satisfaction for their wages, including all expenses, the surveyor three dollars per day, and each chainman and the marker one dollar per day, while they shall be employed in said business, of which fact a certificate signed by said commissioners shall be deemed sufficient evidence.

SEC. 6. *And be it further enacted,* That the sum of thirty thousand dollars be, and the same is hereby appropriated, to defray the expense of laying out and making said road. And the President is hereby authorized to draw, from time to time, on the treasury for such parts, or at any one time, for the whole of said sum, as he shall judge the service requires. Which sum of thirty thousand dollars shall be paid, first, out of the fund of two per cent. reserved for laying out and making roads *to* the State of Ohio, by virtue of the seventh section of an act passed on the thirtieth day of April, one thousand eight hundred and two, entitled, "An act to enable the people of the eastern division of the territory northwest of the river Ohio to form a constitution and State government, and for the admission of such State into the Union on an equal footing with the original States, and for other purposes." Three per cent. of the appropriation contained in said seventh section being directed by a subsequent law to the laying out, opening and making roads *within* the said State of Ohio; and secondly, out of any money in the treasury not otherwise appropriated, chargeable upon, and reimbursable at the treasury by said fund of two per cent. as the same shall accrue.

SEC. 7. *And be it further enacted,* That the President be, and he is hereby requested, to cause to be laid before Congress, as soon as convenience will permit, after the commencement of each session, a statement of the proceedings under this act, that Congress may be enabled to adopt such further measures as may from time to time be proper under existing circumstances.

Approved, March 29, 1806.　　　　TH. JEFFERSON.

UNITED STATES OF AMERICA,　}
　　　　DEPARTMENT OF STATE. }

To all to whom these presents shall come, Greeting:

I certify that hereto annexed is a true copy of an Act of Congress, approved March 29, 1806, the original of which is on file in this Department, entitled: "An Act to regulate the laying out and making a road from Cumberland, in the State of Maryland, to the State of Ohio."

In testimony whereof, I, James G. Blaine, Secretary of State of the United States, have hereunto subscribed my name and caused the seal of the Department of State to be affixed.

Done at the City of Washington, this seventh day of March. A. D. 1891, and of the Independence of the United States the one hundred and fifteenth.

JAMES G. BLAINE.

No. 220.

NINTH CONGRESS—SECOND SESSION.

January 31, 1807.

To the Senate and House of Representatives of the United States:

In execution of the act of the last session of Congress, entitled, "An act to regulate the laying out and making a road from Cumberland, in the State of Maryland, to the State of Ohio," I appointed Thomas Moore, of Maryland, Joseph Kerr, of Ohio, and Eli Williams, of Maryland, commissioners to lay out the said road, and to perform the other duties assigned to them by the act. The progress which they made in the execution of the work, during the last season, will appear in their report now communicated to Congress; on the receipt of it, I took measures to obtain consent for making the road of the

States of Pennsylvania, Maryland and Virginia, through which the commissioners propose to lay it out. I have received acts of the Legislatures of Maryland and Virginia, giving the consent desired; that of Pennsylvania has the subject still under consideration, as is supposed. Until I receive full consent to a free choice of route through the whole distance, I have thought it safest neither to accept nor reject, finally, the partial report of the commissioners.

Some matters suggested in the report belong exclusively to the legislature.

TH. JEFFERSON.

The commissioners, acting by appointment under the law of Congress, entitled "An act to regulate the laying out and making a road from Cumberland, in the State of Maryland, to the State of Ohio, beg leave to report to the President of the United States, and to premise that the duties imposed by the law became a work of greater magnitude, and a task much more arduous, than was conceived before entering upon it; from which circumstance the commissioners did not allow themselves sufficient time for the performance of it before the severity of the weather obliged them to retire from it, which was the case in the first week of the present month (December). That, not having fully accomplished their work, they are unable fully to report a discharge of all the duties enjoined by the law; but as the most material and principal part has been performed, and as a communication of the progress already made may be useful and proper, during the present session of Congress, and of the Legislatures of those States through which the route passes, the commissioners respectfully state that at a very early period it was conceived that the maps of the country were not sufficiently accurate to afford a minute knowledge of the true courses between the extreme points on the rivers, by which the researches of the commissioners were to be governed; a survey for that purpose became indispensable, and considerations of public economy suggested the propriety of making this survey precede the personal attendance of the commissioners.

Josias Thompson, a surveyor of professional merit, was taken into service and authorized to employ two chain carriers and a marker, as well as one vaneman, and a packhorse man and horse, on public account; the latter being indispensable and really beneficial in excelerating the work. The surveyors' instructions are contained in document No. 1, accompanying this report.

Calculating on a reasonable time for the performance of the instructions to the surveyor, the commissioners, by correspondence, fixed on the first day of September last for their meeting at Cumberland to proceed in the work; neither of them, however, reached that place until the third of that month, on which day they all met.

The surveyor having, under his instructions, laid down a plat of his work, showing the meanders of the Potomac and Ohio rivers, within the limits prescribed for the commissioners, as also the road between those rivers, which is commonly traveled from Cumberland to Charleston, in part called Braddock's road; and the same being produced to the commissioners, whereby straight lines and their true courses were shown between the extreme points on each river, and the boundaries which limit the powers of the commissioners being thereby ascertained, serving as a basis whereon to proceed in the examination of the grounds and face of the country; the commissioners thus prepared commenced the business of exploring; and in this it was considered that a faithful discharge of the discretionary powers vested by the law made it necessary to view the whole to be able to judge of a preference due to any part of the grounds, which imposed a task of examining a space comprehending upwards of two thousand square miles; a task rendered still more incumbent by the solicitude and importunities of the inhabitants of every part of the district, who severally conceived their grounds entitled to a preference. It becoming necessary, in the interim, to run various lines of experiment for ascertaining the geographical position of several points entitled to attention, and the service suffering great delay for want of another surveyor, it was thought consistent with the public interest to employ, in that capacity, Arthur Rider, the vaneman, who had been chosen with qualification to meet such an emergency; and whose service as vaneman could then be dispensed with. He commenced, as surveyor, on the 22d day of September, and continued so at field work until the first day of December, when he was retained as a necessary assistant to the principal surveyor, in copying field notes and hastening the draught of the work to be reported.

The proceedings of the commissioners are specially detailed in their general journal, compiled from the daily journal of each commissioner, to which they beg leave to refer, under mark No. 2.

After a careful and critical examination of all the grounds within the limits prescribed, as well as the grounds and ways out from the Ohio westwardly, at several points, and examining the shoal parts of the Ohio river as detailed in the table of soundings, stated in their journal, and after gaining all the information, geographical, general and special, possible and necessary, toward a judicial discharge of the duties assigned them, the commissioners repaired to Cumberland to examine and compare their notes and journals, and determine upon the direction and location of their route.

In this consultation the governing objects were:

1st. Shortness of distance between navigable points on the eastern and western waters.

2d. A point on the Monongahela best calculated to equalize the advantages of this portage in the country within reach of it.

3d. A point on the Ohio river most capable of combining certainty of navigation with road accommodation; embracing, in this estimate, remote points westwardly, as well as present and probable population on the north and south.

4th. Best mode of diffusing benefits with least distance of road.

In contemplating these objects, due attention was paid as well to the comparative merits of towns, establishments, and settlements already made, as to the capacity of the country with the present and probable population.

In the course of arrangement, and in its order, the first point located for the route was determined and fixed at Cumberland, a decision founded on propriety, and in some measure on necessity, from the circumstance of a high and difficult mountain, called Nobley, laying and confining the east margin of the Potomac so as to render it impossible of access on that side without immense expense, at any point between Cumberland and where the road from Winchester to Gwynn's crosses, and even there the Nobley mountain is crossed with much difficulty and hazard. And this upper point was taxed with another formidable objection; it was found that a high range of mountains, called Dan's, stretching across from Gwynn's to the Potomac, above this point, precluded the opportunity of extending a route from this point in a proper direction, and left no alternative but passing by Gwynn's; the distance from Cumberland to Gwynn's being upward of a mile less than from the upper point, which lies ten miles by water above Cumberland, the commissioners were not permitted to hesitate in preferring a point which shortens the portage, as well as the Potomac navigation.

The point on the Potomac being viewed as a great repository of produce, which a good road will bring from the west of Laurel Hill, and the advantages which Cumberland, as a town, has in that respect over an unimproved place, are additional considerations operating forcibly in favor of the place preferred.

In extending the route from Cumberland, a triple range of mountains, stretching across from Jenings' run in measure with Gwynn's, left only the alternative of laying the road up Will's creek for three miles, nearly at right angles with the true course, and then by way of Jenings' run, or extending it over a break in the smallest mountain, on a better course by Gwynn's, to the top of Savage mountain; the latter was adopted, being the shortest, and will be less expensive in hill-side digging over a sloped route than the former, requiring one bridge over Will's creek and several over Jenings' run, both very wide and considerable streams in high water; and a more weighty reason for preferring the route by Gwynn's is the great accommodation it will afford travelers from Winchester by the upper point, who could not reach the route by Jenings' run short of the top of Savage, which would withhold from them the benefit of an easy way up the mountain.

It is, however, supposed that those who travel from Winchester by way of the upper point to Gwynn's, are in that respect more the dupes of common prejudice than judges of their own ease, as it is believed the way will be as short, and on much better ground, to cross the Potomac below the confluence of the north and south branches (thereby crossing these two, as well as Patterson's creek, in one stream, equally fordable in the same season), than to pass through Cumberland to Gwynn's. Of these grounds, however, the commissioners do not speak from actual view, but consider it a subject well worthy of future investigation. Having gained the top of Allegany mountain, or rather the top of that part called Savage, by way of Gwynn's, the general route, as it respects the most important points, was determined as follows, viz.:

From a stone at the corner of lot No. 1, in Cumberland, near the confluence of Will's creek and the north branch of the Potomac river; thence extending along the street westwardly, to cross the hill lying between Cumberland and Gwynn's, at the gap where Braddock's road passes it; thence near Gwynn's and Jesse Tomlinson's, to cross the big Youghiogheny near the mouth of Roger's run, between the crossing of Braddock's road and the confluence of the streams which form the Turkey foot; thence to cross Laurel Hill near the forks of Dunbar's run, to the west foot of that hill, at a point near where Braddock's old road reached it, near Gist's old place, now Colonel Isaac Meason's, thence through Brownsville and Bridgeport, to cross the Monongahela river below Josias Crawford's ferry; and thence on as straight a course as the country will admit to the Ohio, at a point between the mouth of Wheeling creek and the lower point of Wheeling island.

In this direction of the route it will lay about twenty-four and a half miles in Maryland, seventy-five miles and a half in Pennsylvania, and twelve miles in Virginia; distances which will be in a small degree increased by meanders, which the bed of the road must necessarily make between the points mentioned in the location; and this route, it is believed, comprehends more important advantages than could be afforded in any other, inasmuch as it has a capacity at least equal to any other in extending advantages of a highway, and at the same time establishes the shortest portage between the points already navigated, and on the way accommodates other and nearer points to which navigation may be extended, and still shorten the portage.

It intersects Big Youghiogheny at the nearest point from Cumberland, then lies nearly parallel with that river for the distance of twenty miles, and at the west foot of Laurel Hill lies within five miles of Connellsville, from which the Youghiogheny is navigated; and in the same direction the route intersects at Brownsville the nearest point on the Monongahela river within the district.

The improvement of the Youghiogheny navigation is a subject of too much importance to remain long neglected; and the capacity of that river, as high up as the falls (twelve miles above Connellsville), is said to be equal, at a small expense, with the parts already navigated below. The obstructions at the falls, and a rocky rapid near Turkey Foot, constitute the principal impediments in that river to the intersection of the route, and as much higher as the stream has a capacity for navigation; and these difficulties will doubtless be removed when the intercourse shall warrant the measure.

Under these circumstances the portage may be thus stated:
From Cumberland to Monongahela, 66½ miles. From Cumberland to a point in measure with Connellsville, on the Youghiogheny river, 51½ miles. From Cumberland to a point in measure with the lower end of the falls of Youghiogheny, which will lie two miles north of the public road, 43 miles. From Cumberland to the intersection of the route with the Youghiogheny river, 34 miles.

Nothing is here said of the Little Youghiogheny, which lies nearer Cumberland; the stream being unusually crooked, its navigation can only become the work of a redundant population.

The point which this route locates, at the west foot of Laurel Hill, having cleared the whole of the Allegheny mountain, is so situated as to extend the advantages of an easy way through the great barrier, with more equal justice to the best parts of the country between Laurel Hill and the Ohio. Lines from this point to Pittsburg and Morgantown, diverging nearly at the same angle, open upon equal terms to all parts of the Western country that can make use of this portage; and which may include the settlements from Pittsburg, up Big Beaver to the Connecticut reserve, on Lake Erie, as well as those on the southern borders of the Ohio and all the intermediate country.

Brownsville is nearly equi-distant from Big Beaver and Fishing creek, and equally convenient to all the crossing places on the Ohio, between these extremes. As a port, it is at least equal to any on the Monongahela within the limits, and holds superior advantages in furnishing supplies to emigrants, traders, and other travelers by land or water.

Not unmindful of the claims of towns and their capacity of reciprocating advantages on public roads, the commissioners were not insensible of the disadvantage which Uniontown must feel from the want of that accommodation which a more southwardly direction of the route would have afforded; but as that could not take place without a relinquishment of the shortest passage, considerations of public benefit could not yield to feelings of minor import. Uniontown being the seat of justice for Fayette county, Pennsylvania, is not without a share of public benefits, and may partake of the advantages of this portage upon equal terms with Connellsville, a growing town, with the advantage of respectable water-works adjoining, in the manufactory of flour and iron.

After reaching the nearest navigation on the western waters, at a point best calculated to diffuse the benefits of a great highway in the greatest possible latitude east of the Ohio, it was considered that, to fulfill the objects of the law, it remained for the commissioners to give such a direction to the road as would best secure a certainty of navigation on the Ohio at all seasons, combining, as far as possible, the inland accommodation of remote points westwardly. It was found that the obstructions in the Ohio, within the limits between Steubenville and Grave creek, lay principally above the town and mouth of Wheeling; a circumstance ascertained by the commissioners in their examination of the channel, as well as by common usage, which has long given a decided preference to Wheeling as a place of embarcation and port of departure in dry seasons. It was also seen that Wheeling lay in a line from Brownsville to the centre of the State of Ohio and Post Vincennes. These circumstances favoring and corresponding with the chief objects in view in this last direction of the route, and the ground from Wheeling westwardly being known of equal fitness with any other way out from the river, it was thought most proper, under these several considerations, to locate the point mentioned below the mouth of Wheeling. In taking this point in preference to one higher up and in the town of Wheeling, the public benefit and convenience were consulted, inasmuch as the present crossing place over the Ohio from the town is so contrived and confined as to subject passengers to extraordinary ferriage and delay, by entering and clearing a ferry-boat on each side of Wheeling island, which lies before the town and precludes the opportunity of fording when the river is crossed in that way, above and below the island.

From the point located, a safe crossing is afforded at the lower point of the island by a ferry in high, and a good ford at low water.

The face of the country within the limits prescribed is generally very uneven, and in many places broken by a succession of high mountains and deep hollows, too formidable to be reduced within five degrees of the horizon, but by crossing them obliquely, a mode which, although it imposes a heavy task of hill-side digging, obviates generally the necessity of reducing hills and filling hollows, which, on these grounds, would be an attempt truly Quixotic. This inequality of the surface is not confined to the Allegheny mountain; the country between the Monongahela and Ohio rivers, although less elevated, is not better adapted for the bed of a road, being filled with impediments of hills and hollows, which present considerable difficulties, and wants that super-abundance and convenience of stone which is found in the mountain.

The indirect course of the road now traveled, and the frequent elevations and depressions which occur, that exceed the limits of the law, preclude the possibility of occupying it in any extent without great sacrifice of distance, and forbid the use of it, in any one part, for more than half a mile, or more than two or three miles in the whole.

The expense of rendering the road now in contemplation passable, may, therefore, amount to a larger sum than may have been supposed necessary, under an idea of embracing in it a considerable part of the old road; but it is believed that the contrary will be found most correct, and that a sum sufficient to open the new could not be expended on the same distance of the old road with equal benefit.

The sum required for the road in contemplation will depend on the style and manner of making it; as a common road cannot remove the difficulties which always exist on deep grounds, and particularly in wet seasons, and as nothing short of a firm, substantial, well-formed, stone-capped road can remove the causes which led to the measure of improvement, or render the institution as commodious as a great and growing intercourse appears to require, the expense of such a road next becomes the subject of inquiry.

In this inquiry the commissioners can only form an estimate by recurring to the experience of Pennsylvania and Maryland in the business of artificial roads. Upon this data, and a comparison of the grounds and proximity of the materials for covering, there are reasons for belief that, on the route reported, a complete road may be made at an expense not exceeding six thousand dollars per mile, exclusive of bridges over the principal streams on the way. The average expense of the Lancaster, as well as Baltimore and Frederick turnpike, is considerably higher; but it is believed that the convenient supply of stone which the mountain affords will, on those grounds, reduce the expense to the rate here stated.

As to the policy of incurring this expense, it is not the province of the commissioners to declare; but they cannot, however, withhold assurances of a firm belief that the purse of the nation cannot be more seasonably opened, or more happily applied, than in promoting the speedy and effectual establishment of a great and easy road on the way contemplated.

In the discharge of all these duties, the commissioners have been actuated by an ardent desire to render the institution as useful and commodious as possible; and, impressed with a strong sense of the necessity which urges the speedy establishment of the road, they have to regret the circumstance which delays the completion of the part assigned them. They, however, in some measure, content themselves with the reflection that it will not retard the progress of the work, as the opening of the road cannot commence before spring, and may then begin with marking the way.

The extra expense incident to the service from the necessity (and propriety, as it relates to public economy,) of employing men not provided for by law, will, it is hoped, be recognized, and provision made for the payment of that and similar expenses, when in future it may be indispensably incurred.

The commissioners having engaged in a service in which their zeal did not permit them to calculate the difference between their pay and the expense to which the service subjected them, cannot suppose it the wish or intention of the Government to accept of their services for a mere indemnification of their expense of subsistence, which will be very much the case under the present allowance; they, therefore, allow themselves to hope and expect that measures will be taken to provide such further compensation as may, under all circumstances, be thought neither profuse nor parsimonious.

The painful anxiety manifested by the inhabitants of the district explored, and their general desire to know the route determined on, suggested the measure of promulgation, which, after some deliberation, was agreed on by way of circular letter, which has been forwarded to those persons to whom precaution was useful, and afterward sent to one of the presses in that quarter for publication, in the form of the document No. 3, which accompanies this report.

All which is, with due deference, submitted.

ELI WILLIAMS,
THOMAS MOORE,
JOSEPH KERR.

DECEMBER 30, 1806.

Pennsylvania Grants Permission to Make the Road Through Her Territory — Uniontown Restored, Gist Left Out, and Washington, Pennsylvania, Made a Point — Simon Snyder, Speaker of the House — Presely Carr Lane, a Fayette County Man, Speaker of the Senate, and Thomas McKean, Governor — A Second Special Message From President Jefferson, and a Second Report of the Commissioners — Heights of Mountains and Hills — On to Brownsville and Wheeling — An Imperious Call Made on Commissioner Kerr.

An Act authorizing the President of the United States to open a road through that part of this State lying between Cumberland, in the State of Maryland, and the Ohio river.

WHEREAS, by an Act of the Congress of the United States, passed on the twenty-ninth day of March, one thousand eight hundred and six, entitled "An act to regulate the laying out and making a road from Cumberland, in the State of Maryland, to the State of Ohio," the President of the United States is empowered to lay out a road from the Potomac river to the river Ohio, and to take measures for making the same, so soon as the consent of the legislatures of the several States through which the said road shall pass, could be obtained: And whereas, application hath been made to this legislature, by the President of the United States, for its consent to the measures aforesaid: Therefore,

SECTION 1. _Be it enacted by the Senate and House of Representatives of the Commonwealth of Pennsylvania, in General Assembly met, and it is hereby enacted by the authority of the same,_ That the President of the United States be, and he is hereby authorized to cause so much of the said road as will be within this State, to be opened so far as it may be necessary the same should pass through this State, and to cause the said road to be made, regulated and completed, within the limits, and according to the intent and meaning of the before recited Act of Congress in relation thereto; _Provided, nevertheless,_ That the route laid down and reported by the commissioners to the President of the United States, be so altered as to pass through Uniontown, in the county of Fayette, and Washington, in the county of Washington, if such alteration can, in the opinion of the President, be made, consistently with the provisions of an act of Congress passed March 29th, 1806, but if not, then over any ground within the limit of this State, which he may deem most advantageous.

SEC. 2. _And be it further enacted by the authority aforesaid,_ That such person or persons as are or shall be appointed for the pur-

146

pose of laying out and completing the said road, under the authority of the United States, shall have full power and authority to enter upon the lands through which the same may pass, and upon any land near or adjacent thereto, and therefrom to take, dig, cut and carry away such materials of earth, stone, gravel, timber and sand as may be necessary for the purpose of completing, and for ever keeping in repair, said road; *Provided*, That such materials shall be valued and appraised, in the same manner as materials taken for similar purposes, under the authority of this Commonwealth are by the laws thereof, directed to be valued and appraised, and a certificate of the amount thereof shall, by the person or persons appointed, or hereafter to be appointed under the authority of the United States for the purpose aforesaid, be delivered to each party entitled thereto, for any materials to be taken by virtue of this act, to entitle him, her or them to receive payment therefor from the United States.

SIMON SNYDER,
Speaker of the House of Representatives.
P. C. LANE,
Speaker of the Senate.
Approved, the ninth day of April, one thousand eight hundred and seven.
THOMAS M'KEAN.

TENTH CONGRESS—FIRST SESSION.

Communicated to Congress February 19, 1808.

To the Senate and House of Representatives of the United States:

The States of Pennsylvania, Maryland and Virginia having, by their several acts consented that the road from Cumberland to the State of Ohio, authorized by the act of Congress of March 29, 1806, should pass through those States, and the report of the commissioners communicated to Congress with my message of January 31, 1807, having been duly considered, I have approved of the route therein proposed for the said road as far as Brownsville, with a single deviation since located, which carries it through Uniontown.

From thence the course to the Ohio, and the point within the legal limits at which it shall strike that river, is still to be decided.

In forming this decision, I shall pay material regard to the interests and wishes of the populous parts of the State of Ohio, and to a future and convenient connection with the road which is to lead from the *Indian* boundary near Cincinnati, by Vincennes, to the Mississippi, at St. Louis, under authority of the act of April 21, 1806. In this way we may accomplish a continuous and advantageous line of communication from the seat of the General Government to St. Louis, passing through several very interesting points, to the Western country.

I have thought it advisable, also, to secure from obliteration the trace of the road so far as it has been approved, which has been executed at such considerable expense, by opening one-half of its breadth through its whole length.

The report of the commissioners herewith transmitted will give particular information of their proceedings under the act of March 29, 1806, since the date of my message of January 31, 1807, and will enable Congress to adopt such further measures, relative thereto, as they may deem proper under existing circumstances.

TH. JEFFERSON.

FEBRUARY 19, 1808.

———

The undersigned, commissioners appointed under the law of the United States, entitled "An act to regulate the laying out and making a road from Cumberland, in the State of Maryland, to the State of Ohio," in addition to the communications heretofore made, beg leave further to report to the President of the United States that, by the delay of the answer of the Legislature of Pennsylvania to the application for permission to pass the road through that State, the commissioners could not proceed to the business of the road in the spring before vegetation had so far advanced as to render the work of exploring and surveying difficult and tedious, from which circumstance it was postponed till the last autumn, when the business was again resumed. That, in obedience to the special instructions given them, the route heretofore reported has been so changed as to pass through Uniontown, and that they have completed the location, gradation and marking of the route from Cumberland to Brownsville, Bridgeport, and the Monongahela river, agreeably to a plat of the courses, distances and grades in which is described the marks and monuments by which the route is designated, and which is herewith exhibited; that by this plat and measurement it will appear (when compared with the road now traveled) there is a saving of four miles of distance between Cumberland and Brownsville on the new route.

In the gradation of the surface of the route (which became

necessary) is ascertained the comparative elevation and depression of different points on the route, and taking a point ten feet above the surface of low water in the Potomac river at Cumberland, as the horizon, the most prominent points are found to be elevated as follows, viz.:

	Feet.	10ths.
Summit of Wills mountain	581	3
Western foot of same	304	4
Summit of Savage mountain	2022	24
Savage river	1741	6
Summit Little Savage mountain	1900	4
Branch Pine Run, first Western water	1699	9
Summit of Red Hill (after called Shades of Death)	1914	3
Summit Little Meadow mountain	2026	16
Little Youghiogheny river	1322	6
East Fork of Shade Run	1558	92
Summit of Negro mountain, highest point	2328	12
Middle branch of White's creek, at the west foot of Negro mountain	1360	5
White's creek	1195	5
Big Youghiogheny river	645	5
Summit of a ridge between Youghiogheny river and Beaver waters	1514	5
Beaver Run	1123	8
Summit of Laurel Hill	1550	16
Court House in Uniontown	274	65
A point ten feet above the surface of low water in the Monongahela river, at the mouth of Dunlap's creek	119	26

The law requiring the commissioners to report those parts of the route as are laid on the old road, as well as those on new grounds, and to state those parts which require the most immediate attention and amelioration, the probable expense of making the same passable in the most difficult parts, and through the whole distance, they have to state that, from the crooked and hilly course of the road now traveled, the new route could not be made to occupy any part of it (except an intersection on Wills mountain, another at Jesse Tomlinson's, and a third near Big Youghiogheny, embracing not a mile of distance in the whole) without unnecessary sacrifices of distances and expense.

That, therefore, an estimate must be made on the route as passing wholly through new grounds. In doing this the commissioners feel great difficulty, as they cannot, with any degree of precision, estimate the expense of making it merely passable; nor can they allow themselves to suppose that a less breadth than that mentioned in the law was to be taken into the calculation. The rugged deformity of the grounds rendered it impossible to lay a route within the grade limited by law otherwise than by ascending and descending the hills obliquely, by which circumstance a great proportion of the route occupies the sides of the hills, which cannot be safely passed on a road of common breadth, and where it will, in the opinion of the commissioners, be necessary, by digging, to give the proper form to thirty feet, at least in the breadth of the road, to afford suitable security in passing on a way to be frequently crowded with wagons moving in opposite directions, with transports of emigrant families, and droves of cattle, hogs, etc., on the way to market. Considering, therefore, that a road on those grounds must have sufficient breadth to afford ways and water courses, and satisfied that nothing short of well constructed and completely finished conduits can insure it against injuries, which must otherwise render it impassable at every change of the seasons, by heavy falls of rain or melting of the beds of snow, with which the country is frequently covered; the commissioners beg leave to say, that, in a former report, they estimated the expense of a road on these grounds when properly shaped, made and finished in the style of a stone-covered turnpike, at $6,000 per mile, exclusive of bridges over the principal streams on the way; and that with all the information they have since been able to collect, they have no reason to make any alteration in that estimate.

The contracts authorized by, and which have been taken under the superintendence of the commissioner, Thomas Moore (duplicates of which accompany this report), will show what has been undertaken relative to clearing the timber and brush from part of the breadth of the road. The performance of these contracts was in such forwardness on the 1st instant as leaves no doubt of their being completely fulfilled by the first of March.

The commissioners further state, that, to aid them in the extension of their route, they ran and marked a straight line from the crossing place on the Monongahela, to Wheeling, and had progressed twenty miles, with their usual and necessary lines of experiment, in ascertaining the shortest and best connection of practical grounds, when the approach of winter and the shortness of the days afforded no expectation that they could complete the location without a needless expense in the most inclement season of the year. And, presuming that the postponement of the remaining part till the ensuing spring would produce no delay in the business of making the road, they were induced to retire from it for the present.

The great length of time already employed in this business, makes it proper for the commissioners to observe that, in order to connect the best grounds with that circumspection which the importance of the duties confided to them demanded, it became indispensably necessary to run lines of experiment and reference in various directions, which exceed an average of four times the distance located for the route, and that, through a country so irregularly broken, and crowded with very thick underwood in many places, the work has been found so incalculably tedious that, without an adequate idea of the difficulty, it is not easy to reconcile the delay.

It is proper to mention that an imperious call from the private concerns of Commissioner Joseph Kerr, compelled him to return home on the 29th of November, which will account for the want of his signature to this report.

All of which is, with due deference, submitted, this 15th day of January, 1808.

ELI WILLIAMS,
THOMAS MOORE,

NOTE.—It will be observed that Keyser's Ridge, which is unquestionably the highest point on the road, is not mentioned by the commissioners. This is, no doubt, because, at the date of their report, the locality did not bear the name Keyser's Ridge, and was known as a peak of Negro mountain. Soon after the location of the road, one Keyser acquired the property at the ridge, and it took its name from him. It will also be observed that the measurement of heights by the commissioners was made from "a point ten feet above the surface of low water in the Potomac at Cumberland." A table of heights given in a subsequent chapter, the authority for which is not ascertainable, differs from that in the commissioners' report, but their report must be accepted as accurate from their point of measurement. The other table referred to, gives the heights above the Atlantic and above Cumberland, and embraces more hills than the commissioners' report.

Albert Gallatin, Secretary of the Treasury, called upon for Information respecting the Fund Applicable to the Roads mentioned in the Ohio Admission Act — His Responses.

TENTH CONGRESS — FIRST SESSION.

Communicated to the House of Representatives March 8, 1808.

TREASURY DEPARTMENT, March 3, 1808.

Sir: In answer to your letter of the 1st instant, I have the honor to state:

1st. That the 5 per cent. reserved by the act of 30th April, 1802, on the net moneys received for public lands in the State of Ohio, sold since 1st July, 1802, has amounted to the following sums, viz:

From 1st July, 1802, to 30th June, 1803...........................$ 6,220 00
From 1st July, 1803, to 30th June, 1804............................ 8,810 17
From 1st July, 1804, to 30th June, 1805............................ 13,994 30
From 1st July, 1805, to 30th June, 1806............................ 31,442 20
From 1st July, 1806, to 30th June, 1807............................ 28,827 92
From 1st July, 1807, to 31st December, 1807 (estimated).......... 15,000 00

$104,294 59

And that the said 5 per cent. will henceforth probably amount to $30,000 a year.

2d. That, of the $30,000 appropriated by act of 29th March, 1806, there has been expended, in laying out the Cumberland road from Cumberland to Brownsville, about.................$10,000
That there may be wanted to complete the location, about .. 5,000

$15,000

3d. That contracts have been made for opening one-half of the breadth of said road, which, as verbally informed by one of the commissioners, will require about $3,000, leaving, probably, about $12,000 of the appropriation for the further improvement of the road.

4th. That the portion of the road actually located and confirmed, no part of which exceeds an angle of five degrees, extends from the navigable waters of the Potomac, at Cumberland, to the navigable waters of the Monongahela, at Brownsville (Red Stone Old Fort), and it is stated, though no official report has been made to me, at about seventy miles.

5th. That that road can be considered as a national object only if completed as a turnpike, whereby all the flour and other produce of the western adjacent countries may be brought to a market on the Atlantic shores; and the transportation of all the salt and other commodities and merchandise whatever, imported from the Atlantic ports to the western country generally, may be reduced probably one dollar per cwt.

And, Lastly, that the expense of completing that part of the road in such manner, is estimated at $400,000.

I have the honor to be, respectfully, sir, your obedient servant,

ALBERT GALLATIN.

Hon. John Montgomery, of Maryland, Chairman, etc., in Congress.

COMMITTEE ROOM, Dec. 22, 1808.

Sir: The committee appointed on the message of the President, transmitting a report of the commissioners concerning a road from Cumberland to Ohio, have directed me to request that you would cause to be laid before them such information as may be in possession of the Treasury Department respecting the fund applicable by law to "the laying out and making public roads leading from the navigable waters emptying into the Atlantic, to the Ohio," etc. (1) The unexpended balance of the $30,000 appropriated by the act of the 29th of March, 1806; (2) The amount of moneys, exclusive of the above, now in the treasury, and in the hands of the receiver of public moneys, applicable to that object; and (3) an estimate of the probable amount of moneys that will accrue to the fund within the two succeeding years.

I have the honor to be, very respectfully, sir, your obedient servant,

JEREMIAH MORROW.

To the Hon. Secretary of the Treasury.

TENTH CONGRESS — SECOND SESSION.

Cumberland Road.

Communicated to the House of Representatives, February 16, 1809.

TREASURY DEPARTMENT, Dec. 29, 1808.

Sir: In answer to your letter of the 22d instant, I have the honor to state, for the information of the committee:

1st. That the unexpended balance of the appropriation, made by the act of March 29, 1806, for opening a road from Cumberland, on the Potomac, to the river Ohio, amounts to $16,075.15; part of which sum will probably be wanted in order to complete the location and opening of the road. It is probable that about $13,000 will remain applicable to making the road.

2dly. That the total amount received, either at the treasury, or by the receivers of public moneys on account of roads, and calculated at the rate of 5 per cent. on the net proceeds of the sales of lands in the State of Ohio, subsequent to the 30th day of June, 1802, was, on

the 30th day of September last $104,692
leaving, if that mode of calculating be correct, and after deducting the sum appropriated by the above mentioned act.. 30,000

a sum applicable to the road of ....$ 74,692
in addition to the above mentioned unexpended balance of.. 16,075

and making together a sum of ....$ 90,767
But if the amount applicable to roads be calculated at the rate of 2 per cent. only, on the net proceeds of the sales of lands, this will, on the 30th of September last, have produced only ....$ 41,876
from which, deducting the appropriation of.............. 30,000

leaves an unappropriated balance of ....$ 11,876
which, added to the unexpended balance of the appropriation 16,075

makes an aggregate of only.............................$ 27,951

3dly. That the probable receipts on account of that fund may, for the two ensuing years, be estimated at $22,500 a year, if calculated at the rate of 5 per cent., and at $9,000 a year, if calculated at the rate of 2 per cent. on the sales of lands.

I have the honor to be, respectfully, sir, your obedient servant,

ALBERT GALLATIN.

Hon. Jeremiah Morrow, Chairman of the Land Committee.

From 1st July, 1802, to 30th June, 1803, 2 per cent.................$ 2,400 00
From 1st July, 1803, to 30th June, 1804, 2 per cent.................. 3,524 06
From 1st July, 1804, to 30th June, 1805, 2 per cent.................. 5,597 72
From 1st July, 1805, to 30th June, 1806, 2 per cent.................. 11,243 55
From 1st July, 1806, to 30th June, 1807, 2 per cent.................. 9,120 75
From 1st July, 1807, to 30th June, 1808, 2 per cent.................. 9,802 80
Estimated July, 1808, to 31st October, 1808, 2 per cent............. 2,815 60

Total $44,692 48

The sum of $30,000 appropriated per act of 29th of March to be paid therefrom; of which $13,924.85 seems to have been paid.

A. G.

The Life of the Road Threatened by the Spectre of a Constitutional Cavil — President Monroe Vetoes a Bill for its Preservation and Repair — General Jackson has Misgivings — Hon. Andrew Stewart comes to the Rescue.

SPECIAL MESSAGE.

To the House of Representatives: MAY 4, 1822.

Having duly considered the bill, entitled "An act for the preservation and repair of the Cumberland Road," it is with deep regret (APPROVING, AS I DO, THE POLICY), that I am compelled to object to its passage, and to return the bill to the House of Representatives, in which it originated, under a conviction that Congress do not possess the power, under the Constitution, to pass such a law. A power to establish turnpikes, with gates and tolls, and to enforce the collection of the tolls by penalties, implies a power to adopt and execute a complete system of internal improvements. A right to impose duties to be paid by all persons passing a certain road, and on horses and carriages, as is done by this bill, involves the right to take the land from the proprietor on a valuation, and to pass laws for the protection of the road from injuries; and if it exist, as to one road, it exists as to any other, and to as many roads as Congress may think proper to establish. A right to legislate for one of these purposes, is a right to legislate for the others. It is a complete right of jurisdiction and sovereignty for all the purposes of internal improvement, and not merely the right of applying money under the power vested in Congress to make appropriations (under which power, with the consent of the States through which the road passes, the work was originally commenced, and has been so far executed). I am of opinion that Congress do not possess this power—that the States individually cannot grant it; for, although they may assent to the appropriation of money within their limits for such purposes, they can grant no power of jurisdiction or sovereignty, by special compacts with the United States. This power can be granted only by an amendment to the Constitution, and in the mode prescribed by it. If the power exist, it must be either because it has been specifically granted to the United States, or that it is incidental to some power, which has been specifically granted. If we examine the specific grants of power, we do not find it among them, nor is it incidental to any power which has been specifically granted. It has never been contended that the power was specifically granted. It is claimed only as being incidental to some one or more of the powers which are specifically granted. The following are the powers from which it is said to be derived: (1) From the right to establish post offices and post roads; (2) From the right to declare war; (3) To regulate commerce; (4) To pay the debts and provide for the common defence and general welfare; (5) From the power to make all laws necessary and proper for carrying into execution all the powers vested by the Constitution in the government of the United States, or in any department or officer thereof; (6) And lastly, from the power to dispose of and make all needful rules and regulations respecting the territory and other property of the United States. According to my judgment, it cannot be derived from either of these powers, nor from all of them united, and in consequence it does not exist. Having stated my objections to the bill, I should now cheerfully communicate at large the reasons on which they are founded, if I had time to reduce them to such form as to include them in this paper. The advanced stage of the session renders that impossible. Having, at the commencement of my service in this high trust, considered it a duty to express the opinion that the United States do not possess the power in question, and to suggest for the consideration of Congress the propriety of recommending to the States an amendment to the Constitution, to vest the power in the United States, my attention has been often drawn to the subject since, in consequence whereof, I have occasionally committed my sentiments to paper respecting it. The form which this exposition has assumed is not such as I should have given it had it been intended for Congress, nor is it concluded. Nevertheless, as it contains my views on this subject, being one which I deem of very high importance, and which, in many of its bearings, has now become peculiarly urgent, I will communicate it to Congress, if in my power, in the course of the day, or certainly on Monday next.

JAMES MONROE.

General Jackson, in his famous veto of the Maysville Road bill (May 27, 1830), refers to the Cumberland Road, and to the above message of President Monroe, in the following terms:

"In the administration of Mr. Jefferson we have two examples of the exercise of the right of appropriation, which, in the consideration that led to their adoption, and in their effects upon the public mind, have had a greater agency in marking the character of the power than any subsequent events. I allude to the payment of fifteen millions of dollars for the purchase of Louisiana, and to the ORIGINAL APPROPRIATION FOR THE CONSTRUCTION OF THE CUMBERLAND ROAD; the latter act deriving much weight from the acquiescence and approbation of three of the most powerful of the original members of the confederacy, expressed through their respective legislatures. Although the circumstances of the LATTER CASE may be such as to deprive so much of it as relates to the actual construction of the road of the force of an obligatory exposition of the Constitution, it must nevertheless be admitted that so far as the mere appropriation of money is concerned, they present the principle in its most imposing aspect. No less than twenty-three different laws have been passed through all the forms of the Constitution, appropriating upwards of two millions and a half of dollars out of the national treasury in support of that improvement, with the approbation of every president of the United States, including my predecessor, since its commencement. The views of Mr. Monroe upon this subject were not left to inference. During his administration, a bill was passed through both houses of Congress, conferring the jurisdiction and prescribing the mode by which the federal government should exercise it in the case of THE CUMBERLAND ROAD. He returned it with objections to its passage, and in assigning them, took occasion to say that in the early stages of the government he had inclined to the construction that it had no right to expend money except in the performance of acts authorized by the other specific grants of power, according to a strict construction of them; but that on further reflection and observation his mind had undergone a change; that his opinion then was: 'that Congress had an unlimited power to raise money, and that in its appropriation they have a discretionary power, restricted only by the duty to appropriate it to purposes of common defence and of general, not local, National, not State benefit;' and this was avowed to be the governing principle through the residue of his administration."

On the 27th of January, 1829, the Hon. Andrew Stewart, of Pennsylvania, in a vigorous speech on the floor of Congress, repelled the proposition that the general government was lacking in power and authority to make and preserve the road, from which the following extracts are taken:

"Mr. Stewart expressed his regret that gentlemen had deemed this a fit occasion to draw into discussion all the topics connected with the general power over the subject of internal improvements. If repeated decisions, and the uniform practice of the government could settle any question, this, he thought, ought to be regarded as settled. The foundation of this road (the National or Cumberland) was laid by a report made by Mr. Giles, the present Governor of Virginia, in 1802, and was sanctioned the next session by a similar report, made by another distinguished Virginian (Mr. Randolph), now a member of this House—it was the offspring of Virginia, and he hoped she would not now abandon it as illegitimate. Commenced under the administration of Mr. Jefferson, it had been sanctioned and prosecuted by every president, and by almost every Congress, for more than a quarter of a century. * * * *

"Without roads and canals, of what avail was it to the people of the West to possess a country, abounding with all the essential elements of wealth and prosperity—of what avail was it to have a country abounding with inexhaustible mines of coal and ore; to possess a fruitful soil and abundant harvests, without the means of transporting them to the places where they were required for consumption? Without a market, the people of the West were left without a motive for industry. By denying to this portion of the Union the advantages of internal improvements, you not only deprive them of all the benefits of governmental expenditures, but you also deprive them of the advantages which nature's God intended for them. Possessing the power, how, he asked, could any representative of the interior or western portions of this Union vote against a policy so essential to the prosperity of the people who sent him here to guard their rights, and advance their interests? * * * *

"The right of this government to construct such roads and canals as were necessary to carry into effect its mail, military, and commercial powers, was as clear and undoubted as the right to build a post office, construct a fort, or erect a lighthouse. In every point of view the cases were precisely similar, and were sustained and justified by the same power." * * * *

The power, said Mr. S., "to establish post offices and post roads," involves the power and duty of transporting the mail, and of employing all the means necessary for this purpose. The simple question, then, was this: Are roads necessary to carry the mail? If they were, Congress had expressly the right to make them, and there was an end to the question. Roads were, he contended, not only necessary to carry into effect this power, but they were absolutely and indispensably necessary; you cannot get along without them, and yet we are gravely told that Congress have no right to make a mail road, or repair it when made! That to do so would ruin the States and produce consolidation — ruin the States by constructing good roads for their use and benefit; produce consolidation by connecting the distant parts of the Union by cheap and rapid modes of inter-communication. If consolidation meant to confirm and perpetuate the Union, he would admit its application, but not otherwise. But we are told that the *States* will make roads to carry the mails. This was begging the question. If the States would make all the roads required to carry into effect our powers, very well; but if they did not, then we may undoubtedly make them ourselves. But it was never designed by the framers of the Constitution that this government should be dependent on the States for the means of executing its powers: "its means are adequate to its ends." This principle was distinctly and unanimously laid down by the Supreme Court in the case already referred to: "No trace," says the Chief Justice, "is to be found in the Constitution of an intention to create a dependence of the government of the Union on the States for the execution of the powers assigned to it — its means are adequate to its ends. To impose on it the necessity of resorting to means it cannot control, which another government may furnish or withhold, would render its course precarious, the result of its measures uncertain, and create a dependence on other governments, which might disappoint the most important designs, and is incompatible with the language of the Constitution." And this was in perfect harmony with the constant and uniform practice of the government. * * *

Mr. S. begged gentlemen to turn their attention for a moment to the statute book, and see what the practice of the government had been; what had been already done by Congress in virtue of this power of "establishing post offices and post roads." In 1825 an act had been passed, without a word of objection, which went infinitely further than the bill under consideration. His colleague (Mr. Buchanan) was then a member of this House, and no doubt, voted for it. His eloquence was then mute — we heard nothing about States rights, spectres, and sedition laws. This bill, regulating the post office establishment, not only created some thirty or forty highly penal offences, extending not only over the Cumberland Road, but over every other road in the United States, punishing with severest sanctions, even to the taking away the liberty and the lives of the citizens of the States, and requiring the State courts to take cognizance of these offences and inflict these punishments. This was not all: this act not only extended over all the mail roads, but all other roads running parallel with them, on which all persons are prohibited, under a penalty of fifty dollars, from carrying letters in stages or other vehicles performing regular trips; and authorizing, too, the seizure and sale of any property found in them for the payment of the fines. The same regulations applied to boats and vessels passing from one town to another. Compare that bill with the one under debate. This bill had two or three trifling penalties of ten dollars, and was confined to one road of about one hundred and fifty miles in extent, made by the United States, while the other act, with all its fines and forfeitures, pains and penalties, extended not only to all the mail roads in the United States, but also to all parallel roads; yet no complaint was

then heard about the constitutionality of this law, or the dreadful consequences of carrying the citizens hundreds of miles to be tried. Under it no difficulties had ever been experienced, and no complaint had ever been heard. There had been no occasion for appointing United States Justices and creating federal courts to carry this law into effect, about which there was so much declamation on this occasion: this was truly choking at gnats and swallowing camels. To take away *life* by virtue of the post office power for robbing the mail, is nothing; but to impose a fine of ten dollars for wilfully destroying a road which has cost the government a million of dollars, is a dreadful violation of State rights! An unheard of usurpation, worse than the sedition law, and went further towards a dissolution of the Union than any other act of the government. Such were the declarations of his colleague; he hoped he would be able to give some reason for thus denouncing this bill, after voting for the act of 1825, which carried this same power a hundred times further than this bill, both as regards the theatre of its operations, and the extent of its punishments. * * * *

Having thus established, and, as he thought, conclusively, the right to construct roads and canals for mail and military purposes, he came next to say a few words on the subject of those which appertained to the express power of "regulating commerce with foreign nations and *among the several States.*" This power carried with it, as a necessary incident, the right to construct commercial roads and canals. From this grant Congress derived exactly the same power to make roads and canals that it did sea-walls, light-houses, buoys, beacons, etc., along the seaboard. If the power existed over the one it existed over the other in every point of view; the cases were precisely parallel; it was impossible to draw a distinction between them. This power was essential to every government — there was no government under the sun without it. All writers on national law and political economy considered the right to construct roads and canals as belonging to the commercial power of all governments. * * *

There were great arteries of communication between distant divisions of this extensive empire, passing through many States or bordering upon them, which the States never could and never would make. These works were emphatically national, and ought to be accomplished by national means.

He instanced the road now under consideration — it passed through Maryland, Pennsylvania and Virginia, yet neither of these States would have given a dollar to make it. It passed mostly through mountainous and uninhabited regions. He adverted to the Potomac, Ohio, and Mississippi rivers. Important as these were to all the States, yet they were the internal concerns of none — they were mere boundaries to which the States would give nothing, while they had so many objects exclusively internal requiring all their means. For these reasons he was utterly opposed to the project of dividing the surplus revenue of the general government among the several States; this would be to surrender the national means which the people had confided to this purpose to mere local and sectional objects, while those truly national would remain forever unprovided for. He did not claim for this government the power to make roads and canals for all purposes. The powers of this government and of the States were distinct and well defined. To the national government belonged, under the Constitution, the power of making national roads and canals for national purposes. To the States belonged the power of providing for state and local objects. The roads and canals projected and executed by the States and private companies were often highly important in a national point of view; and to such, in his opinion, this government ought always to afford aid in a proportion corresponding with the interest the nation had in their accomplishment. When individuals were willing to go before and vest millions of their private funds in works strictly and truly national, connecting the remote sections of the Union together (of which we had two distinct examples, one in this district and the other in a neighboring city, Baltimore), could this government, charged with the care and guardianship of all the great interests of the nation, look on with cold indifference? Was it not our duty to lend a helping hand to encourage, to cheer, and to sustain them in their noble and patriotic efforts? * * * *

Mr. Stewart said he would now proceed to answer, as briefly as possible, some leading arguments urged by gentlemen in opposition to the bill under consideration. His colleague (Mr. Buchanan) had said that this bill proposed a greater stretch of power than the sedition law. This was an argument "ad captandum vulgus." He would not do his colleague the injustice to suppose that he was so ignorant of the Constitution of his country as seriously to address such an argument to the understanding of this House. The bill under consideration was necessary to carry into effect the express power of transporting the mail. What power of this government was the sedition law intended to carry into effect? None. It was therefore not only clearly unconstitutional on this ground, but it went directly to abridge the freedom of the press, and, of course, was a plain and palpable violation of that provision in the Constitution, which declares that "Congress shall make no law abridging the freedom of speech or of the press." Now, if his colleague could show any provision in the Constitution in the slightest degree impugning the right of Congress to pass this bill, then he might have some excuse for offering such an argument, otherwise he had none. The gentleman had, in a very labored effort, endeavored to prove that this government had no kind of jurisdiction or control whatever over this road. Yet his own amendment recognized the existence of the very power which he denies. By his amendment he proposes what? That this government shall cede the roads to the States, with the power to erect gates and collect as much toll as was necessary to keep it in repair. But his whole argument went to prove that Congress did not possess the very power which his amendment assumed and proposed to the States. The gentleman's amendment, and his speech therefore, were at open war with each other, and would perhaps both perish in the conflict. Certainly, both could not survive—one or the other must fall.

The gentleman, proceeding in his argument, had assumed premises which nobody would admit, and then, with an air of great triumph, he drew conclusions which even his own premises would not support. He takes for granted that this government, with all its mail, military, and commercial powers, has no more right to make a road to carry these powers into effect, through a State, than any individual possessing none of these powers would have. Thus, having assumed what was utterly inadmissible, he triumphantly inquires whether an individual, having obtained leave to make a road through another's land, could put up gates and exact toll? The gentleman says, surely not. But he said, surely yes, unless expressly prohibited by the contract. Suppose, by permission, I build a mill, said Mr. S., upon that gentleman's estate, and construct a bridge and turnpike road to get to it, have not I as much right to demand toll at the bridge as at the mill? Most undoubtedly; so that the gentleman's premises and his conclusions were alike fallacious and unsound. This position had been taken by both the gentlemen from Virginia (Mr. Barbour and Mr. Archer), to whom he would make the same reply.

A most extraordinary argument had been advanced against military roads: the public enemy may get possession of them in war!! Was it possible that an American statesman could, at this time of day, urge such an argument? It might be addressed to a set of timid savages, secure in the midst of the wilderness. The enemy get possession of our roads, and therefore not make them! Such cowardly arguments would deprive us of every possible means of defence. The enemy, it might be said with equal propriety, may get our ships, our forts, our cannon, our soldiers, and therefore we ought not to provide them. What would the brave freemen of this country say to the men who would deny them roads to travel on, lest the enemy might take them from us in war? They would reply, with Spartan magnanimity, "Let them come and take them." * * *

A great deal has been said on the subject of jurisdiction; that, if it existed at all, it must be exclusive; that it could not attach to soil, and much metaphysical refinement of this sort, which had little to do with the subject. On this point, the only sound and practical rule was, that this government had a right to assume such jurisdiction over their roads as was necessary for their preservation and repair by such means as should be deemed most expedient, leaving everything beyond that to the States. Thus far the Constitution declared the legislation of Congress to be "the supreme law of the land, anything in the constitution and laws of any State to the contrary notwithstanding." This left to the laws of the States, the right to punish all offences and other acts committed upon the road, in the same manner as though they had occurred in any other part of their territory. Such had been the uniform practice of the government in executing all its powers up to the present time, and no complaint had ever been made or inconvenience experienced.

It has been universally conceded on all hands in this debate, that the consent of the States could not confer any jurisdiction or powers on this government beyond what it had derived from the Constitution. This was too clear a proposition to admit of doubt. Yet the names of Jefferson, Madison, Monroe, and Gallatin, were introduced and relied on. Did gentlemen forget that Mr. Gallatin was the very first man that ever suggested the plan for making the Cumberland road, and that it had been sanctioned and actually constructed under the administrations of Jefferson, Madison, and Monroe? Their opinions were thus reduced to practice, which was the best evidence in the world—"By their fruits shall ye know them."

At the session of the year 1831, the Pennsylvania Legislature passed a bill, which was approved April 4th, of that year, by George Wolf, governor, the preamble to, and the first, and part of the second, and all of the tenth sections of which read as follows:

"Whereas, that part of the Cumberland Road lying within the State of Pennsylvania is in many parts in bad condition for want of repairs, and as doubts have been entertained whether the United States have authority to erect toll gates on said road, and collect toll; and as a large proportion of the people of this commonwealth are interested in said road, and its constant continuance and preservation; therefore,

SECTION 1. *Be it enacted by the Senate and House of Representatives of the commonwealth of Pennsylvania, in general assembly met, and it is hereby enacted by authority of the same;* That as soon as the consent of the government of the United States shall have been obtained, as hereinafter provided, WILLIAM F. COPLAN, DAVID DOWNER, of Fayette county, STEPHEN HILL, BENJAMIN ANDERSON, of Washington county, and THOMAS ENDSLEY, of Smithfield, Somerset county, shall be, and they are hereby appointed commissioners, a majority of whom shall be sufficient to transact business, who shall hold their offices for three years after the passage of this act, after which the right of appointing said commissioners shall vest in the governor of this commonwealth, to build toll houses, and erect toll gates at suitable distances on so much of the Cumberland Road as lies within the State of Pennsylvania; *Provided,* that if any one or more of the commissioners should die, resign, or refuse to serve, the Governor shall appoint one or more other commissioners to fill the vacancies so happening; *And provided, also,* that nothing herein contained shall be construed to prevent the Governor from re-appointing the commissioners named in this act, if he thinks proper.

SEC. 2. That for the purpose of keeping so much of the said road in repair as lies within the State of Pennsylvania, and paying the expense of collection and other incidental expenses, the commissioners shall cause to be erected on so much of the road as passes within this State at least six gates, and that as soon as said gates and toll-houses shall be erected, it shall be the duty of the toll collectors, and they are hereby required to demand and receive for passing the said gates, the tolls hereafter mentioned; and they may stop any person riding, leading or driving any horses, cattle, sulky, chair, phæton, cart, chaise, wagon, sleigh, sled or other carriage of burden or pleasure from passing through the said gates, until they shall respectively have paid for passing the same, that is to say: (Here follow the rates).

SEC. 10. That this act shall not have any force or effect, until the Congress of the United States shall assent to the same, and until so much of the said road as passes through the State of Pennsylvania, be first put in a good state of repair, and an appropriation made by Congress for erecting toll-houses and toll-gates thereon, to be expended under the authority of the commissioners appointed by this act: *Provided,* The legislature of this State may at any future session thereof, change, alter or amend this act, provided that the same shall not be so altered or amended, as to reduce or increase the rates of toll hereby established, below or above a sum necessary to defray the expenses incident to the preservation and repair of said road, for the payment of the fees or salaries of the commissioners, the collectors of tolls, and other agents. *And provided further,* That no change, alteration, or amendment, shall ever be adopted, that will in any wise defeat or affect, the true intent and meaning of this act.

Ohio was a little in advance of Pennsylvania in accepting the road, and less exacting in her terms. The legislature of that State, on the 4th of February, 1831, passed an act authorizing the acceptance, without requiring that the road should be put in repair as a condition precedent. On the 23d of January, 1832, Maryland, by an act of her legislature, agreed to accept the road upon the same condition required by Pennsylvania, and on the 7th of February, 1832, Virginia accepted in an act similar to that of Ohio. On the 3d of July, 1832, Congress declared its assent to the above mentioned laws of Pennsylvania and Maryland in these words: "To which acts the assent of the United

States is hereby given to remain in force during the pleasure of Congress," and on the 2d of March, 1835, assented to the act of Virginia with a similar limitation.

JANUARY 19, 1835.

REFERRED TO THE COMMITTEE OF THE WHOLE HOUSE, TO WHICH IS COMMITTED BILL No. 221.

To the Senate and House of Representatives of the United States in Congress assembled:

The undersigned beg leave to represent that they have been appointed commissioners, under the act of the Legislature of Pennsylvania, to accept from the general government so much of the Cumberland Road as lies within the limits of that State, and erect toll gates as soon as it is put in such a state of repair as is required by the provisions of that act. That they have every disposition to relieve the government from the burden of the road, so soon as they can feel themselves justified, under the law, in doing so; but they beg leave to respectfully represent that the road has not yet been put in that condition that would enable them to accept of it.

On some parts no more than six inches, and west of the Monongahela river, three inches only of metal have been put upon it, and it is apparent that this will be totally insufficient to preserve it under the heavy travel upon that road. Besides, the bridges throughout the whole road remain untouched. Under these circumstances, it is impossible for us, in the discharge of our duty, to accept of it; and we would most earnestly urge upon Congress the propriety of making such an appropriation as will complete the repairs in a substantial manner, as required by the act of our own legislature. We will not undertake to prescribe the amount which may be necessary; but, to satisfy your honorable bodies that we are disposed to go as far as the faithful discharge of our duty will permit, we hereby pledge ourselves, so soon as Congress shall make an appropriation of so much money as may be estimated by the department as necessary for that purpose, to accept of the road, and have toll gates erected without delay. We, therefore, beg leave most respectfully to submit to the wisdom of your honorable bodies to determine whether it will be better to make the necessary appropriation to justify us in accepting the road, and relieving the government from all future charge, or to keep it in its present state, subject to annual appropriations for its preservation, as heretofore.

THO. ENDSLEY.
STEPHEN HILL.
DAVID DOWNER.
WILLIAM F. COPLAN.
BENJAMIN ANDERSON.

January 7, 1835.

To the Honorable the Senate and House of Representatives of the United States in Congress assembled:

The undersigned beg leave to represent that they have been appointed commissioners, under the act of Assembly of the State of Maryland, to report to the Governor and Council of said State when that part of the Cumberland Road which lies within the limits of said State shall have been put in that state of repair contemplated by the act of Congress, and the act of Assembly of the State of Maryland, agreeing to receive the road and to keep it in repair; that they will with great pleasure report the road to the Governor and Council the moment they can with propriety do so. And they beg leave to represent that they feel authorized to say that the Governor and Council will, with great pleasure, authorize them to receive the road whenever it shall be put in that condition which would justify the State in accepting it. They further represent that the road has not yet been put in that condition that would justify them in advising the State to receive it. On some parts of the road no more than three and a half inches of metal has been put, and it is evident that this covering will be totally insufficient to preserve it in a fit state for use under the heavy travel which is constantly passing over it. The bridges also, throughout the whole distance, remain in a ruinous and dilapidated condition. They further respectfully represent that the new location from Cumberland, through the narrows of Wills creek and along Braddock's run, a distance of upwards of six miles, has had but three and a half inches of metal upon it; and the bridge over Wills creek and the bridges over Braddock's run were to be permanent stone structures, by the act of Assembly of Maryland, authorizing the President to change the location of the road. The undersigned are also advised that it is contemplated by the superintendent to put up wooden structures for bridges, in lieu of the stone bridges required by the act

of Assembly of Maryland, authorizing the change in the location of the road, which would be in direct violation of that act. They further represent that the floors of wooden bridges must be removed every two or three years, and the whole structure of the bridges themselves must be built every twenty or twenty-five years.

Under these circumstances it would be impossible for the undersigned, in the discharge of their duty, to recommend to the State the acceptance of the road. And they would most earnestly but respectfully urge upon Congress the propriety of making such an appropriation as will be sufficient to complete the repairs on the old road, and to finish the new location in a substantial manner, as contemplated and required by the act of the Legislature of Maryland. The undersigned will not undertake to prescribe the sum which may be necessary for this purpose; but, to satisfy your honorable bodies that they are disposed to go as far as the faithful discharge of their duty will permit, they hereby pledge themselves that so soon as Congress shall make an appropriation of so much money as may be estimated by the department as necessary for the completion of the repairs of the old road, and the finishing of the road on the new location, together with the construction of permanent stone bridges, they will forthwith report to the Governor and Council the state of the road, and recommend that the State receive such part of the road as may be completed, and to collect tolls on it to keep it in repair, thereby relieving the United States from any further expense for repairs on such part. They further beg leave most respectfully to submit to the wisdom of your honorable bodies to determine whether it will be better to make the necessary appropriation to enable them to recommend the road as in a fit condition to be received by the State, and thus relieve the government from any further burden, or to let it remain in its present state, subject to appropriations for its preservation, as heretofore.

JOHN HOYE,
MESHECK FROST,
Commissioners of the State of Maryland.

On April 1, 1835, Pennsylvania accepted the road in the following brief terms, embodied in the third section of an act of her legislature of that date: " The surrender by the United States of so much of the Cumberland Road as lies within the State of Pennsylvania is hereby accepted by this State, and the commissioners to be appointed under this act are authorized to erect toll gates on the whole or any part of said road, at such time as they may deem it expedient to do so."

Maryland, Virginia, and Ohio also accepted the road, and thenceforth it was, and remains, under the control of the several States through which it passes.

Plan of Repairs — The Macadam System adopted — Mr. Stockton offers his services — Capt. Delafield made Superintendent — The Road in a bad condition — Permission asked to deviate from instructions, and refused — Capt. Gievey lifted the old road bed indiscriminately — First defects to be remedied — Lieut. Mansfield at Uniontown — Plan emphasized in notices for contracts — Free passage for water a first consideration.

ENGINEER DEPARTMENT,
WASHINGTON, July 23, 1832.

Lt. J. K. F. Mansfield, Corps of Engineers:

SIR: By direction of the Secretary of War, you have been assigned, temporarily, to the superintendence of the repairs of the Cumberland Road east of the Ohio river; and in the discharge of your duties in this capacity, you will be governed by the following instructions:

1st. Respecting the parts to be repaired. The extreme limits within which your operations will be confined are, the point of intersection of the road with the western boundary line of the State of Pennsylvania, and Cumberland, in the State of Maryland; the dividing line between these States will be considered as dividing the line of the road to be repaired into two divisions, and the division within the State of Pennsylvania will be subdivided into six equal sections, and that within the State of Maryland, into two; then, having made a thorough examination of each of these sections, with a view to make yourself acquainted with their exact condition, you will classify them in the order of their condition, placing the worst first, the next worst second, and so on, making the best the last. You will then make an estimate for the repairs of each of these sections, to ascertain how far the appropriation, which is one hundred and fifty thousand dollars, will go toward repairing the whole road. Separate contracts will then be made for executing the repairs, commencing with No. 1, and passing regularly through the sections, as classified, to the best section; and these repairs will be prosecuted with as much despatch as the nature of the case will allow. Should you deem it advisable, in letting out these sections, to retain any portion of them which may seem to require but slight repairs, and which repairs could be executed with greater economy by having overseers and laborers to act under your immediate direction, you are at liberty to do so, bearing in mind, however, that whenever the repairs of the road can be made with equal economy, it is the wish of the department that they should be made by contract. As soon as one or more of these sections are finished, you will notify the commissioners appointed to receive this road by the laws of Pennsylvania and Maryland, approved, that of the former on the 4th day of April, 1831, and that of the latter on the 4th day of January, 1832, that these sections are ready to be turned over to the State, and you will accordingly turn them over.

2d. Respecting the mode of repairs. In order to insure efficient and permanent repairs, they are to be made on that which is called the Macadam system; that is to say, the pavement of the old road must be entirely broken up, and the stones removed from the road; the bed of which must then be raked smooth, and made nearly flat, having a rise of not more than three inches from the side to the center, in a road thirty feet wide; the ditches on each side of the road, and the drains leading from them, are to be so constructed that the water cannot stand at a higher level than that which is eighteen inches below the lowest part of the surface of the road; and, in all cases, when it is practicable, the drains should be adjusted in such a manner as to lead the water entirely from the side ditches. The culverts are to be cleared out, and so adjusted as to allow the free passage of all water that may tend to cross the road.

Having thus formed the bed of the road, cleaned out the ditches and culverts, and adjusted the side drains, the stone, reduced to a size not exceeding four ounces in weight, must be spread on with shovels, and raked smooth. The old material should be used only when it is of sufficient hardness, and no clay or sand must be mixed with the stone.

In replacing the covering of stone, it will be found best to lay it on in strata of about three inches thick, admitting the travel for a short interval on each layer, and interposing such obstructions from time to time as will insure an equal travel over every portion of the road; taking care to keep persons in constant attendance to rake the surface when it becomes uneven by the action of the wheels of carriages. In those parts of the road, if any, where materials of good quality cannot be obtained from the road in sufficient quantity to afford a course of six inches, new stone must be procured to make up the deficiency to that thickness; but it is unnecessary, in any part, to put on a covering of more than nine inches. None but limestone, flint or granite, should be used for the covering, if practicable; and no covering should be placed upon the bed of the road till it has become well compacted and thoroughly dried. At proper intervals, on the slopes of hills, drains or paved catch-waters must be made across the road, when the cost of constructing culverts would render their use inexpedient. These catch-waters must be made with a gradual curvature, so as to give no jolts to the wheels of carriages passing over them; but whenever the expense will justify the introduction of culverts, they will be used in preference; and in all cases where the water crosses the road, either in catch-waters or under culverts, sufficient pavements and overfalls must be constructed to provide against the possibility of the road or banks being washed away by it.

The masonry of the bridges, culverts, and side walls, must be repaired, when it may be required, in a substantial manner, and care must be taken that the mortar used be of good quality, without admixture of raw clay. All the masonry to be well pointed with hydraulic mortar, and in no case must the pointing be put on after the middle of October; all masonry finished after this time will be well covered, and pointed early in the following spring. Care must be taken, also, to provide means for carrying off the water from the bases of walls, to prevent the action of frost on their foundations; and it is highly important that all foundations in masonry should be well pointed with hydraulic mortar to a depth of eighteen inches below the surface of the ground.

As the laws on the subject of this road do not seem to justify a deviation from the original location, you will be careful to confine your operations to the road as you find it located; but, as it is believed that its axis may be dropped without adding much to the expense in those places where its inclination with the horizon exceeds four degrees, you are authorized, under the exercise of a sound discretion, to make this change.

In making your contracts, it must be understood that you are to have the general supervision of their execution, and that it will be your duty to see that all labor and materials (provided for by them) be applied in the most faithful and substantial manner. These contracts must provide in their specifications for all the work that can be anticipated, and should it happen that additional stipulations are afterwards found to be necessary for either workmanship or supplies not originally provided for, the facts must be reported to this department, and, with its approbation, if obtained, new contracts will be made for the additional services and supplies required; and it must be distinctly understood by the contractors that no payment will be made for work not provided for by their contracts.

Mr. L. W. Stockton, of Uniontown, has been engaged on this road and is intimately acquainted with every part of it, as well as with the adjacent country; and, as he has offered his services, you would do well to call upon him and avail yourself of them in any capacity that may seem to you best.

As soon as it can be done, a drawing of the whole road, with details of construction, will be forwarded, to be filed in this office.

You will take up your headquarters at any point on the road where your services may appear to you to be most needed; and, as soon as you shall have completed such an examination of the road as will place you in possession of the information necessary to draw up the specifications to your contracts, you will invite proposals for those contracts through the public prints. These contracts will be closed with as little delay as the interest of the road will allow, when the work will be commenced, and the contracts, together with the proper estimates, forwarded to this office. For the mode of making these estimates, keeping your accounts, and conducting your correspondence with this office, you are referred to the regulations of the Engineer Department.

Captain Delafield has been assigned to the permanent superintendence of the repairs of this road, and has been directed to join you on or before the 1st of October next. You will, therefore, immediately on his arrival, turn over to him these instructions, together with all the papers and public property that may be in your possession relating to the road. As soon as you shall have completed the necessary examinations on the road, you will commence and continue the repairs simultaneously in both States.

You will make application for such instruments and funds as may appear necessary to enable you to execute the foregoing instructions.

I am, &c.,

C. GRATIOT,
Brigadier General.

CUMBERLAND, MD., August 1, 1832.

Sir: I have this evening returned from a general reconnoissance of the road in this State. I find the road in a shocking condition, and every rod of it will require great repair; some of it is now almost impassable. I purpose leaving here to-morrow, on a particular measurement and survey of the road as it is, and the requisites to put it in complete repair.

The object of this communication is to request to be permitted to deviate, according to circumstances, from so much of my instructions as requires the old bed in all cases to be lifted, and the rise in the middle three inches; for there are parts of the road where the top of the old bed is full low, and where it will be more expensive, and less firm, to remove the old bed and fill in with earth, than to bring stone and Macadamize on the top of the old bed to the thickness of nine inches; and there are cases on the sides of the mountains where a greater rise than three inches, such, for instance, as some parts of it now have, which is more advantageous than a less one to confine the water to the gutters in cases of torrents, and thereby preventing a general sweep over the whole road, which would carry off the smallest stuff of a Macadamized road.

The repairs made by Mr. Giesey, about two years since, have the radical fault resulting from having lifted the old road indiscriminately, and not giving sufficient rise to the center for a mountainous country.

I have the honor to be, sir,

Very respectfully, your most obedient,

J. K. F. MANSFIELD,
Lieut. of Engineers.

Gen. Chas. Gratiot, Chief Engineer.

ENGINEER DEPARTMENT.

WASHINGTON, August 9, 1832.

Sir: Your letter of the 1st instant, requesting permission to deviate, according to circumstances, from so much of the instructions of the department to you, on the subject of the repairs of the Cumberland Road, as requires the old road in all cases to be lifted, and the rise in the middle to be made three inches, has been under consideration, and I have to inform you that this permission cannot be granted.

In withholding the sanction of the department to any deviation from the prominent features of your instructions on the subject of these repairs, it may, perhaps, be proper to state, for your information, the views of the department on this subject.

By referring to the report of Mr. Weaver, a printed copy of which you have in your possession, who made an examination of the Cumberland Road in 1827, you will perceive that the mode of constructing it was that of digging a trench, or of sinking the bed of the road below the natural surface of the ground; that this trench was filled with large stones, and that these were covered with stones a size smaller, and so on. By this construction, it was intended that the weight of the carriages passing over the road should be supported by the large stones, and that the smaller stones were only intended to present an even surface for the easy passage of vehicles over it. The great objections to this construction are, that the bed being lower than the surface of the ground on each side, the ditches can hardly ever be sunk sufficiently deep to intercept the passage of water from the ground adjacent to the road to the ditch or trench in which the road is made; this water, by keeping the bed constantly wet, would cause the heavy stones of the first layer to sink into the ground, and thus break up the surface of the road, and allow the free passage of water through the covering itself. In the winter, the frost acting upon the bed, rendered wet by the free passage of water to it in every direction, would heave the stones to such a degree that the road in a little time would be perfectly impassable; and if any evidence, in addition to that presented by the testimony of the most experienced and approved road builders, were necessary to convince the department that the present dilapidated state of the road under your charge is owing entirely to the operation of the causes above alluded to, it is believed that that evidence is found in the report made by Capt. Delafield, who inspected the repairs of this road made by Mr. Giesey. By pursuing the course suggested in your letter, it is believed that these objections and difficulties would still obtain, and that in a little time, however faithfully the repairs might be made on the top of the large stones, the road would be in as bad order as it is at present, since the great cause of these evils would remain, viz.: that of having the bed which supports the stones, and which in fact should

be the real support of the traffic on the road, lower than the neighboring ground.

It is the intention of the department that the defects of the first construction of the road shall be remedied in its repair, and as it is believed that the adoption, as nearly as practicable, of the Macadam system, in all its important features, presents the only means of effecting this remedy, and as this system forms the basis of your instructions, it is recommended that they be departed from as little as possible.

It is by no means the intention of the department to take from you all discretion in the discharge of your duties; such a course would defeat the object had in view in sending an officer of engineers on the road; but it is believed to be highly important that the exercise of this discretion should be limited to an extent that will insure the adoption of such principles and rules as cannot fail to render these repairs permanent. For these principles and rules, you are referred to Mr. Macadam's work on the construction and repairs of roads, a copy of which is in your possession. In removing the metal from the old road, whenever hollows present themselves in the old bed, it is recommended that they be filled with earth; indeed, the whole bed of the road should be elevated, and its form given to it, before any of the covering of stone be replaced. The earth necessary for this may be taken from the ditches, or even from the sides of the road, where it can be done without encroaching upon the privileges of persons residing on the road. I am, &c., &c.,

C. GRATIOT.

Lt. J. K. F. Mansfield,
　　Corps of Engineers, Uniontown, Pa.

EXTRACTS FROM NOTICES FOR CONTRACTS.

PLAN OF REPAIRS.

The plan for repair is to lift the pavement of the old road in all cases, and deposit the stone off the bed; then to repair the culverts, clear the drains, ditches, and culverts, so as to admit the free passage of water, and graduate the bed of the road, so that, when well packed by travel or other means, it will be three inches higher in the middle than at either side, for a bed of thirty feet. Having thus formed the bed of the road, the hard stone (if there be any) of the old road, broken to a size not exceeding four ounces, is to be placed on the bed of the road to a breadth of twenty feet, and a thickness not exceeding nine inches, and in cases where there is a deficiency of the old material, limestone or whinstone is to be procured to supply the deficiency to the required thickness of nine inches. Catch-waters and hollow-ways to be permanently constructed on the sides of hills, and at other places where it will be thought necessary by the superintending engineer, but in no case to exceed one in every twelve rods. In those sections where pieces of hitherto Macadamized road are included, the sand is to be taken off, and, before new metal is added, the surface loosened with a pick. The metal added to be three inches thick in the cases heretofore Macadamized.

JOS. K. F. MANSFIELD,
Lieutenant Corps of Engineers.

ENGINEER DEPARTMENT,

WASHINGTON, August 27, 1832.

Sir: I have to acknowledge the receipt of your letter of the 24th inst., inclosing two printed advertisements for proposals to contract for the repairs of the Cumberland Road under your charge.

In answer, the department would call your attention to your remarks under the head "Plan of Repairs," and would suggest that, instead of removing the stones from the bed of the road before the drains, ditches, and culverts are put in repair, to allow the free passage of water from the road, this latter operation should be first attended to, to the end that the removal of the stone from the road might be effected without the fear of being annoyed by the accumulation of water from heavy rains. Besides, thus preparing the drains, ditches, &c., in the first place, would enable the bed to become perfectly dry by the time the stones are prepared to be replaced.

I am, &c.,

C. GRATIOT

Lt. J. K. F. Mansfield,
Corps of Engineers, Uniontown, Pa.

Lieut. Mansfield superseded by Capt. Delafield—The Turning of Wills Mountain—Contractors not Properly Instructed—Capt. Delafield suggests a Change of Plan, and enforces his Views by Copious Quotations from Macadam—He is Permitted to exercise his own Discretion—Too much sand between Uniontown and Cumberland—Operations at Wills Creek suspended—A Collision with the Chesapeake and Ohio Canal Company—The difficulty adjusted, and operations resumed.

ENGINEER DEPARTMENT,

WASHINGTON, October 5, 1832.

Sir: On the arrival of Captain Delafield, of the engineers, on the Cumberland Road in Pennsylvania and Maryland, you will hand to him the enclosed communication, which assigns to him the superintendence of the repairs of that road which have heretofore been conducted under your supervision. You will, also, turn over to him all the funds, books, papers, and public property in your possession appertaining to this road, and close your account with it.

Very respectfully, &c.,

By order:

WM. H. C. BARTLETT,
Lieut. and Assistant to Chief Engineer.

Lieut. J. K. F. Mansfield,
Corps of Engineers, Uniontown, Pa.

Sir: The surveys of a route for turning Wills mountain by the valley of Braddock's run and Wills creek are progressing, being retarded only by the weather. I have examined the whole route, and can confirm the most satisfactory account you may have heard of it. The ground over which the road will pass is a uniform inclined plane, requiring very few culverts, two small bridges over Braddock's run of about fifteen feet span each, with side hill in no other part than about 300 yards in the "Narrows" of Wills creek, where a most simple and expedient plan will be to use the level and smooth bottom of the creek for the road, by building a wall not to exceed ten feet in height, thus throwing the stream on the opposite bank, peculiarly well formed for this construction, being a low bottom of alluvion. The idea of cutting into the mountain would be expensive, and no better than throwing the creek from its present bed.

On the arrival of Mr. Pettit, I shall divide the road into four sections, giving him one. The present condition of the road is most unpromising. Nearly every contractor has formed his bed in the valley made by the removal of the old pavement, the consequence of which is, that, with the mild season and rainy weather, the bed is not drained, nor can it be, until the side roads are cut down to the bottom of the stone strata—a measure I directed as the only means of correcting the evil. Time, and the headstrong obstinacy of some of the contractors, have prevented much of the work being so attended to. All the contracts made by Lieut. Mansfield distinctly specify that the road for 30 feet in width shall be graded in such manner as to avoid this difficulty; yet in carrying the contracts into effect, the superin-tendents have, in no instance, instructed the contractors in the proper course. They have, in most instances too, permitted the stone to be broken on the road; the consequences of this are, much sand and dirt in the metal, and a bed graded without proper attention. This is the more remarkable, as in my report on the work executed two years since by one of the present superintendents, these errors were pointed out as serious evils, yet they are not corrected. It must be expected, therefore, that all that part of the road now under construction will be very indifferently made, and by no means such as the Macadam system calls for. By the time the superintendents acquire a knowledge of their business, the present contracts will be completed. Instead of giving out any more of the work under the present system, as I had contemplated and advertised, I shall postpone doing so until I am better assured that the work can be properly executed. I look anxiously for Mr. Pettit, trusting his intelligence may correct some of the defects in the section he will be called upon to superintend.

To instruct the superintendents in their duties, I shall be compelled to have printed a manual or primer, with a few lithographic sections, that the sight may aid the mind in a proper understanding of the business. To persevere in the present plan, where neither contractors, superintendents, nor laborers, understand their business, is highly inexpedient, and I shall forthwith commence maturing a system that must be productive of more good with less money, or it were better to leave the work undone, for I am satisfied that durability can not be looked for under the present system.

My first business will be to draw the operations to a close, and then endeavor to bring about the correction. You will be apprised of my views before carrying any of them into effect, observing that, in anticipation of a change, I have suspended making the contracts alluded to in my communication of the 27th ultimo.

Respectfully, your obedient servant,

RICH'D DELAFIELD,
Captain of Engineers.

Brig. Gen. Charles Gratiot,
Chief Engineer.

Baltimore, May 6, 1833.

Sir: The instructions of the department of the 23d July last, relating to the method of repairing the Cumberland Road east of the Ohio, are founded upon principles upon which I differ in opinion, and beg leave to request your reconsideration, involving, as they do, an expenditure of not less than $250,000, when compared with what I judge to be the most judicious method of making the repairs.

It is in relation to the propriety of breaking up the old bed of the road in all cases. I apprehend the department was not aware that the bed is a substantial, yet rough pavement, and not formed of loose, detached masses of quarry stone thrown together, without order. It is important to consider this particular when examining the authorities on road making.

My own views are that it is decidedly preferable to retain the old pavement in all cases where its continuity is unbroken, even mending

small parts that may be deranged, and Macadamizing over it. In this, I think, I am borne out by Macadam, Dean, Telford, and Farey, whose ideas on the subject are annexed, as extracted from "Macadam on Roads."

The only two arguments against the method I propose are, first, that the metal will grind to dust by being placed over large stone. In answer to which, I say, that the road passing through a rocky country, even after removing the pavement, there still remains a rocky foundation; and where the pavement is well bedded in sand or clay, we have all the elasticity necessary from the clay or sand bed through the pavement. In support of which, see the sample of metal taken from the road through Uniontown, where the under strata have not worn or crushed an iota, presenting angles as sharp as the day they were first placed there. Were the metal placed upon an unyielding rock, it would doubtless soon grind to dust; but placing it upon a pavement laid in sand or gravel, preserves the elasticity so necessary for this kind of road. Second: That large stone, placed under Macadam metal, will work to the surface. This is doubtless true when detached pieces are surrounded by the metal, but with a pavement the case is very different. I find pieces of this Cumberland Road, repaired as far back as 1827, by Mr. Ewing, over the old pavement, in perfect order to this day; as, also, some parts done in this way by Giesey in 1829, that are much better than any of the repairs he made at the same time; and a piece through Uniontown, by the authorities of the place, in 1830, remains in perfect order.

I have been led to reflect upon this subject from learning that the Ohio road had cut through and was impassable at certain places during the months of February and March, and seeing the state of the road under my supervision between Cumberland and Wheeling, comparing the parts repaired last season, those under Giesey, Ewing, and the town authorities, with the old pavement that has stood sixteen years without a cent of money in repair, and to this day is a very good wagon road, rough, it is true, yet never cutting through during the fall, winter, or spring, where the pavement is continuous. To throw away so firm a foundation I cannot think advisable, and beg you to reflect upon the subject and favor me with your views.

The road in Ohio has worn six years (nearly) without repairs, and was impassable this spring. The old Cumberland Road has worn sixteen years, and mile after mile has never been known to cut through at any season. Parts of it covered with Macadamized metal, and worn for five years, are in fine order, and present a very smooth surface, never having cut through. Other parts, where the old pavement has been removed and Macadamized, were impassable during the spring after three years' wear. We have to bear in mind the impossibility of keeping the ditches and drains open in the mountains during the winter. Ice forming in the drains will, of course, throw the melting snows on the surface of the road, which is destructive to a Macadamized road on clay or sand, whereas, if on the old pavement, it has strength enough to resist the travel until either dried by frost, or sun. This is a consideration that the English road-makers had not to consider with the same weight. As to keeping the drains open, and the road surface free from water in the winter, I conceive it impracticable in the mountains; hence the further propriety of preserving a foundation that will secure a firm road at all seasons, even if the wear should prove some five or ten per cent. more rapid, which I do not even think will be the case on the plan suggested of Macadamizing upon a pavement, and not on an unyielding, rocky bottom. Respectfully, your obedient servant,

RICHARD DELAFIELD,
Captain of Engineers.

Brig. Gen. C. Gratiot,
Chief Engineer.

EXTRACTS FROM "MACADAM ON ROADS," MADE BY CAPTAIN DELAFIELD IN SUPPORT OF HIS VIEWS RELATING TO THE PAVEMENT FORMING THE BED OF THE "CUMBERLAND ROAD EAST OF THE OHIO."

Page 39.—"It would be highly unprofitable to lift and relay a road, even if the materials should have been originally too large. The road between Cirencester and Bath is made of stone too large in size. In this case I recommend cutting down the high places," &c.

Page 40.—"A part of the road in the Bath district is made of freestone, which it would be unprofitable to lift. Other cases of several kinds have occurred where a different method must be adopted, but which it is impossible to specify, and must be met by the practical skill of the officer, and who must constantly recur to general principles."

Page 42.—"The price of lifting a road, &c., leaving the road in a finished state, has been found in practice to be from 1d. to 2d. per superficial yard, lifted four inches deep."

Page 47.—"It is well known to every skillful and observant road-maker, that if strata of stone of various sizes be placed on a road, the largest stones will constantly work up." (This is in no manner applicable to a pavement, and a road made even in the manner he alludes to was lifted only four inches deep.—R. D.)

Page 105.—"How deep do you go in lifting the roads? That depends upon circumstances, but I have generally gone four inches deep. I take up the materials four inches, and, having broken the large pieces, I put them back again."

"Does the plan which you have mentioned, of breaking up the roads, apply to gravel roads, or only to those roads composed of hard stones? In gravel roads, and in some other roads, it would be impossible to break them up to advantage; and, in several places, I should think it unprofitable to lift a road at all. I did not order the road near Reading to be lifted, but I directed, whenever a large piece of flint was seen, it should be taken up, broken, and put down again. I am speaking of a gravel road now."

Page 107.—"There are other cases besides that of gravel, in which I should think it unprofitable to lift a road. The road between ———— and ———— is made of very soft stone, and is of so brittle a nature, that if it were lifted it would rise in sand, and there would be nothing to lay down again that would be useful. I should not recommend lifting of freestone roads, for the same reason, because it would go so much to sand that there would be very little to lay down again. I will explain what I have done to the road between Cirencester and Bath. I was obliged to lift a little of the sides of the road, in order to give it shape, but in the center of the road we 'shoved it.' It was before in the state which the country people call gridirons: that is, it was in large ridges, with long hollows between, and we cut down the high part to a level with the bottom of the furrows, and took the materials and sifted them at the side of the road, and returned what was useful to the center."

(So far we have the views of Mr. Macadam. From the same work I continue to quote.—R. D.)

Page 153.—"Considering the very great traffic upon White-chapel road, is it your opinion (addressed to Mr. Farey) that it would be advantageous to pave any part of that road? I think it would be desirable to pave it within some feet of the footpath," &c.

Page 158.—"In the neighborhood of London the materials that are to be procured are of too tender and brittle a nature to endure the wear of the heavy carriages. I, therefore, am of the opinion that it would be proper to pave the sides of all the principal entrances into London."

Page 166.—"James Walker says, 'The traffic upon the Commercial rail road, both up and down, is very great. I am quite sure that the expense of this road would have been very much greater, probably much more than doubled, if it had not been paved. The road has been paved for about sixteen years. and the expense of supporting it has been small. During the thirteen years that the East India dock branch has been paved, the paving has not cost £20.'"

Page 167.—"But as the paving is always preferred for heavy carriages," &c.

Page 172.—"The thickness ought to be such, that the greatest weight will not effect more than the surface of the shell, in order to spread the weight which comes upon a small part only of the road over a large portion of the foundation."

Page 173.—"If the foundation is bad, breaking the bottom stone into small pieces is expensive and injurious, upon the principle I have above described, for the same reason that an arch formed of whole bricks, or deep stones, is preferred to one of the same materials broken into smaller pieces, for, in some countries, the materials will admit of the foundation of the road being considered as of the nature of a flat arch, as well as being supported by the strata directly under it. But the error of laying stones in large pieces upon the surface is more common and more injurious."

Page 183.—"James Dean says, 'Near to great towns it would be highly advantageous if the center of the road, for about twelve feet in width, were to be paved with hard, well-squared stones, nine inches deep.'"

Page 188.—"Thomas Telford, Esq., says, 'The improvements made in North Wales I beg leave to submit as models for the roads through hilly countries. Great pains have been taken in constructing firm and substantial foundations for the metallic part of the roadway.'"

Page 189.—"There has been no attention paid to constructing a good and solid foundation for the roadway."

Page 192.—"Are you of the opinion that it would be advisable or practicable to procure, from any particular part of the country, better materials, so as to form perfect roads without the necessity of paving them? That these materials could be procured, is evident; but I am satisfied that the most economical and preferable mode would be by the means of paving."

ENGINEER DEPARTMENT.

WASHINGTON, May 8, 1833.

Sir: Your communication of the 6th instant, submitting your views in regard to lifting the old bed in prosecuting the repairs of the Cumberland road east of the Ohio, and requesting a reconsideration of so much of the instructions of the department of the 23d July last as relates to this matter, has just been received. That part of the instructions alluded to, which requires that the old bed shall, in all cases, be taken up, will be considered as suspended, and you are hereby authorized to exercise your discretion in this particular.

Very respectfully, &c.,

C. GRATIOT, Brig. General.

Capt. R. Delafield,
Corps of Engineers, Uniontown, Pa.

UNIONTOWN, PA., June 11, 1833.

Sir: I find upon an examination of the National Road, under your superintendence, from Cumberland to this place, that too great a portion of sand and other perishable stone has been allowed to be put on it. In almost the whole distance, little or no regard has been paid to the keeping the side drains open, at least sufficiently so to carry the water freely from the road. The culverts are too few and small, particularly on the long slopes; and the manner of constructing the hollow-ways and catch-waters is defective. These errors of construction cause the water, in many places, to pass over the road, to its rapid destruction. I am aware of the difficulties you have to contend with under the contract system, and that to this cause most of the evils complained of may be traced. As it is all important that they should be remedied, as soon as practicable, you will enforce the early completion of the several contracts, according to their conditions, after making due allowance for the stoppage arising from your order for suspending operations during last winter. On the completion of the road, should it be found not to possess the requisite properties to secure its permanency, you will make such additions under your own agency as will place it in the condition contemplated by the government, before turning it over to the States. Not less than six inches of lime or sandstone should be put upon the surface, and where lime is exclusively used, the thickness should not be less than nine inches. The side ditches should, when practicable, be at least eighteen inches below the bed of the road; and when this cannot be done, culverts, 2'x3', should be constructed at convenient distances to carry off the water, which, in no instance, should be allowed to rise above the level of the bed of the road. The catch-waters should be constructed in such a manner, that while they subserve the purposes for which they are intended, they should admit the passage of vehicles without jolting; and, in every case, with a view to prevent their being washed into deep gullies. As this frequently happens when they are constructed with broken stone, it will be proper to pave them with shingle stones, if to be had; or, when this cannot be obtained, with limestone firmly imbedded in the road. It should especially be observed that, before breaking up the road for the reception of the metal, the ditches should be first prepared, and then the culverts. This will keep the roadway dry for travel, and better prepare it for the reception of its covering. As it is found impracticable to keep the travel from the center of the road, and the deep ruts that are formed, then, as a consequence, I would recommend, instead of the present system of blocking, that rakers should be constantly employed to preserve the transverse profile. If it does not come within the spirit of the contract, that this labor should be performed by the contractors, you will hire men to do it yourself. This operation, in addition to the draining system before recommended, will, it is presumed, preserve the road from further ruin, and place it in a condition to receive its last coat of limestone. Finally. while studying due economy in your administration of the affairs of the road, you should constantly bear in mind that the wishes of the government are to have a superior road, both as regards workmanship, and the quality of the materials used in its construction. With this understanding, it is expected that you will avail yourself of all the facilities within your reach to effect, in a satisfactory manner to yourself and the public at large, the great end proposed—the construction of a road unrivaled in the country. These are the views and special instructions of the Secretary of War.

I am, respectfully, &c.,

C. GRATIOT, Brig. General.

Capt. R. Delafield,
Corps of Engineers, Uniontown, Pa.

ENGINEER DEPARTMENT,
WASHINGTON, July 16, 1833.

Sir: You will forthwith cause all operations to cease on that part of the new location of the Cumberland Road on the east of Wills creek. You shall in a few days receive further instructions on this subject. Very respectfully, &c.,

WM. H. C. BARTLETT,
Lieut. and Assistant to Chief Engineer.

Capt. R. Delafield,
Corps of Engineers, Uniontown, Pa.

ENGINEER DEPARTMENT,
WASHINGTON, July 20, 1833.

Sir: On the 16th you were advised to delay any further action as to the location of the Cumberland Road until you were again written to.

Mr. Purcell reports to the Board of the Chesapeake and Ohio Canal Company that the road being at the site now chosen will occasion an increased cost to the Canal Company of upwards of $16,000. It is very desirable to avoid this state of things, for, as their charter claims precedence, it would necessarily create a demand upon the government commensurate with the injury sustained.

Major Eaton, president of the Canal Company, will direct Mr. Purcell, the engineer, to proceed forthwith to Cumberland, with you, to ascertain the best mode of making the location by which to avoid any injury or increased expense to the Canal Company. You are instructed to confer freely with Mr. Purcell, holding the object suggested steadily in view, and give such direction to the location of the road as may best attain this object. This done, you will forward a plan of the route agreed on, and a minute detail of everything, particularly what increased expense to the Canal Company will probably be occasioned. On receiving your report, the case will be considered here, and you be advised immediately of the course to be pursued.

Very respectfully, &c., &c.,

By order:

WM. H. C. BARTLETT,
Lieut. and Assistant to Chief Engineer.

Capt. R. Delafield,
Corps of Engineers, Uniontown, Pa.

PHILADELPHIA, July 26, 1833.

Sir: The order of your department of the 16th instant was received by me at Cumberland, and its injunctions forthwith carried into effect. The communication of the 20th has since been received, explanatory of that order. In relation to locating that part of the National Road that might probably interfere with the Canal Company, measures were taken to procure from the Company such information as would enable me to locate the road without coming in contact with any part of the Canal route; and, so far as the information was furnished, I have endeavored so to do. I enclose copies of the letter and information received from the president of the company, in reply to a request for such information as would enable me to "ascertain at what point the Chesapeake and Ohio Company contemplate erecting their dam across Wills creek, and to what height it will be raised above low water. The information desired is for enabling me to locate the bridge for the road at a point, and elevate its arches to such a height that the interest of the Canal Company will not be effected; and that I may at the same time, fulfill the objects contemplated by the law authorizing the new location."

In reply to which you will perceive "the location of the canal is that recommended by General Bernard, and the Board of Internal Improvement, over which he presided," and that it was proposed to feed the canal at Cumberland, and below by a dam to be erected across the Potomac about a mile above Cumberland. The water of the Potomac was to be carried over Wills creek twenty-one or two feet above ordinary water in the creek.

Such is the information furnished me by the president of the Ca-

nal Company, and by which I have been governed in the location of the road. On the eastern side of Wills creek the grading is finished to the site of the bridge; on the western side I have directed no work to be executed that can have any bearing upon this point.

You perceive it has been my study to avoid conflicting with the interests of the Canal Company; but, from the want of knowing the exact location of their works, will occasion to them an increased expense, as reported by Mr. Purcell, of 16,000 dollars if the bridge is constructed at the point now chosen. If, then, the Company will cause the Canal to be located through the gap of Wills mountain, and give me bench marks from which to ascertain the cuttings and embankments they propose making, I will then locate the road on such ground as not to interfere in any manner with their operations, and such as shall be most advantageous for the public interest. I judge the communication of the department was written under the impression that an interference with the works of the Canal Company was unavoidable, and that some compromise of advantages and disadvantages would necessarily have to be made. Such, however, I do not conceive to be the case.

I have located as high up the creek as would give room for a six horse team to turn off and on a bridge at right angles with the stream with facility. If the Canal Company make choice of this ground, I have but to make a bridge oblique with the current, and thus avoid the work of the Canal Company. To ascertain this, it is essential that the Canal Company should make choice of the ground and locate their works; after having so done, if they will favor me with plans and sections, with bench marks of reference of the part in the valley of the creek, the road shall be made not to interfere with their interest, which has always been looked upon by me as claiming precedence.

I have here pointed out a course for the consideration of the department, differing materially from the one ordered by the letter of the 20th instant. First, in consideration of its not being acquainted with the nature of the case, and, next, with its requiring me to perform a service in no way necessary to a proper understanding of the interests of the Government connected with the road; to do which, surveys, levels, calculations of excavation and embankment must be made, that the time of neither myself nor the officers associated with me could accomplish.

What I ask is, information from the Company as to their own works solely. It will suffice for all purposes connected with the location of the road.

Be pleased to address me at New Castle, and on any matter relating to the section of the road near Cumberland requiring immediate attention, a copy of the communication forwarded to Lieutenant Pickell, at that place, would prevent any delay; Lieutenant P. being the officer to whom I have assigned this particular section of the road.

Respectfully, your obedient servant,

RICH'D DELAFIELD.
Captain of Engineers.

Brig. Gen. Charles Gratiot,
Chief Engineer.

WASHINGTON, D. C., May 10, 1832.

Sir: Your letter to Mr. Ingle, the clerk of the Chesapeake and Ohio Canal Company, has been handed over to me, and I am authorized, on the part of the president and directors, to express to you our thanks for the considerate regard you have paid to the location adopted by the Chesapeake and Ohio Canal Company, for the part of their work which will pass through Cumberland. The location adopted is that recommended by General Bernard, and the Board of Internal Improvement, over which he presided.

When the proposed change of the Cumberland Road immediately above the town was under consideration of the Committee on Roads and Canals, I suggested the very precaution you now practice, which was to see that no conflict would arise in hereafter conducting the canal over its long established route, by a conflict with the location of the improved road, the value of which I know well how to appreciate. The hill above Cumberland, which it is proposed to avoid, was the worst between that place and Wheeling, if reference had to be had to the inclination of its surface. General Bernard proposed to feed the canal at Cumberland, and for some distance below it, as far, at least, as the mouth of the South branch, by means of a dam to be erected at a ledge of rocks crossing the Potomac about a mile above Cumberland. The dam was to be elevated so high as to conduct the canal over Wills creek at Cumberland, with an elevation of twenty-one or twenty-two feet above ordinary water in the creek. This was to be effected by an aqueduct across the creek. I presume at this season of the year the ledge of rocks is visible above Cumberland. Enclosed I send you extracts from General Bernard's report, which accompanied the President's message to Congress of December 9, 1826, and is now a congressional record. From that you may perhaps infer all that is essential to your purpose of avoiding a collision with the rights of the Chesapeake and Ohio Canal Company, who have adopted for the location of the canal General Bernard's report.

C. F. MERCER,
President of the Chesapeake and Ohio Canal Company.

EXTRACTED—PAGE 55, DOC. No. 10, 19TH CONGRESS, 2D SESSION.—EXECUTIVE PAPERS.

"The difficulties of this passage (down Wills creek) are great, and continue for more than a mile. The ground then becomes favorable (i. e., in descending Wills creek from the west), permitting the canal to pass at the outskirts of Cumberland, to join with the eastern section. Adjoining Cumberland, the canal will receive a feeder from the Potomac for a supply below, and more especially to complete what is necessary in relation to the first subdivision of the eastern section.

"This feeder is proposed to be made navigable, in order to accommodate the trade of the Potomac above Cumberland. Its length is one mile, its width at the water line thirty feet, its depth four feet. At its point of departure from the Potomac, a basin is formed in the bed of the river, by means of a dam erected at the first ledge above Cumberland.

"This basin, comprehending an extent of about eight miles, will afford a constant supply of water, and also accommodate the canal trade of the Potomac. The levees around the basin, the dam, the guard lock of the feeder, and its aqueduct over Wills creek, are included in the estimate of this subdivision.

"In the table of quantities and cost, this feeder is made to cost a very large sum (two or three words illegible in the MS.) if the dam above Cumberland is supposed to be ever changed from the above location. The aqueduct over Wills creek is computed to cost $41,601; the length of the aqueduct, seventy yards; the number of arches, three; the span of the arch, thirty feet; the height of the piers, sixteen feet."

The above is a true copy.   C. F. MERCER.
May 10, 1833.

ENGINEER DEPARTMENT.

WASHINGTON, August 10, 1833.

Sir: The Secretary of War has just returned to this place, having passed over the Cumberland Road east of the Ohio. He feels great interest in this road, and is anxious that the operations on it shall be so directed as to obtain the best possible results. His confidence in your ability induced him to select you as its superintendent, knowing that under your management his wishes would be realized; and deeming it a work of much greater importance than that with which you are occupied on the Delaware, he has expressed a wish that by far the greater portion of your time should be passed upon the road. You will, therefore, repair to Cumberland without loss of time, ascertain the exact location of the Chesapeake and Ohio canal along the valley of Wills creek, and so adjust that of the road as shall remove the present difficulties, and avoid any interference with the interests of the Canal Company. This being done, you will communicate to the department the result.

Very respectfully, &c.,
WM. H. C. BARTLETT.

Capt. R. Delafield,   Lt. and Ass't to Ch. Eng'r.
Corps of Engineers, New Castle, Del.

ENGINEER DEPARTMENT.

WASHINGTON, September 12, 1833.

Sir: Your letter of the 9th instant, enclosing a plan and sections of part of Wills' creek, exhibiting the location of the National Road "as now constructed;" the ground selected by the engineer of the Chesapeake and Ohio Canal Company for its canal, and the new location of the National Road, in consequence of the Canal Company having made choice of the route upon which the road was constructed,

has been received. The plan has been submitted, with the approval of this department, to the Secretary of War, and by him adopted; and the construction of the road on the new location will, therefore, be proceeded with.   I am, sir, &c.,
C. GRATIOT,
Capt. R. Delafield,   Brig. General.
Corps of Engineers, Cumberland, Md.

CUMBERLAND ROAD, AT STODDARD'S, MD.,
September 17, 1833.

Sir: I enclose herewith plan and sections of part of the Cumberland Road between Cumberland and Frostburg, where an alteration has just been made in the location, by which a very steep hill is avoided, and the distance decreased.

By the new route there is a slope of $18\frac{2}{16}$ feet in a distance of 1,600; by the old road the slope was 53.9' in 700 feet on one side of the hill, and 35.7' in 900 feet on the other side.

This is now undergoing construction. The foundation of the center pier of the bridge over Wills creek is raised above water.

Respectfully, your obedient servant,
RICH'D DELAFIELD,
Brig. Gen. Charles Gratiot,   Captain of Engineers.
Chief Engineer.

ENGINEER DEPARTMENT,

WASHINGTON, September 25, 1833.

Sir: Your letter of the 17th inst., enclosing a plan and sections of part of the Cumberland Road between Cumberland and Frostburg, where you had made an alteration in the location, thereby avoiding a steep hill, and decreasing the distance, was duly received; and I have to inform you that the alteration referred to has been approved.   I am, &c.,
C. GRATIOT,
Capt. R. Delafield,   Brig. General.
Corps of Engineers, Cumberland, Md.

On with the work — Wooden Bridges proposed for the new location up Wills Creek and Braddock's Run — The War Department holds that Wooden Superstructures would be a Substantial Compliance with the Maryland law — New instructions issued from Wheeling — The old bed to be retained — Two classes of work — Frauds by Contractors — Form for Contracts forwarded from Brownsville — Report and Estimate called for by the Senate — The law of Congress renders a change of plan necessary — The Secretary of War greatly interested in the Road — Cumberland to Frostburg.

ENGINEER DEPARTMENT,

WASHINGTON, June 25, 1834.

Sir: In addition to the views of the department, communicated to you this morning, I now have to request that you will proceed to apply the funds available for the Cumberland Road east of the Ohio, with the utmost despatch consistent with the public interest. It is greatly to be desired that the repairs of this road may be completed before the termination of the coming fall.

I am, &c.,   C. GRATIOT,
Capt. R. Delafield,   Brigadier General.
Corps of Engineers, New Castle, Del.

CUMBERLAND, Md., July 23, 1834.

Sir: I beg leave to call your attention to the act of the Legislature of Maryland, giving its consent to change the location of the National Road near this place, to turn Wills mountain by the route of Wills creek and Braddock's run, in which it is provided that certain bridges shall be constructed of stone, and to compare this act with that of the last session of Congress, and inform me whether or not I will be justified in constructing the bridges with stone abutments and wing-walls, and *wooden* superstructures. There is a necessity growing out of the cost, the law requiring the road to be finished with $300,000.

From the most advantageous offers received, the bridge over Wills creek will not cost less than $15,000, constructed of stone, and if built of wood, planed, and painted with three coats of white lead, roofed with shingles, will cost not to exceed $7,000. There are two other bridges on the same new route to be constructed, the ratio of expense of which will not materially vary. *   *   *

Respectfully, your obedient servant,

RICH'D DELAFIELD,
Captain of Engineers.

Brig. Gen. Charles Gratiot,
   Chief Engineer.

CUMBERLAND, July 24, 1834.

Sir: I have just finished comparing the numerous offers for work to be done on the 16 miles of road immediately west of this place. There is great competition among very excellent and responsible men of the country, as well as from the railroad and canal below us.

The offers for the bridge render its construction with stone next to impracticable, under the law, to finish the road with $300,000. They are as follows: $22,000, $21,930, $23,323, $22,680, $24,000.

To construct the abutments I have offers at $3.80 cents per perch; that would, with the superstructure of wood, make the whole cost not to exceed $6,500 to $7,000. We cannot with propriety expend so large a sum for a stone bridge, with such limited means. I strongly recommend a wooden superstructure if compatible with existing laws under which we act, and beg to be advised as requested in my letter of yesterday.

Respectfully, your obedient servant,

RICH'D DELAFIELD,
Captain of Engineers.

Brig. Gen. Charles Gratiot,
   Chief Engineer.

ENGINEER DEPARTMENT.

WASHINGTON, July 29, 1834.

Sir: It has just been determined by the War Department that the substitution of wood for stone, in the superstructures of the bridges on the new piece of road around Wills hill would be deemed by the State of Maryland a substantial compliance with the requirements of her law giving assent to the change from the old to the present location of that part of the road. You will, therefore, build the abutments of those bridges in a good and durable manner, of the best stone to be had in your immediate neighborhood, and make the superstructure of wood. These last, when completed, must be well covered, and painted in the best manner. This is communicated in answer to your two letters of the 23d and 24th instant, on the subject, which are at hand. I am, &c.,

C. GRATIOT.

Capt. R. Delafield,
   Corps of Engineers, Cumberland, Md.

COPY OF INSTRUCTIONS SENT BY THE SUPERINTENDENT OF THE CUMBERLAND ROAD, EAST OF THE OHIO, TO EACH OF HIS ASSISTANTS ON THE LINE OF THE ROAD.

WHEELING, May 29, 1834.

Sir: In conducting the operations for repairing the section of the road under your supervision, during the present season, two very important alterations will be made in the system of last year.

The first is to retain, in all cases, the old bed or pavement, breaking down with sledges the prominent or projecting pieces into the ruts and holes, and smoothing the grade with quarry chips, or stone broken on the face of the road with sledge-hammers, slightly covering the bed so prepared with the earth from the ditches, observing to put no more earth than is barely sufficient to prevent the metal coming in contact with the large stone of the bed.

Where there is no stone in the old bed, restore the grade with the best and hardest material to be found in the vicinity, making it a point to have stone to fill the large holes. This formation of the bed for the metal on top of the old bed will enable large and sufficient ditches to be formed for carrying off the water. The most particular attention must be given to these ditches, as upon them depends the preservation of the road.

All the earth taken from the ditches, side roads, and slopes, not

required to make good the grade and side roads, must be thrown down the hill side, and on no account whatever upon the slope of a side hill cutting, from whence it soon washes back into the ditches. The minimum size of the ditches should not be less than three feet wide on top, one foot deep, and one foot wide in the bottom; the whole depth to be below the bed of the road. Rock and peculiar side slopes can alone prevent this being practiced.

The side slopes must be cut to a slope of 45, with berms, as a minimum; and as low as 60 wherever it is practicable.

Wherever earth is required for a filling to make good the side roads, require that it be taken from some near side slope or other point that will improve such part of the road. The minimum side road is to be five feet; wherever the natural ground will permit, cause it to be increased to admit of summer roads, placing the ditches outside of such increased side road.

The second alteration is, to have the whole work done by contract, instead of job work and day labor, as was practiced last year.

To effect this, the greatest precaution is necessary to specify what work has to be done on each chain of four rods of the road, the particular grade for such portion, the depth and size of the ditches, the side roads and slopes, and from whence the required earth is to be taken to restore the grade, and where the surplus earth is to be taken from the ditches, drains, side slopes, &c.

In the delivery of stone for the metal, the contract must provide that the stone be delivered and broken on the side roads in rectangular piles or strings of such dimensions as you require on the several parts of the road, and the measurement made of the cubic contents of the stone thus prepared; from which measurement you will ascertain the number of perches, by previously having a mass, containing five perches of stone, as it comes from the quarry, as compactly piled as can be without the use of a hammer, taking large and small indiscriminately. Have this mass broken to the size of four ounces; ascertain the cubic contents of the bulk it shall produce, the fifth part of which you will take as a perch, and the unit of measurement for paying for the number of perches to be delivered.

The metal is to be thrown on the road at such favorable periods as you shall designate, after it has been measured, and not until the contractor has prepared the required quantity for half a mile at a time.

You will require the contractor to commence the grade at one end of the piece he is to repair, and continue regularly through, not permitting him to seek the parts requiring least work to execute first; and when delivering stone, to commence the delivery at a point giving a mean distance for hauling from the quarry; a mean rate of payment is then equitable, otherwise it would not be.

The work on your section may be divided into two distinct classes: the one, where nothing has as yet been done; and the other, the part graded and stone prepared for the metal during the past season.

On the first class, you will make contracts to grade, deliver, and put on three perches of limestone where the old bed remains firm, and four perches where the old bed has disappeared, requiring the grade to be finished by the 15th of October; and if the metal is all prepared by that date, to be put on by the 1st of November, the contractor continuing to rake the road, change the travel, and preserve the whole work in order, until the succeeding 1st of April. Should the contractor, however, not be able to prepare the metal to put it on the road by the 1st of November, then he is to preserve the grade of the road in order until the first favorable state of the weather after the 15th of March ensuing, when he is to put on the metal, raking and smoothing the surface for twenty days after the whole metal shall have been put on the road.

You will observe that the contract is to call for preserving the road in either case during the winter; in one case, by adding metal, raking, &c., and in the other, by breaking with a sledge stone to fill the ruts, covering such stone in the spring lightly before putting on the metal.

The second class of work is the unfinished part of last year's operations, upon which you will be time to put three and a half additional perches per rod on such parts as were covered last year, and four perches per rod on such as had none, requiring that it be put on by the 1st of November, and be preserved, raked, &c., until

the succeeding 1st of April, during the winter filling ruts made by travel with additional metal, to be prepared and ready at convenient points on the road.

For the culverts you will make a contract with one person for all that may be necessary on half your section, and with a second person for the other half, the work to be paid by the perch of twenty-five cubic feet, measured by the plan and dimensions you shall designate for each locality, and according to which plan the work must be constructed. For this work you will require the stone to be of good proportions, with parallel beds and faces, and not smaller than two cubic feet in each piece, in no case ever permitting a stone to be placed "on edge," a very common practice, destructive of good masonry. The covering stone to be of such additional dimensions as you shall judge necessary for each locality. The bottoms of the culverts to be paved or flagged with stone, and such an apron constructed at each end as to guard against the ends being undermined by the passage of the water.

The repairs of the masonry of the bridges and walls on Wheeling Hill it is very desirable to effect by contract, if practicable. On Wheeling Hill the object may be effected by requiring the masonry to conform with that already executed, particularly in regard to the size and quality of the stone, paying for it by the perch measured in the wall when finished, reserving the one-fifth of the value from monthly payments as security for the faithful execution of the whole work. The repairs of the bridge may be executed in like manner, specifying the masonry of the bridge now building over Wheeling Creek as the standard, excepting stones placed on edge.

It is desirable to postpone the repair of all masonry to the latest date, excepting only such parts as are necessary to perfect the grade; you will make your contracts accordingly. The masonry of the culverts and some of the bridges must be finished in time, including the filling to make good the roadway, to permit the contractor for grading to comply with his agreement. The usual one-fifth of the value of work done being retained until the expiration of the time for completing the whole work, when this sum is to be applied either to carry into effect the remaining provisions of the agreement, as stipulated to be executed, or paid to the contractor, if the work has been faithfully executed according to the tenor of the agreement.

You will make all your payments by checks drawn on the bank through which I shall make your remittances, taking duplicate receipts for moneys thus paid, attached to a bill giving the quantity, rate, cost, and date of the receipt of the article clearly and distinctly expressed.

Your check book must be added up, and the balance in bank ascertained every Saturday evening, which balance must be reported in the weekly reports to be forwarded to me, as required last season.

The balance of your account, as appears by your ledger account with me, must also form an item in the weekly report. The assistant engineer will make an inspection of these books, and report to me, whenever he comes on your section of the road.

The receipted vouchers you will forward to the office at Brownsville, of all payments made during the week at the end of such week, reserving the duplicate until called for by myself or the assistant engineer.

So soon as you are apprised by me of funds being available you will immediately advertise by hand bills, and through the public prints, that contracts will be made for repairing the section of road under your supervision, and that proposals for executing the work will be received for twenty days from the date of your advertisement, for repairing each mile of the road according to stipulations and particular information, to be had on enquiring of you on or after such date as you are enabled to collect it. Let the advertisements express that the repairs consist principally in grading the road over the old bed, cleaning out the ditches and drains, restoring the side roads to their width of five feet and covering the road thus prepared with limestone broken to four ounce pieces, in such quantities as shall be specified for each rod, varying from two to four perches per rod, and keeping the whole until the first of April next, by which date the contracts are to be completed.

To ascertain the work to be done on the different mile sections, and on the particular parts of each mile, you will, the instant funds are available, make a measurement of the road, noting the work to be done on each chain (as specified in the previous parts of this communication) in the most minute detail.

This statement, reduced as much as practicable to a tabular form, you will cause to be printed, as the information to be given to persons upon which to make their proposals, and it will be embodied in or attached to the articles of agreement as a specification of the work to be done.

As you will find it convenient to have the prepared metal piled in uniform masses, admitting of the application of a gauge to ascertain whether or not the required quantity is in the pile, you will cause such gauges to be made with slopes of 45 degrees and in no instance permit a measurement of stone to be made without having previously verified the dimensions of the gauge. The necessity for this you will perceive by reflecting that the end of the gauge may be cut off and the angles altered to make a material difference in the quantity, without being perceptible to the eye.

The following are some of the frauds heretofore practiced, and now enumerated that you may look cautiously to their not being practiced upon your section of the road:

1st. Diminishing the size and altering the angle of the gauge.

2d. Loosening the pile of metal just before the measurement, to increase its bulk.

3d. Concealing or covering up in the piles of metal large masses of stone or other matter.

4th. Breaking stone of a softer or otherwise inferior quality than the sample agreed upon.

5th. Breaking the metal to a larger size than that agreed upon.

6th. Removing the prepared metal from one point to another after it has been measured.

7th. Taking metal from the face of the road, of the first or second stratum, to make it appear the desired quantity has been broken to fill the gauge.

8th. On parts of the road where limestone has already been delivered, wagoners, with a partial load, passing from the quarries to the point of delivery, have been detected in stealing a piece from several piles, thus making a full load from what has already been paid for.

Very many other frauds have been detected upon receiving and paying for stone perches before breaking. No corrective offers for the many that may be practiced under this system. It is, therefore, in no case, to be adopted. Always measuring the stone after it is broken, and reserving one-fifth of its value until the whole agreement has been fully and faithfully complied with, are the best securities against fraudulent practices.

Immediately after concluding the contracts on your section for the season, you will forward me a statement of the funds required to carry them into effect, and the times such funds will probably be required. Respectfully, your obedient servant,

RICH'D DELAFIELD,
Captain of Engineers.

PHILADELPHIA, December 28, 1834.

Sir: The enclosed letter of the 29th May was prepared as the instructions for Lieutenant Vance, conducting the operations on the seventh division of the road, and a copy thereof was forwarded to the officer of each division, with directions to conform thereto on their respective sections, suiting the phraseology to their divisions.

On the 27th June, on being made acquainted with the particulars of the act of Congress making the appropriation for the year's service, the following instructions were communicated to the officers of the several divisions, slightly changed to suit each particular division:

"*Sir:* Funds having been made available for continuing the repairs of the Cumberland Road, east of the Ohio, you will cause the preparatory measures to be taken immediately, and notice given as required by my letter of the 29th of May, a copy of which has been forwarded to you from Brownsville.

"The act of Congress grants a specific sum for finishing the repairs of the road; you will, therefore, in your arrangements, provide for the stone bridges on the new road, and three and a half perches of stone to the rod on the surface of the road as metal; the latter to be furnished by the 31st of December, and kept raked and additional metal put on until the 15th day of February ensuing; the masonry of the bridges to be finished by the 15th of October, with proposals of the terms for finishing the same work by the 30th day of June, 1835.

"The form of a contract has also been forwarded to you from Brownsville, which, with the letter of instructions accompanying it, connected with the tenor of this communication, you will make your guide in the management of the section of road confided to your supervision.

"You will observe the form of the contract provides for work that may not occur in your division. You will, in preparing the form to be printed, be cautious to suit the same to your particular division, as to distance, &c., &c. Mile sections are desirable for subdividing the road, and as the portion to be given under contract to an individual; on your division other subdivisions will be found more convenient, and your attention must, in consequence, be given to make the phraseology of the instrument conform with the facts of the case.

"Hereafter, you will commence and continue your weekly reports to me. Apprise me of the date you limit the reception of proposals, that I may be with you at the time.

"RICH'D DELAFIELD, Captain of Engineers."

The instructions to the officer of the third division required him to provide for the work to be done on his division not exceeding three and a half perches of stone to a rod on the surface of the road as metal, reducing the quantity to two or one perch, as might be requisite to keep the whole in repair until finally completed.

For a copy of the form of contract forwarded to the officers of the several divisions, see the contracts on file in your office, for the *fourth* division of the road.

I enclose the statement called for by the letter of your department of the 9th instant.

Respectfully, your obedient servant,
RICH'D DELAFIELD,
Captain of Engineers.

Brig. Gen. Charles Gratiot,
Chief Engineer.

REPORT AND ESTIMATE FOR THE CUMBERLAND ROAD, EAST OF THE OHIO, UNDER A RESOLUTION OF THE SENATE OF THE UNITED STATES, CALLING FOR THE CONDITION OF THE MASONRY, THE THICKNESS OF METAL ON VARIOUS PARTS, &c., &c., DECEMBER, 1834.

The plan of repair adopted and continued for this road to July, 1834, was that of Macadam, with nine inches of metal in three strata.

The provisions of the act of Congress of the last session made a change in the plan of operation necessary. The sum of $300,000 was appropriated to finish the repairs of the road from Cumberland to Wheeling, a distance of one hundred and thirty-two miles, of which fifty-four miles had not been commenced.

To conform with the provisions of the law, it became necessary to confine the expenditure of this sum to the most indispensable parts of the system, and adopt a less expensive and less permanent repair; abandoning the plan of finishing the mountain division with limestone throughout, and to a width of twenty feet; confining the metal on the more expensive parts of these divisions to a width of from twelve to fifteen feet, instead of twenty; abandoning further repairs to the masonry of the parapets of the bridges; depositing the stone that had been prepared for this purpose on the side roads, and leaving the side walls on Wheeling Hill in their unfinished state; limiting the stratum of metal to be put on this season to three perches and a half, on an average, per rod, on the whole line of the road; transporting the stone that had previously been collected for an additional thickness of metal to parts that had not been supplied with any; substituting wooden bridges for stone over Wills creek and Braddock's run, and abandoning altogether the construction of any bridge over Dunlap's creek. The repairs thus modified are fast drawing to a close, when the road will present parts covered with thicknesses of metal varying from three to nine inches, as follows:

First division, in Maryland, sixteen miles, one hundred and sixty rods, including new location, is covered with three inches of metal.

Second division, in Maryland, sixteen miles, one hundred and ninety-four rods, is covered with six inches of metal.

Third division, in Pennsylvania, two hundred rods, is covered with four inches and a half of metal.

Third division, in Pennsylvania, twenty-five miles, one hundred rods, to a width of from twelve to fifteen feet, is covered with nine inches of metal.

Fourth division, in Pennsylvania, one mile, seven rods, is covered with three inches of metal.

Fourth division, in Pennsylvania, fourteen miles, one hundred and twenty-three rods, to a width of from twelve to fifteen feet, is covered with six inches of metal.

Fifth division, in Pennsylvania, eighteen miles, nine rods, is covered with three inches of metal.

Sixth division, in Pennsylvania, twenty-one miles, two hundred and seventy-three rods, is covered with three inches of metal.

Seventh division, in Virginia, five miles, is covered with three inches of metal.

Seventh division, in Virginia, nine miles, two hundred and sixteen rods, is covered with six inches of metal.

The number of inches of metal put on that part which has been located anew, the first six miles of the first division, being three inches, and the number of inches of metal put upon that part of the road which lies between the Monongahela and the Ohio, the fifth, sixth, and seventh divisions, being three inches of metal on forty-four miles and two hundred and eighty-two rods, and six inches of metal on nine miles and two hundred and sixteen rods.

To make this a permanent and substantial road, such that the heavy transportation wagons shall not force their wheels through the metal into the bed, not less than the original contemplated thickness of three strata of three inches each, or the same number of strata of three perches and a half of stone each, appears sufficient. That three inches of metal will not suffice to bear up the travel passing over this road, is proved by the experience of the last two years. Nor will six inches answer the purpose on all parts of the road, during a long or continued wet spell of weather, when, from absorption alone, the solidity and contiguity of the metal has become weakened and lessened. On the crests of the hills it will be solid, with a thickness of six inches, when, in the valley and grades under one degree, the evidence of its insufficiency are apparent. Nothing less than the three strata of three inches each has been found sufficient; the last stratum being unequally applied according to the firmness and dryness, and the slope or grade of the bed. Such was judged necessary for a Macadam road from Cumberland to Wheeling, and the results tend to confirm the necessity of a thickness of nine inches on an average, to secure the object contemplated by the instructions of the Chief Engineer.

The condition of the masonry on the whole line of the road is in an unfinished state, so far as regards many of the parts upon which repairs have been commenced; and where nothing had been done toward repairing the bridges, many of their side-walls or parapets are in a dilapidated state, or torn down to the level of the roadway. In repairing the road under the last act of Congress, no more masonry was undertaken than the construction of culverts to drain the road, and repairing such parts as were necessary to perfect the roadway twenty feet in width; all other parts were left in the unfinished and decayed state in which they were when the appropriation of the year caused an abandonment of further repairs to this part of the work.

To carry into effect the repairs originally contemplated, and to secure the uniform strength throughout the whole line of the road equivalent to nine inches of metal, the following sums will be necessary, after applying the means now on hand, and which are pledged for the work commenced and contracted for in July last.

By reference to the annexed statement, it will be perceived that the price per perch for delivered stone prepared as metal on the road varies from ninety-three cents to $2.50, and is stated for each section throughout the whole line of the road. Three quarries supply upward of twenty miles of the road, there being none nearer or accessible. Quarries of the best limestone are numerous and not remote from the road between Wheeling and the eastern base of Laurel hill; from thence to Frostburg they are few in number, situated in deep ravines, and remote from the road; from Frostburg to Cumberland they are comparatively numerous and of easy access. It will be seen that the price agrees with the difficulty of procuring the stone, and in the ratio above stated, from ninety-three cents to $2.50 per perch.

Gen. Lewis Cass, Secretary of War, transmits a Report — More about the Wooden Bridges for the New Location near Cumberland — The War Department thinks they will do — John Hoge stoutly Objects — The Governor of Maryland takes a hand against Wooden Bridges — John Hoge to the Front Again — The Pennsylvania Commissioners make another demand that the Road be put in Repair.

WAR DEPARTMENT, January 3, 1835.

Sir: Herewith I have the honor to transmit a report from the Chief Engineer, which furnishes the information called for by the resolution of the House of Representatives of the 12th ultimo. respecting the Cumberland Road east of the Ohio.

Very respectfully, your most obedient servant.
LEW. CASS.

Hon. John Bell,
Speaker of the House of Representatives.

ENGINEER DEPARTMENT,
WASHINGTON, January 3, 1835.

Sir: I have the honor to hand you the information called for by the House of Representatives on the 12th ultimo, relating to the Cumberland Road east of the Ohio,

And remain, sir, very respectfully, your obedient servant,
C. GRATIOT,
Chief Engineer.

The Hon. Lewis Cass,
Secretary of War.

Sir : In making the repairs of the Cumberland Road east of the Ohio river, it was deemed expedient, in the fall of 1832, to change that part of the old location which is immediately west of Cumberland, in the State of Maryland, for the purpose of turning Wills hill. By this an abrupt rise of several hundred feet would be avoided. A survey, preparatory to this change, was made, and the result submitted to Congress, in the session of 1832–'33; the proposed change was authorized, and the location, as exhibited on the drawing of the survey, adopted. This change of location involved the construction of a bridge over the mill-race in the town of Cumberland, and another over Wills creek, as well as other bridges of minor importance, with several culverts. The Legislature of the State of Maryland passed an act giving assent to the change in question, with the proviso, however, "that the part of the road embraced in this change should be made of the best material, upon the Macadam plan, and that a good, substantial stone bridge should be made over the mill-race, in the town of Cumberland, and over Wills creek at the place of crossing, and that substantial stone bridges and culverts should be made wherever the same may respectively be necessary along the line of said road."

In the estimates which were prepared, and submitted at the commencement of the last session of Congress for its action, the sum proposed for the completion of the repairs of the entire road from Cumberland to the Ohio river, contemplated the erection of the bridges on the new location, in conformity to the requirements of the law of Maryland just referred to. But, as is known to you, more than one-half of this sum was stricken from the bill, which embodied the whole amount of the estimate. The act appropriating the remainder requires that the whole of the repairs shall be completed for this diminished sum. Under these circumstances, it becomes necessary to change the plan upon which it was proposed to execute the work, and the object of this communication is to ascertain the extent to which the department may be allowed to carry this change on the new part of the road embraced by the law of Maryland. If the bridges alluded to be built of stone, the expense will be much greater than the sum allotted to that section would bear: whereas, if the abutments be built of stone, and the superstructure of wood, the same ends would be attained as would result from bridges built entirely of stone, but the letter of the Maryland law would be departed from. Good wooden superstructures, well covered and painted, would last, with a little care, at least forty years, and perhaps longer. To abandon this new location, and return to the old road, would be to sacrifice a large amount of money already expended on the former, which is now in a state of forwardness, and would soon be finished. Besides, a bridge must, in any event, be constructed over Wills creek, and every consideration of convenient and easy traveling conspires to render its location on the new line of the road desirable.

The officer charged with the repairs of the road is now engaged in giving out the work to contract, and making other arrangements necessary to a speedy application of the funds. It is, therefore, very desirable that an early decision may be had of this question, and it is accordingly respectfully requested.

I have the honor to be, &c.,

C. GRATIOT, Brig. Gen.

Hon. Secretary of War.

I approve of the course recommended by General Gratiot with regard to the bridges—the abutments to be of stone, and the superstructure of wood—believing that such a course would be deemed by Maryland a substantial compliance with the law, under the circumstances of the case.

JOHN FORSYTH,

July 28, 1834. Act. Sec'y of War.

CUMBERLAND, August 5, 1834.

Sir : I was this day informed that the bridge across Wills creek, on the new location of the Cumberland road up Braddock's run, is to be built of wood. By the act of the Legislature of Maryland, authorizing the President to change the location of the road, it is enacted that the road may be located up Wills creek through the narrows, provided the bridges were all built of stone. I am decidedly of the opinion that, by the provisions of that law, the President had no right to change the location of the road unless he strictly complied with every provision and requisition of said law. You will, on examination of the act of Maryland, passed at December session, 1832, chapter 55, see that the bridges are to be all built of stone. I sincerely hope you will, on examining the law, and reflecting on the subject, direct the bridges to be built in strict compliance with the law authorizing the change in location; it would, in all probability, save money and time.

I am sure the State will not receive the road without the stone bridges. I shall be gratified to hear from you on this subject by return mail.

Your most obedient,

General C. Gratiot. JOHN HOYE.

ENGINEER DEPARTMENT,

WASHINGTON, August 14, 1834.

Sir : Your communication in behalf of the citizens of Cumberland, remonstrating against the erection of bridges of wooden superstructures over Wills creek, &c., addressed to me under date of 6th instant, is received. The measure to which the citizens of Cumberland object, grows, of necessity, out of existing circumstances; and the bridges will have to be built in the manner and of the materials named in the instruction of the department to the superintendent of the road, or the new location to turn Wills hill must be abandoned. The people of Cumberland are doubtless aware that estimates were submitted to Congress last fall for funds sufficient to put up the structures over Wills creek in conformity with the law of Maryland, to which you refer; and it is hoped that they are also aware that these funds were reduced more than one-half in amount, and that the act appropriating the residue imposes the task of completing all the repairs on the whole road east of the Ohio, with the sum rendered available by it.

You will perceive, sir, that there was no other course left to the department than to change the plan and system of repairs.

The bridges which it is proposed to construct will, with care, last at least forty years.

Very respectfully, &c.,

C. GRATIOT,

Brig. Gen. and Chief Engineer.

B. S. Pigman, Esq., Cumberland, Md.

EXECUTIVE DEPARTMENT,

ANNAPOLIS, September 10, 1834.

Sir : By an act of the General Assembly, passed at December session, 1832, (of which, at your request, an authenticated copy was transmitted to you on the 29th day of March, 1833), the consent of this State was given to a change of the location of a part of the Cumberland or National Road within our limits, upon certain conditions; among which, "that a good and substantial stone bridge shall be made over the mill-race in the town of Cumberland, and over Wills creek at the place of crossing, and that substantial stone bridges or culverts shall be made wherever the same may respectively be necessary along the line of said road."

By the same act, John Hoye and Meshach Frost, Esqrs., and the superintendent for the time being of the said road, appointed by the President of the United States, were appointed commissioners "to report the said National Road, when finished and repaired within the limits of this State, to the Governor and Council."

A communication has been received from John Hoye, Esq., in which he states that "the War Department has now directed and contracted to have all the bridges on said new location built of wood."

I beg leave to call your attention to this subject, in the fullest confidence that there has been some mistake or misapprehension on the part of some of the agents or persons employed upon the work in question, and that you will cause the terms and conditions upon which the consent of the State was given to the proposed improvements to be respected and carried into effect.

With great respect, I have the honor to be,

Your obedient servant,

Hon. Lewis Cass, JAMES THOMAS.

Secretary of War.

WAR DEPARTMENT,

WASHINGTON, September 12, 1834.

Sir : I have had the honor to receive your letter of the 10th instant, respecting the construction of the bridge on the National Road near Cumberland, and for your information I beg leave to enclose the accompanying report from the Engineer Department, which explains the course which has been taken, and the necessity of it. I trust that you will find that the act of the State of Maryland has been substantially complied with, and certainly so far as the means within this department permitted.

Very respectfully, &c.

His Excellency James Thomas,   LEW. CASS.
  Governor of Maryland, Annapolis.

ENGINEER DEPARTMENT,
      WASHINGTON, September 12, 1834.

Sir: In answer to your inquiries of this morning respecting certain bridges on the Cumberland Road, in the State of Maryland, I have the honor to submit the following statement:

In applying the money appropriated by Congress at the session of 1831 and '32, for the repairs of the Cumberland Road east of the Ohio river, it was deemed highly important to change the location of that part of the road immediately west of Cumberland to turn Wills mountain, as, by that means, a rise of several hundred feet, within a few miles, would be avoided. A survey was accordingly made, and submitted to Congress, and the change was approved. The State of Maryland assented, provided the part of the road embraced in the change should be "made of the best materials, upon the Macadam plan, and that a good and substantial stone bridge should be made on the mill-race, in the town of Cumberland, and over Wills creek at the place of crossing, and that substantial stone bridges and culverts should be made wherever the same may respectively be necessary along the line of said road."

Estimates were prepared last fall for the entire completion of the repairs of the road from Cumberland to the Ohio. These estimates, which contemplated the construction and erection of bridges, in strict conformity with the law of Maryland giving her consent to the change of location, were submitted to Congress at the commencement of its recent session, and amounted to six hundred and fifty-two thousand one hundred dollars. Full and ample explanations accompanied these estimates, so there could have been no misunderstanding respecting them. A bill of appropriation was introduced, embracing their entire amount. This amount, after much discussion, was reduced to less than one-half, to-wit: $300,000, and the bill became a law, containing a section which requires that as soon as the sum of $300,000, or as much thereof as is necessary, shall be expended on the road agreeably to the provisions of this act, the same shall be surrendered to the States, respectively, through which the road passes; "and the United States shall not thereafter be subject to any expense for repairing said road." Under these circumstances, it was plain that the system of repairs upon which the estimates were predicated could not be executed, and a change became necessary. The stone bridges referred to in the law of Maryland constituted a heavy item in the estimates, and it was entirely out of the question to build them without absorbing more of the appropriation than the absolute requirements of other sections of the road would admit. There being no obligation to finish the new location further than that imposed by the very great advantage resulting from its adoption, the question arose whether it would be best to abandon it, and return to the old road or not. After adopting every expedient, consistent with a faithful execution of the law, to diminish the expenses on other portions of the road, it was found that a sufficient sum would be left to construct this new portion of the best material, on the Macadam plan, and to build the abutments and piers of all the bridges on it of good stone, and in the best manner, provided the superstructures were made of wood. This was the best that could be done; and when it was considered that these superstructures, being made of the best materials, would, when covered and well painted, last, with a little care, from thirty to forty years, it was recommended to the acting Secretary of War, during your absence, to adopt them in preference to surrendering all the benefits that will result from the new road. The acting Secretary, considering that the approval of the measure would, under this state of things, be a substantial compliance with the law of Maryland, directed instructions to that effect to be issued to the superintendent of the road, which was accordingly done.

With great respect, &c.,

By order: WM. H. C. BARTLETT,
         Lieut. and Assist. to Chief Engineer.
The Hon. Secretary of War.

CUMBERLAND, December 12, 1834.

Sir: As one of the commissioners appointed by the Legislature of Maryland to report to the Governor and Council of said State when that part of the National Road within the limits of this State shall have been repaired agreeably to the provisions of the law of the State agreeing to receive that part of the road lying within the limits of this State; and a further act of the Legislature of Maryland, authorizing the President of the United States to change the location of a part of said road within the limits of Maryland, the change of location was authorized to be made on certain and positive conditions that the bridges over Wills creek and Braddock's run should all be permanent stone bridges; and the road to be constructed with the best materials, on the Macadam plan (see the law of Maryland, passed December session, 1832, chapter 55). The plan of the bridges has been changed by the superintendent to wooden bridges, in direct violation of the engagements with this State. The President had no right to change the location of the road, unless the law of this State authorizing the change was fully complied with.

The metal on the new location is not more than three and a half inches, and every wagon that passes over it, when the road is wet, cuts entirely through the stone, and turns up the clay. I am advised that there is a part of the road, fourteen miles west of Cumberland, which has had but three and a half inches of metal put on it over the original pavement. I am gratified to have it in my power to state that, from observation, and the best information I have been able to collect, the last appropriation for the road has been most judiciously expended. I believe that it is the first that has been well laid out.

I must say that we cannot report in favor of this State receiving the road until the permanent stone bridges are erected, and the road in that state of repair contemplated by the law.

I beg leave to refer you to my letter to General C. Gratiot, dated in August last, which, with my communication to his excellency James Thomas, Governor of Maryland, a copy of which, I presume, he communicated to your department during the last summer, you will please to consider a part of this communication. I should have addressed you at an earlier period, but was prevented by severe indisposition.

I remain, with respect, your most obedient,

JOHN HOYE.

Hon. Lewis Cass,
  Secretary of War, Washington City.

NOVEMBER 17, 1834.

Sir: The undersigned commissioners, appointed by the Governor of Pennsylvania to erect gates and superintend the collection of tolls on the Cumberland Road "after it shall be put in a good state of repair by the United States," respectfully represent:

That, from a full and careful examination of the subject, they are satisfied that they are not authorized, by the terms of the law under which they are appointed, to accept the road from the United States, or erect gates for the collection of tolls, until provision is made by Congress for completing the repairs on the plan already adopted by the agents of the United States, and sanctioned by several appropriations to carry it into effect. Without this it is evident that a considerable portion of the road, which has received but a single stratum of stone, will be left in a condition so weak and imperfect as soon to become again totally impassable for a considerable portion of the year.

The law of Pennsylvania expressly requires that, before the road is accepted by the Commissioners, it must be put in good and complete repair by the United States. To this act and all its provisions, Congress, on the 3d of July, 1832, gave its assent; an appropriation was made, and a plan of repair was accordingly adopted by the agents of the government, and two subsequent appropriations made by Congress to carry this plan and compact into effect. The complete repair of the road is made by the compact a condition precedent to be performed by the United States. It is not performed, as appears by the report of the agents of the United States, and, until it is, the Commissioners appointed by the State cannot be justified in accepting the road or exacting tolls. Besides, it is evident that the tolls established, even if raised to the maximum, will be totally inadequate to the preservation and repair of the road, unless first put in a state of complete and substantial repair. This, a statement of a single fact will fully demonstrate. It appears by a report lately received from the superintendent of that part of the road which lies between Hagerstown and Cumberland, that the tolls there collected amount to $312 per mile per annum; of this $45 is required to pay gate keepers and superintendents, leaving $267 for repairs. The tolls on that part of the road are more than three times as high as those proposed on this, so that the amount of tolls applicable to the repair of this road will not exceed $89 per mile per annum, a sum barely sufficient to preserve the road after it is put in the best possible state of repair. The undersigned do not presume to prescribe a plan of repair; they are satisfied with that adopted and partly executed by the agents of the United States; and they now distinctly declare and pledge themselves, that so soon as Congress shall appropriate the sum required by the Secretary of War to complete the repair of the road on the plan adopted in his report at the last session, we will, with all possible despatch, proceed to erect the gates, and relieve the United States from all further charge or expense on account of said road, after the appropriation so made shall be expended.

Very respectfully, your most obedient servants,

THOMAS ENDSLEY.
DANIEL DOWNER.
WILLIAM F. COPLAN.
STEPHEN HILL.
BENJAMIN ANDERSON.

Hon. Lewis Cass,
Secretary of War.

Note.—The bridges near Wills creek were in the end built of stone.

The Iron Bridge over Dunlap's Creek at Brownsville — Interesting facts relating to its projection and construction — The first step — Several respectable Gentlemen of Brownsville call the attention of the Government's Agent to the subject.

NATIONAL ROAD, 85⅝ MILES FROM CUMBERLAND,
August 15, 1832.

Sir: Yesterday, as I passed through Brownsville, I was waited on by several of the most respectable gentlemen of that place, who were anxious to have me examine the bridge over Dunlap's creek, between Brownsville and Bridgeport, to see its condition, and to give my opinion as to its renewal. Accordingly, I observed that I thought the bridge would not stand a twelve-month, and that I did not feel myself authorized to renew it, as the bridge had never been made by the government, but recommended that they write to the department for a decision; and, agreeably to their request, observed that I would likewise report the actual condition of the bridge. Consequently, I enclose to the department a leaf from my note book, giving a rough sketch of the bridge, and pointing out its defects. The reason why this bridge was not originally constructed by the government, as well as a bridge over the Monongahela river, are better known to the department than I am able to conjecture.

I have to observe that a company is now constructing a substantial bridge over the Monongahela river, across from Bridgeport, thereby making the bridge over Dunlap's creek an important link in the road; and that a bridge, to ensure the purpose of a common highway, would not be suitable for the only connecting point between two important and increasing towns.

I have the honor to be, sir,

Very respectfully, your most obedient servant,

J. K. F. MANSFIELD,
Lieutenant Corps of Engineers.

Gen. C. Gratiot,
Chief Engineer.

THE SUBJECT TO BE EXAMINED.

ENGINEER DEPARTMENT,
WASHINGTON, August 20, 1832.

Sir: Your letter of the 15th inst., informing the department that you had, at the request of the citizens of Brownsville, made an examination of the bridge over Dunlap's creek, with a view to an opinion on the question of its removal, and transmitting a rough sketch of the bridge as it at present exists, is received.

In consequence of the views presented in your letter, it will be necessary to make a thorough examination of this bridge to ascertain whether it is sufficiently substantial to answer all the purposes of the road, by putting proper repairs upon it, or whether it will be necessary to remove it entirely, and to build a new one.

You will accordingly make this examination, and with your report on the subject you will transmit such drawings and explanatory notes as may be necessary to present a full and clear view of the repairs, or new bridge, as the case may be, accompanied by the proper estimates for their execution.

You will also ascertain, by the best oral testimony that can be obtained in the vicinity of the bridge, whether it is on the line of the road as originally located, and make known the fact in your report.

The Secretary of War has been written to on the subject, and, as soon as his decision is known at the department, you will be instructed accordingly.

I am, &c., &c.,
C. GRATIOT.

Lieut. J. K. F. Mansfield.
Corps of Engineers, Uniontown, Pa.

AN EXAMINATION MADE, AND AN ADVERSE DECISION RENDERED.

UNIONTOWN, PA., August 24, 1832.

Sir: I have the honor to acknowledge the receipt of the letter of the department on the subject of the bridge over Dunlap's creek, at Brownsville, and to state that I have completed the examination of the road to the Virginia line, and have already given out notices for contracts, two of which are enclosed for the perusal of the department.

I am, &c.,
J. K. F. MANSFIELD,
Lieutenant Corps of Engineers.

Gen. Charles Gratiot,
Chief Engineer.

ENGINEER DEPARTMENT,
WASHINGTON, October 11, 1832.

Sir: You were informed by letter from the department, under date of 20th August last, that the Secretary of War had been written to on the subject of building a new bridge over Dunlap's creek in the place of that which is at present in the line of the Cumberland Road, between Brownsville and Bridgeport, and which was referred to in your communication to the Chief Engineer of the 15th of August last. I now have to inform you that the Secretary of War has decided that the bridge in question cannot be built at the expense of the government, under the law making appropriation for the repairs of the Cumberland Road east of the Ohio river.

Very respectfully, &c.,
By order: WM. H. C. BARTLETT,
Lieut. of Engineers, and Assistant to Chief Engineer.

Lieut. J. K. F. Mansfield,
Corps of Engineers, Uniontown, Pa., or Capt. Delafield.

THE DECISION REVERSED, AND THE BRIDGE TO BE BUILT.

ENGINEER DEPARTMENT,
WASHINGTON, May 13, 1833.

Sir: The Secretary of War has determined that a new bridge shall be built across the mouth of Dunlap's creek, in the line of the Cumberland Road; you will, therefore, be pleased to submit a plan, and estimate, with as little delay as practicable, with the view to the erection of this bridge during the present year.

I am, sir, &c.,
C. GRATIOT,
Brig. General.

Capt. R. Delafield,
Corps of Engineers, Uniontown, Pa.

A SERIOUS QUESTION AS TO LOCATION ARISES — A REQUEST THAT BARRIERS BE USED ON THE ROAD.

Extract from a letter dated BROWNSVILLE, May 14, 1834.

Sir: To establish the location of Dunlap's creek bridge, I desire the field notes of the commissioners, if on file in your office, and Mr. Shriver's notes of location. From these, I am inclined to believe it will appear that the most favorable route for the bridge was pointed out by the commissioners, and the route over the bridge now used, no part of the National Road, but a county bridge, that we have no right to interfere with. May I request such information as is within your reach on this subject?

The road may be called a very excellent turnpike between this and Frostburg, at the present time; so smooth that already the stage proprietors have commenced the use of a "rough lock," that materially injures the surface. Some defects are clearly observable, growing out of the constant travel and wear of the center of the road from the prohibition to use barriers to change the travel.

Without being permitted to use barriers of logs, stumps and stones, it is out of our power ever to make a perfect Macadamized road, and far from being as good as the expenditure should produce. Such a system has been resorted to on every road I have seen made, and every officer associated with me concurs in the opinion that we cannot succeed without using them. Permit me to ask a reconsideration of the order prohibiting their use.

Respectfully, your obedient servant,

RICH'D DELALFIELD,
Captain of Engineers.

Brig. Gen. Charles Gratiot,
Chief Engineer.

THE USE OF BARRIERS PERMITTED—A ROAD BEGINNING AT UNIONTOWN, AND ENDING AT WASHINGTON.

ENGINEER DEPARTMENT,

WASHINGTON, May 20, 1834.

Sir: Your communication, dated the 14th instant, was duly received. In conformity with your request, a detail of two officers, as your assistants on the Cumberland Road, has been applied for. Herewith is transmitted a book containing, as stated, "the notes of a location of the United States western road, beginning at Uniontown, and ending at the turnpike near Washington," which is the only document among the papers transferred from the Treasury Department to this office, relating to the Cumberland Road, embraced in the notes, required to be forwarded to you.

(On the subject of regulating the travel so as to preserve the surface of the road from injury mentioned in your letter, you will again resort to the use of barriers, wood only, to be used for the purpose, and placed only on one side of the road at the same time, provided the object can thus be accomplished, and so elevated as to be very conspicuous, that the travel by night may not be endangered by the barriers).

I am, &c.,

C. GRATIOT,
Brig. General.

Capt. R. Delafield,
Corps of Engineers, Brownsville, Pa.

A BIG APPROPRIATION, BUT THE BRIDGE ABANDONED.

ENGINEER DEPARTMENT,

WASHINGTON, June 25, 1834.

Sir: Three hundred thousand dollars have just been appropriated for the repairs of the Cumberland Road east of the Ohio. You will perceive by the law, a printed copy of which is herewith enclosed, that the intention is that this sum shall complete the repairs. You will, therefore, take your measures accordingly, and put the road in as good condition as this sum will admit of. The new section to turn Wills hill will be completed on the plan already commenced, but the plan of operations on the other sections must be modified to suit the requirements of the law. The iron bridge over Dunlap's creek will be abandoned. Your project, when matured, will be transmitted for the approval of the department.

Very respectfully, &c.,

WM. H. C. BARTLETT,
Lieut. and Assistant to Chief Engineer.

By order:

Capt. R. Delafield,
Corps of Engineers, New Castle, Del.

ANOTHER AND FINAL CHANGE—THE BRIDGE TO BE BUILT ON THE SITE OF THE OLD ONE.

ENGINEER DEPARTMENT,

WASHINGTON, August, 14, 1834.

Sir: I have to acknowledge the receipt of your communication, dated 31st ultimo, in reference to the bridge over Dunlap's creek, on the Cumberland Road, east of the Ohio. The subject of rebuilding this bridge was brought to the notice of the Secretary of War during the summer of 1832, when he refused to take any action in the matter, on the ground that it was a county bridge, which should be repaired or rebuilt by the county authorities, as the United States, in adopting a system of repairs, had undertaken to repair only that which they had originally constructed. It was thought on the other side, that notwithstanding the United States had not built this bridge, yet, as they had enjoyed the free benefit of it, and as it lay on the tacitly acknowledged line of the road, they were bound, under the act of Congress authorizing the repairs of the road to work on every part of it without reference to original constructors or proprietors. In this state of the case, it was submitted to Mr. Taney, then Attorney General, who decided verbally in favor of the latter view, and instructions in conformity thereto were issued to the superintendent of the road, requiring him to cause the bridge to be either repaired or rebuilt. This question having been settled, the next is, whether Dunlap's creek can be crossed at any other point than where the county bridge now stands. It is the opinion of the department that it cannot. It would seem there is no evidence on record that any location was ever finally fixed upon by the commissioners, and reported by them to the President, for the part of the road in the immediate vicinity of this creek; but the fact that the road was actually made in its present location, and used ever since its original construction, without any opposition, is strong proof that this route was adopted by the Government; at all events, in the absence of all other evidence, the department feels constrained to act upon this. Now, the appropriations having been made for the repairs of the road, and not for constructing any part of it, except the new section to turn Wills hill, it is not perceived how any part of the funds can be applied to the new location proposed by you. These views having been submitted to the acting Secretary of War, he concurs in them. Your operations will, therefore, be confined to the old road on which the bridge must be located. Very, &c.,

C. GRATIOT,

Capt. Richard Delafield,
Corps of Engineers, Brownsville, Pa.

PROPOSALS FOR CARRYING THE MAILS.

WASHINGTON CITY, September 26, 1831.

We will agree to convey the mail on route No. 1,031, from Philadelphia to Pittsburg, daily in four-horse post coaches, agreeable to advertisement, for the yearly compensation of seven thousand dollars.

Or we will make the following improvements: To convey two daily mails from Philadelphia to Pittsburg: First mail to leave Philadelphia at two o'clock A. M. and arrive at Pittsburg in two days and five hours, so as to arrive in Pittsburg at seven o'clock A. M., and extend the route to Wheeling so as to arrive, including route 1,170, at Wheeling the third day by nine o'clock P. M., from the first of April to first of December, and, from first of December to first of April, to Pittsburg in three and Wheeling in four days; and return from Wheeling by Washington, Pittsburg, and Chambersburg, to Philadelphia within the same time; changing the mail as follows: at Lancaster, Harrisburg, Chambersburg, Bedford, Somerset, Mount Pleasant, and at any other office that is or may be established on the route. The second mail to leave Philadelphia at seven A. M., or immediately after the arrival of the New York mail, and reach Pittsburg in three days and five hours, so as to arrive in Pittsburg by noon, changing the mail at all way offices.

We will agree to carry the mail on route No. 1,198, from Bedford to Washington, Pa., via White House, Somerset, Donegal, Mount Pleasant, McKean's, Old Stand, Robbstown, Gambles, and Parkinson's Ferry, to Washington, Pa., as advertised, for the yearly compensation of twenty-nine hundred dollars.

We do agree to carry the mail on route No. 1,230, from Bedford, Pa., to Cumberland, Md., three times a week in coaches, from the first of April to the first of October, and once a week on horseback from the first of October to the first of April, so as to connect with the Winchester mail at Cumberland, and the Great Eastern and Western mail at Bedford, which is much wanted during the summer season, for the yearly compensation of thirteen hundred dollars.

JAMES REESIDE,
SAMUEL R. SLAYMAKER,
J. TOMLINSON.

To the Hon. WM. T. BARRY,
Postmaster General.

CONTRACT.

This contract, made the fifteenth day of October, in the year one thousand eight hundred and thirty-one, between James Reeside, of Philadelphia, Samuel R. Slaymaker, of Lancaster, and Jesse Tomlinson, of Philadelphia, contractors for carrying the mail of the United States, of one part, and the Postmaster General of the United States of the other part, witnesseth, that said parties have mutually covenanted as follows, viz.: The said contractors covenant with the Postmaster General:

To carry the mails from Pittsburg to Harriottsville, Cannonsburg, Washington, Claysville, West Alexander, and Triadelphia, Va., to Wheeling and back, daily, in four-horse post coaches, the first mail to be changed at each county town through which it passes; the second mail at every office on the route; and to furnish armed guards for the whole, when required by the department, at the rate of six thousand and seven hundred and fifty dollars for every quarter of a year, during the continuance of this contract; to be paid in drafts on postmasters on the route above mentioned, or in money, at the option of the Postmaster General, in the months of May, August, November, and February.

That the mails shall be duly delivered at, and taken from each postoffice now established, or that may be established on any post route embraced in this contract, under a penalty of ten dollars for each offence; and a like penalty shall be incurred for each ten minutes' delay in the delivery of the mail after the time fixed for its delivery at any postoffice specified in the schedule hereto annexed; and it is also agreed that the Postmaster General may alter the times of arrival and departure fixed by said schedule, and alter the route (he making an adequate compensation for any extra expense which may be occasioned thereby); and the Postmaster General reserves the right of annulling this contract, in case the contractors do not promptly adopt the alteration required.

If the delay of the arrival of said mail continue until the hour for the departure of any connecting mail, whereby the mails destined for such connecting mails shall miss a trip, it shall be considered a whole trip lost, and a forfeiture of one hundred dollars shall be incurred; and a failure to take the mail, or to make the proper exchange of mails at connecting points, shall be considered a whole trip lost; and for any delay or failure equal to a trip lost, the Postmaster General shall have full power to annul this contract.

That the said contractors shall be answerable for the persons to whom they shall commit the care and transportation of the mail, and accountable for any damage which may be sustained through their unfaithfulness or want of care.

That seven minutes after the delivery of the mail at any postoffice on the aforesaid route named on the annexed schedule, shall be allowed the postmaster for opening the same, and making up another mail to be forwarded.

The contractors agree to discharge any driver or carrier of said mail whenever required to do so by the Postmaster General.

That when the said mail goes by stage, such stage shall be suitable for the comfortable accommodation of at least seven travelers; and the mail shall invariably be carried in a secure dry boot, under the driver's feet, or in the box which constitutes the driver's seat, under a penalty of fifty dollars for each omission; and when it is carried on horseback, or in a vehicle other than a stage, it shall be covered securely with an oil cloth or bear skin, against rain or snow, under a penalty of twenty dollars for each time the mail is wet, without such covering.

Provided always, That this contract shall be null and void in case the contractors or any person that may become interested in this contract, directly or indirectly, shall become a postmaster or an assistant postmaster. No member of Congress shall be admitted to any share or part of this contract or agreement, or to any benefit to arise thereupon; and this contract shall, in all its parts, be subject to its terms and requisitions of an act of Congress, passed on the 21st day of April, in the year of our Lord one thousand eight hundred and eight, entitled, "An act concerning public contracts."

And it is mutually covenanted and agreed by the said parties that this contract shall commence on the first day of January next, and continue in force until the thirty-first day of December, inclusively, which will be in the year one thousand eight hundred and thirty-five.

In witness whereof, They have hereunto interchangeably set their hands and seals the day and year first above written.

(Signed.)   JAMES REESIDE.   (Seal.)
         SAM'L R. SLAYMAKER. (Seal.)
         JESSE TOMLINSON.   (Seal.)

Signed, sealed and delivered in the presence of

     ROB'T D. CARSON.
     JACOB SHEARER.

BOND.

Know all men by these presents, That James Reeside, as principal, and Richard Morris and David Dorrance, as sureties, are held and firmly bound unto the Postmaster General of the United States of America, in the just and full sum of two thousand nine hundred dollars, value received, to be paid unto the Postmaster General or his successors in office, or to his or their assigns; to which payment, well and truly to be made, we bind ourselves, our heirs, executors, and administrators, jointly and severally, firmly by these presents. Sealed with our seals, dated the seventeeth day of December, in the year of our Lord one thousand eight hundred and thirty-one.

The condition of this obligation is such that whereas the above bounden James Reeside, by a certain contract bearing date the fifteenth day of October, in the year of our Lord one thousand eight hundred and thirty-one, covenanted with the said Postmaster General to carry the mail of the United States from Bedford to Washington (Pennsylvania), as per contract annexed, commencing the first day of January, one thousand eight hundred and thirty-two, and ending the thirty-first day of December, which will be in the year one thousand eight hundred and thirty-five.

Now, if the said James Reeside shall well and truly perform the covenants in the said indenture expressed on his part to be performed, and shall account for all penalties, and shall promptly repay all balances that may at any time be found due from him, then this bond is to be void; otherwise to remain in full force.

(Signed.)   JAMES REESIDE,   (Seal.)
         RICHARD MORRIS,   (Seal.)
         DAVID DORRANCE, (Seal.)

Signed, sealed and delivered in the presence of
     (Signed.)   R. C. WHITESIDE.

A true copy from the original on file in the General Postoffice.
     MW. ST. CLAIR CLARKE, Secretary.

CLAIM FOR EXTRA ALLOWANCE.

WASHINGTON CITY, December 28, 1831.

Sir: For the four years which I have been your contractor for transporting the great Eastern mail from New York to Philadelphia, it has happened almost every week, and several times in a week, that arrivals from foreign countries have brought thousands of ship letters to the office of New York just before the time for my departure, and the importance of their being forwarded without delay to the Southern cities has required my detention from one to two hours beyond the ordinary time for me to leave New York. This detention I have been required to gain in speed, and that increased speed has required me always to keep on that route two extra teams of horses, at an extra expense of not less than one thousand dollars per year for each team. During the first year your predecessor made me an extra allowance for this expense, but during the last three years I have received nothing for it. I now submit the subject to you, in the expectation that you will allow the claim; it is certainly but just that I should be relieved, at least in part, of this burden, for the last three years it has subjected me to an expense of not less than six thousand dollars, which I hope you will direct to be paid to me, at least in part, if you do not think me entitled to the whole. I have also, within the same time, transported to New York all the large mail bags which are made in Philadelphia and sent to New York, not with mails, but to be used in New York, and to be sent from New York to other places. These within three years will amount to about five hundred pounds a week, as will appear from accounts of the manufacturers in your office. Wherever I could procure transportation for those bags in wagons, I have uniformly paid $2.50 per hundred pounds for carrying them, rather than overload my coaches in which we carry the great mail. For this service, I hope you will not consider my claim unreasonable, if I charge ten dollars per week for three years. All of which is submitted to your sense of justice for decision.

Very respectfully, your obedient servant.

         JAMES REESIDE.

HON. WM. T. BARRY.

Endorsement—Allowed. Allow $4,500. The residue of the claim is reserved for future consideration. Allow the remaining $1,500.

COULDN'T AFFORD TO CARRY NEWSPAPERS.

WASHINGTON, July 12, 1832.

Sir: When we entered into contract with you to run two daily mails between Philadelphia and Pittsburg, one with unexampled rapidity, and the other in three and one-half days, we had no idea whatever of carrying the newspaper mail in our most rapid line, nor do we suppose it was ever contemplated by the department. It was our intention and we so expressed it in all our conversation with you, and with the superintendent of mail contracts, to carry the principal letter mail only in the most rapid line, not believing it practicable to carry the heavy load of newspapers sent to the West with sufficient rapidity to reach Pittsburg in the shortest time specified. Indeed, if we could have supposed that it would ever become necessary to carry the newspapers with that rapidity, we should not have undertaken it for less that fifteen thousand dollars a year beyond what we now receive; but experience soon taught us that great complaints were made against the department and ourselves when the newspapers were not received as soon as the letters, and that these complaints were not confined to Pittsburg, but extended all over the West. To satisfy the public, and sustain the credit of both the department and ourselves as its servant, we made the experiment of trying to carry the newspapers with our most rapid line. We have partially succeeded, but with very great loss. For three days in the week we are compelled to exclude all passengers, to the loss of not less than one hundred dollars a day. We are willing to perform our contract to the full extent of its meaning, but we must relinquish carrying the newspaper mails by our most rapid line, unless we can in part be remunerated for it. If, however, the Postmaster General is willing to silence the public clamor, which is so great when we carry them in our slow line, we will carry all the newspaper mails, together with the letter mail, in our most rapid line to Pittsburg and Wheeling, in the shortest time specified in our contract, and so arrange the connection of the Baltimore mail at Chambersburg with our swift line, as to carry the newspapers as well as letter mail, from Baltimore to Pittsburg in two days, for the additional allowance of ten thousand dollars per year, from the first of April last. The increased expense to us will not be less than fifteen thousand dollars a year, and for our own credit and for the credit of the department, we will make one-third of the sacrifice and perform the service for ten thousand dollars a year. We would gladly do it for a less sum if we could afford it, but we cannot, and at that rate our sacrifice will be as much as we can bear. It would be much more gratifying to us if the public would be satisfied without it, but they will not, and our own feelings will not suffer us to perform a service in which we cannot give satisfaction to the public.

Very respectfully, your obedient servants,

JAS. REESIDE.
SAM'L R. SLAYMAKER.

To the Hon. W. T. BARRY,
Postmaster General.

A true copy from the original on file in the General Postoffice.

(The above letter is marked "Granted.")

MW. ST. CLAIR CLARKE. Secretary.

MR. REESIDE DEFIES ALL COMPETITORS.

PHILADELPHIA, January 25, 1833.

Dear Sir: Your favor dated the 22d inst. has just come to hand, which I have examined with much care, but must confess myself at a loss to come to the exact meaning it is extended to convey.

That there is at present, and has been for some time back, an express carried on horseback between this city and New York, is a fact which is well known, and which is publicly acknowledged by the newspapers in New York. That it is impossible to carry the whole of the great Eastern mail through in coaches or otherwise with the same speed as a small package can be carried through on horseback is a fact that requires no comment.

Not having pointed out this matter clearly in your letter whether it was the wish of the department that a certain portion of mails should be sent by express to New York at an earlier hour than it now does.

Should it be the latter, I would at once assure the department of the impossibility of having it carried through in as short a time as it is now carried by express on horseback.

In either case the department may rest assured of my willingness and determination to use every exertion in order to meet the views and wishes of the department. Should you desire it to be sent by express, I have no hesitation in saying that I can have it sent through in a shorter time than it can be done by any other individual in the country. This will be handed to you by Mr. Ewing, whom I have sent on with directions to ascertain from you personally your views of this matter, and who will give you all the information respecting the express that has been sent from this place to New York alluded to in your letter.

With respect, your obedient servant, JAMES REESIDE.

N. B. I will say to a certainty I will go from this city to New York in six hours, or faster than any other one can do it.

JAMES REESIDE.

To Hon. O. B. BROWN,
Superintendent of Mail Contracts,
Washington, D. C.

TEAMS READY FOR THE NATIONAL ROAD.

TRENTON, February 25, 1833.

Dear Sir: You will perceive by the enclosed that I have attended to your directions as far as practicable. It is their own exposition of the matter, and such as they gave me.

I neglected to mention to you in my letter of yesterday that the cause of the private express beating that of the Government alluded to in Mr. Mumford's letter, was owing to but one cause.

Their express came through from Washington.

The Government express from Philadelphia, after the arrival of the steamship, giving the newspaper express the start of six hours in advance of that of the Government. The lateness of the succeeding arrivals originated from the cause mentioned in the enclosed letter. No mail having arrived from the South, they supposed, from the lateness of the arrival of the express the following night, that there would not be any more.

This was caused by the late arrival of the steamboat, and no preparation was made on the road for taking it on. This is their excuse; whether it will pass current is for you to determine. I have just received a letter from Mr. Washington on the subject. He attaches the blame to Thompson's bad horse, &c.

I think we shall be able to get the mail through in time to connect with the boat, should the roads not get worse than they now are.

The mail arrived in Philadelphia this morning at 6 o'clock. I have good reasons for believing that it will continue, unless a change should take place in the roads.

The mail has left Jersey City the last few days at a few minutes past three o'clock P. M., and will continue to leave at that hour unless you direct otherwise: that is three o'clock.

The teams intended for the National Road are here to-night, and start to-morrow for the West; they are twelve in number, Jersey stock. Yours respectfully,

D. EWING.

COLONEL JAMES REESIDE.

P. S. No opposition express for the last four days. Your express horses are in good order, with but two exceptions. D. E.

COPY OF AN ACCOUNT AGAINST COL. JAMES REESIDE.

COL. JAMES REESIDE,   To HUTCHINSON & WEART, *Dr.*
1833.

January 31.—To one horse on express	$ 5 00
February 1. " two horses "	10 00
" 2. " two horses "	10 00
" 3. " two horses "	10 00
" 3. " horses and gig, Eastward, making arrangements for regular express	5 00
March 7.—To two horses on express	5 00
" 7. " running express one month and four days, from February 4 to this date, inclusive, between Trenton and New Brunswick	1,885 71
	$1,970 71

The above is a true copy from our books, so far as relates to expresses, and has been paid to us by Col. Reeside.

HUTCHINSON & WEART.

MR. GALLATIN DEFINES HIS ATTITUDE AS TO THE LOCATION OF THE ROAD, AND GIVES INSTRUCTIONS TO DAVID SHRIVER, SUPERINTENDENT.

When the road was authorized to be constructed by Congress, Mr. Gallatin was Secretary of the Treasury, and a citizen of Fayette county, Pennsylvania. His home was "Friendship Hill," in Spring-hill township, near New Geneva, about fifteen miles south of Union-town, afterward the home of Hon. John L. Dawson. It was intimated in various quarters that Mr. Gallatin was desirous of having the road located through or near his place, and that he used his official influence to further his desire in this regard. The following letter, however, to his old friend David Acheson, of Washington, Pennsylvania, shows that the intimations mentioned were without foundation:

NEW YORK, September 1, 1808.

DAVID ACHESON, ESQ., Washington, Pa.

Dear Sir: On receipt of your letter respecting the Western Road, I immediately transmitted it to the President at Monticello. I was under the impression that he had previously directed the Commissioners to examine both routes and to report to him. It seems, however, that it had not then been yet done. But on the 6th ultimo he wrote to them to make an examination of the best route through Washington to Wheeling, and also to Short Creek, or any other point on the river offering a more advantageous route towards Chillicothe and Cincinnati, and to report to him the material facts with their opinion for consideration.

That it is the sincere wish of the President to obtain all the necessary information in order that the road should pursue the route which will be of the greatest public utility no doubt can exist. So far as relates to myself, after having, with much difficulty, obtained the creation of a fund for opening a great western road, and the act pointing out its general direction, it is sufficiently evident from the spot on the Monongahela which the road strikes, that if there was any subsequent interference on my part it was not of a selfish nature. But the fact is that in the execution of the law I thought myself an improper person, from the situation of my property, to take the direction which would naturally have been placed in my hands, and requested the President to undertake the general superintendence himself. Accept the assurance of friendly remembrance, and of my sincere wishes for your welfare and happiness.

Your obedt servant,

ALBERT GALLATIN.

TREASURY DEPARTMENT, March 9th, 1813.

Sir: You will herewith receive the plot of the road as laid by the Commissioners from the 21st mile to Uniontown.

I approve of having a stone bridge across Little Youghiogheny, and the measures necessary to secure masons should be adopted, but the site cannot be fixed until you have examined whether any alterations in the course be practicable. In that respect I beg leave to refer you to my former letters. As soon as your examination of the ground has taken place, and the alterations you may have found practicable shall have been received and approved, public notice may be given inviting proposals to contract for completing the road as far as Big Yioughiogheny river; an additional appropriation of $140,000 having been made by Congress. You will therefore perceive that in every point of view your examination of the ground is the first object to attend to.

I have the honor to be, respectfully, sir,

Your obt. servant,

ALBERT GALLATIN.

D. Shriver, jr., Cumberland, Md.

TREASURY DEPARTMENT, April 17th, 1813.

Sir: Your letter of the 3d inst. has been duly received. The principal object in finally fixing the course of the road is its perma-

nency and durability without the necessity of perpetual and expensive repairs. To select, therefore, the best ground which that mountainous country will afford, avoiding, as far as practicable, cutting along the side of steep and long hills, always exposed to be washed away, appears to be one of first importance. The other considerations, subordinate to the selection of the best ground, but to be also attended to, are, the expense of making the road, the shortness of the distance and the accommodation (by intersecting lateral roads) of important settlements not on the line of the road.

As an erroneous location would be an irreparable evil, it is better that the contracts for the ensuing twenty miles should be delayed, than to make them before you have had time to take a complete view of the ground. Examine it well before you decide and make your first report. This is more important because it is probable that I will be absent when that report is made, and that it will be decisive, as the acting secretary, to whom the subject will be new and the localities unknown, cannot have time to investigate it critically, and will probably adopt it on your responsibility. If a decisive advantage should arise from an alteration in the last sections already contracted for, and the contractors assent to it, you may, in your report, propose such an alteration. You are authorized for the purpose of facilitating your review of the road, without neglecting the duties of general superintendence, to employ John S. Shriver, or some other able assistant, with a reasonable compensation. You have not stated what this should be, but it is presumed that you will not, in that respect, exceed what is necessary for obtaining the services of a well qualified person. You are authorized to draw for a further sum of twenty thousand dollars; whenever this is nearly exhausted you will apply for a new credit.

With respect to details, they are left at your discretion. You are sensible of the great confidence placed in your abilities and integrity, and I am sure you will not disappoint our expectations.

With perfect consideration and sincere wishes for your welfare, I have the honor to be, sir,

Your obedient servant,

ALBERT GALLATIN.

TREASURY DEPARTMENT, April 20th, 1813.

Sir: You are authorized to employ a surveyor to view the most proper road from Brownsville to Washington in Pennsylvania, and thence to examine the routes to Charlestown, Steubenville, mouth of Short Creek and Wheeling, and report a correct statement of distance and ground on each. If the county road as now established from Brownsville to Washington is not objectionable, it would be eligible to prefer it to any other which might be substituted. The surveyor thus employed will meet with every facility by applying to the gentlemen at Washington who have this alteration in the western road much at heart.

I am respectfully, sir, your obedient servant,

ALBERT GALLATIN.

D. SHRIVER, JR., Cumberland, Md.

TREASURY DEPARTMENT, April 23rd, 1811.

Sir: Mr. Cochran has signed his contract and bonds for the third and fourth sections of the road at the price agreed on, that is to say, at the rate of twenty-two dollars and fifty cents per rod for the third section, and of sixteen dollars and fifty cents per rod for the fourth section.

I now enclose the contracts and bonds for the first and second sections; that for the first in the name of Henry McKinley, and at the rate of twenty-one dollars and twenty-five cents per rod. The proposal of Mr. Reade was at the rate of thirteen dollars for a road covered with a stratum of stones twelve inches thick, all the stones to pass through a three-inch ring. He did not stay here or return here to complete the business and was not present when the road was altered to a stratum of stones fifteen inches thick. The same additional price, viz: one dollar and a half per rod, is allowed him for that alteration which was by agreement given to all the other contractors, making fourteen dollars and a half as set down in the contract, instead of thirteen. The contracts and bonds are in every respect (the names of sections and difference of price only excepted) verbatim the same as both those signed by Mr. Cochran, and they were as you will perceive all executed by me, and signed by the President. After they shall have been signed by the contractors respectively, they will each keep a copy of their own contracts, and you will return the other copy, together with the bond (both being signed by the contractors respectively) to this office.

If either of the contractors should for any reason whatever refuse to sign the contract, you will return the same to this office, notify the person thus refusing that he is not considered as a contractor, forbid his doing any work, and immediately advertise in Cumberland that you will receive proposals for making the section of the road thus not contracted for. You will afterward transmit the proposals which may accordingly be made.

I also enclose a copy of the contracts for your own use in order that you may in every case be able to secure the additions agreed on.

I have the honor to be with consideration, sir,
Your obedient servant,
ALBERT GALLATIN.

The dates were the only blanks left in the contracts and bonds and must be filled at the time of signing, by the contractors.
A. G.

Mr. DAVID SHRIVER, JR., Cumberland, Md.

TREASURY DEPARTMENT, April 30th, 1811.

Sir: Your letter of the 22d inst. has been received. The President has confirmed the alteration in the first section of the road. It will be proper to have a short endorsement to that effect entered on the contract with Mr. McKinley, and signed by him and yourself.

You are authorized to contract for the bridges and mason work on the terms mentioned in your letter, with the exception of the bridges across Clinton's Fork of Braddock's Run, which may perhaps be avoided by the alteration which you contemplate, and which, if necessary, we may, perhaps, considering other expenses, be obliged to contract of cheaper materials. It is left to your discretion to contract for the other mason work as above stated, either with Mr. Kinkead or with the road contractors.

If you shall find it necessary to employ a temporary assistant, you are authorized to do it, provided he shall be employed and paid only when actually necessary. I should think that one dollar and twenty-five, or at most, fifty cents, a day, would in that part of the country be ample compensation.

Respecting side walls no decisive opinion can be given until you shall have matured your ideas on the subject, and formed some estimate of the extent to which they must be adopted and of the expense.

I have the honor to be respectfully, sir,
Your obedient servant,
ALBERT GALLATIN.

Mr. DAVID SHRIVER, JR.,
Superintendent of the Cumberland Road, Cumberland, Md.

LETTER FROM EBENEZER FINLEY.

RELEASE, September 1, 1891.

HON. T. B. SEARIGHT,

My much respected friend: In our conversation the other day, I spoke from memory entirely, as I had no statistics from which to quote. Your father bought the stone tavern house at Searights from Joseph Frost. It was unfinished when your father bought it. I knew Joseph Frost, but have no recollection of the family he came from. Your father was a single man, when he bought the house, but married shortly after.

In relation to Mr. Stewart's and Mr. Benton's colloquy about the National Road, Mr. Stewart said that "hay stacks and corn shocks would walk over it." Mr. Benton replied that "he could not conceive how hay stacks and corn shocks could walk over this bowling green road." "Ah!" rejoined Mr. Stewart, "I do not expect to see them walk in the shape of stacks and shocks, but in the shape of fat cattle, hogs, horses and mules from the Western and Southern States." This was in a discussion in Congress, over an appropriation bill for repairing the road. Another conversation with you at some time, would be very much enjoyed by your unworthy scribbler.

P. S. Now, Colonel, since writing the above, many things have come crowding on my memory, and I will mention some of the principal hotels with which I was more or less acquainted. I frequently traveled over the National Road in my younger days. I went often to Cumberland and occasionally to Baltimore. I will begin at Big Crossings (Somerfield). Coming this way, Thomas Brown kept a tavern on the hillside. Next Daniel Collier, then Inks, and next Widow Tantlinger (Boss Rush's place). Next James Sampey at Mt. Washington, then several stopping places before reaching the Stewart stone house, a hotel that was not largely patronized by travelers on the road. Next the Chalk Hill house and then Jimmy Snyder's. Next the first house to the left as you come to Monroe, built by Mr. Deford. Then several other hotels before you come to Uniontown. In Uniontown, the Walker House (now Feather's) was well patronized. Then James Seaton's and Thomas Brownfield's wagon stands. Next the Cuthbert Wiggins wagon stand (later Moxley's), and next the Searight house. Over the hill, next was a house kept by Samuel Woolverton and Hugh Thompson. Then the Robert Johnson (later Hatfield) stone house. Next old Peter Colley, father of Abel, Solomon and John Colley. Then the Bowman house, kept by John Gribble, and next the Brubaker house. Then the first house to the left as you go into Brownsville, kept by Darra Auld, and next the Workman House. But I presume you have all these. Respectfully,
EB. FINLEY.

LETTER FROM THOMAS A. WILEY, A NATIVE OF UNIONTOWN, WHO RODE THE PONY EXPRESS.

BALTIMORE AND OHIO R. R. CO.,
GEN. TICKET AGENT'S OFFICE,
BALTIMORE, July 16, 1892.

T. B. SEARIGHT, ESQ.— *Dear Sir:*—I have been receiving from some one the *Jeffersonian Democrat*, a paper published in my old favorite Uniontown, and have read with great pleasure your publication of things that transpired along the National Road. I knew a great many of the old wagoners, stage drivers and tavern keepers you mention. When I was working for the stage company the Baltimore and Ohio railroad was only completed to Frederic, Maryland, and I used to travel the old pike very often. I hope to be able to come once more to Uniontown before I go hence, where nearly all the rest have gone, and would delight in a long talk with you about old times on the road. In looking over the paper you sent me I scarcely see any names that I used to know in Uniontown. When last in Uniontown I met William Wilson, Ewing Brownfield and Greenberry Crossland, and did not get a chance to see my old friend and shopmate, Philip Bogardus. He and I worked for the Stockton stage company. The shops were on Morgantown street. I understand that since I was out my old friend, Bogardus, has passed away. I recollect the lady he married was a Miss Lincoln, and I also recollect his boy, Winfield Scott. I have been with the Baltimore and Ohio company since October 10th, 1852, and am still in its service. Again thanking you for the paper you sent me, I close, in the hope that God will bless you and spare your life and mine, that we may meet in old time-honored Uniontown, and talk over the glories of the old pike.
Yours most respectfully,
THOMAS A. WILEY.

The United States

To J Thrower D^r

Novr 2 To 4 Sheets Antiquarian drawing paper $6·00
 To 8/12 doz blank note books at (6 p^r doz) — 4·00
 To 1 Stick indian ink ———————— 0·75
 To 1 bunch crow quills ———————— 0·50
 To 1 bottle ink ———————————— 0·25
             $11 50

Received November 30th 1825 of Jonathan Knight
Commissioner for locating the U S. road from
Zanesville Ohio to the seat of government
in Missouri Eleven dollars and fifty cents,
in full of the above account, and which I
am to pass to the credit of the appropriation for
procuring the necessary survey plans and Estimates,
on the subject of Road & Canals

         J Thrower

I certify that the above articles were necessary
to the location of the U S. road from Zanesville
to Columbus.

         J Knight
         Comm^r

The United States,

1825.   To Thomas Plant Dr

For services in transportation on
the Location of the U.S. road west
of Zanesville from the 4th of Augt
to the 5th of Novr inclusive 94
days at $2. per day $188.00

Received Nov 5th 1825 of Jonathan Knight
Commissioner for Locating the U.S. road from Zanesville
to the seat of Government of Missouri One hundred
& Eighty Eight dollars in full of the above account.
$188.00   Duplicate, Thomas Plant

I certify that the above was necessary to
the location of the U.S. road from Zanesville
to Columbus.
                          Knight
                          Commr

1807. Act of April 9th gives the State's consent to the making of the road within its limits, provided the route be changed to pass through Uniontown and Washington; also gives the United States authorities full power to enter upon lands, dig, cut and carry away materials, etc., for the purpose of completing and *forever* keeping in repair said road. Pamphlet Laws, page 185.

1828. February 7th. Joint resolution authorizes the Government of the United States to erect toll gates, enforce the collection of tolls, and to do and perform every other act and thing which may be deemed necessary to insure the PERMANENT repair and preservation of the road. Andrew Shultz, Governor, Nerr Middleswarth, Speaker of the House of Representatives, Daniel Sturgeon, Speaker of the Senate. Pamphlet laws, page 500.

1831. Act of April 11th. Preamble: "Whereas, that part of the Cumberland Road lying within the State of Pennsylvania is in many parts in bad condition for want of repairs, and as doubts have been entertained whether the United States have authority to erect toll gates on said road and collect toll, and as a large proportion of the people of this commonwealth are interested in said road, ITS CONSTANT CONTINUANCE AND PRESERVATION, therefore, etc." The act then goes on and authorizes the erection of at least six gates, designates classes and persons exempt from toll, provides for the erection of directors (boards ordering teams, etc., to pass to the right), establishes rates of tolls, regulates the manner of collecting the same, etc. Pamphlet Laws, page 419. For a judicial construction of this act, see case of Hopkins vs. Stockton, 2 Watts and Sargeant, page 163.

1835. Act of April 1st requires supervisors of highways to make paved valleys or stone culverts where other roads intersect the Cumberland Road and this act also signifies the State's acceptance of the road from the General Government. Pamphlet Laws, page 102.

1836. Act of June 13th provides for payment of half toll by persons carrying the United States mail, and fixes penalties for attempts to defraud the State of toll. Pamphlet Laws, page 534. This act declared inoperative by the Supreme Court of the United States, in so far as it levies toll on mail coaches.

1837. Act of April 4th exempts persons hauling coal for home consumption from payment of tolls. Pamphlet Laws, page 353.

1839. Act of February 5th in form of a joint resolution requires Commissioners to give bond in the sum of $6,000. Pamphlet Laws, page 637. Changed by subsequent acts.

1839. Act of June 17th, in form of a joint resolution, fixes the compensation of Commissioners at $3 per diem, not to exceed one hundred and fifty days in any one year. Pamphlet Laws, page 679. Changed by subsequent acts.

1840. Act of March 24th authorizes the appointment of one Commissioner by the Governor for a term of three years, at a compensation of $3.00 per diem, requiring him to give bond in the sum of $10,000, to keep an account of receipts and expenditures, and publish the same; and further provides for auditors to adjust accounts. Pamphlet Laws, page 207. Partially repealed by subsequent acts.

1843. Act of April 5th authorizes Commissioners to stop mail coaches to enforce payment of tolls. Pamphlet Laws, page 164. This act held to be void by the Supreme Court of the United States, and supplied by act of April 14th, 1845, *postea.*

1845. Act of April 14th (Omnibus Bill).

"Preamble: Whereas, it has lately been decided by the Supreme Court of the United States, that the acts of assembly of this Commonwealth, relating to the collection of tolls on that part of the Cumberland Road which is within this State, passed June 13th, 1836, and April 5th, 1843, do not authorize the collection of any amount of tolls whatever for the passage upon said road of any stage, coach, or other vehicle carrying passengers with their baggage and goods, if such stage, coach, or other vehicle, is at the same time carrying any of the mails or property of the United States; and whereas, the said court sanctions the power of Pennsylvania to provide for the repairs of said road by a general assessment of tolls upon persons traveling thereon, which it is deemed just and right should be paid; and whereas, also, it is found to be impracticable to keep said road in good repair and out of debt by the tolls collectable under the existing laws of this Commonwealth, as interpreted by said Court, therefore," &c. This act then goes on and in section 12 imposes a toll of not less than two nor more than fifteen cents, as shall be fixed and determined by the Commissioner, upon every person riding or traveling in any vehicle carrying the United States mails, for every fourteen miles over which such person shall have been a passenger or traveler, and in proportion for shorter distances, provided that no toll shall be demanded from any guard to the mails, agent of the postoffice, bearer of dispatches for the General or State Government, nor any naval or military officer of the United States or this State, traveling in the discharge of official duty. Section 13 provides the manner of collecting tolls under this act. Section 14 imposes a penalty of fifty dollars on any driver who neglects to report at every gate the number of passengers in his carriage or coach. Section 15 provides that in case of refusal of passengers to pay or neglect of drivers to report, collectors shall charge in a book all unpaid tolls and sue for the same. Section 16 provides that in every case where a collector may be unable from omission or neglect of drivers or passengers to ascertain the number of passengers liable to toll under this act, he may charge and recover for so many as the carriage shall be capable of carrying. Section 17 provides a penalty of twenty dollars for every fraudulent attempt to evade the payment of toll imposed by this act. Pamphlet Laws, pages 430-1. This act is still in force, though mail coaches (rather hacks) have been carrying passengers and freights for many years without paying toll.

1847. Act of March 16th authorizes the Governor to appoint a Commissioner on each side of the Monongahela river, at a salary of $350 each. Pamphlet Laws, page 477. Subsequently repealed.

1848. Act of April 8th provides for the appointment of trustees by the courts of Somerset, Fayette and Washington counties (one in each), said trustees to appoint one or more Commissioners. Pamphlet Laws, page 523. Repealed.

1850. Act of May 3d authorizes the Commissioner and the Court of Quarter Sessions to determine what travel and transportation shall be in part or in whole exempt from toll; also authorizes the imposition of toll upon persons using the road who do not pass through the gates thereon, and prescribes the manner of collecting the same; also authorizes the Commissioner to change the location of gates, and to sell and convey toll houses and grounds, and to purchase sites. Pamphlet Laws, page 682. This act remains in force.

1856. Act of April 22, authorizes the Courts of Fayette and Washington counties to appoint superintendents. Pamphlet Laws, page 523. Prior to the date of this act, the officer in charge of the road was invariably called Commissioner. This act repealed as to that portion of the road east of the Monongahela by Act of May 1, 1861. *Postea.*

1861. Act of May 1, authorizes the Governor to appoint one person as Superintendent for so much of the road as lies within the counties of Fayette and Somerset, and repeals part of the act of April 22, 1856, *supra.* Pamphlet Laws, page 678.

1864. Act of April 13th, requires Superintendents to appropriate fifty per cent. of the tolls to the payment of old debts. Pamphlet Laws, page 408. Repealed.

1865. Act of March 21, repeals so much of the act of April 13th, 1864, *supra,* as requires Superintendents to apply fifty per cent. of tolls to the payment of old debts, and provides that *bona fide* holders of certificates of indebtedness for repairs shall be allowed credit for tolls on their certificates. Pamphlet Laws, page 474.

1865. Act of November 27th, provides for the adjudication and payment of certain claims against the road. Appendix to Pamphlet Laws of 1866, page 1,226.

1867. Act of January 7th, repeals outright *in toto* the act of April 13th, 1864, *supra.* Pamphlet Laws, page 1,543.

1868. Act of March 20th, authorizes and *requires* the Superintendent to repair the road, and keep it in repair, where it passes through any town or borough forming a street thereof in the

174

county of Fayette. Pamphlet Laws, page 444. In force.

1877. Act of April 4th, authorizes the Governor to appoint a Commissioner for that portion of the road lying between the Monongahela river and the line of the State of West Virginia for a term of three years from the termination of the term of incumbent, at a salary of $3.00 per diem, not to exceed $300 per annum, to account under oath to the auditors of Washington county. Pamphlet Laws, page 53.

1893. Act of June 2d, appropriates $1,500 to repair the great stone bridge at the Big Crossings. Pamphlet Laws, page 213.

The following communications and statements show the unexpended balances in 1834 of appropriations made by Congress in preceding years, for constructing the road through the State of Indiana:

WASHINGTON, Jan. 20th, 1835.

Sir:—I have the honor to transmit herewith a report from the Chief Engineer respecting the unexpended balance of the appropriation for the Cumberland Road in Indiana, in answer to the resolution of the House of Representatives, of the 17th instant.

Very respectfully, your most obedient servant,

MAHLON DICKERSON,

Acting Secretary of War.

To HON. JOHN BELL,

Speaker of the House of Representatives.

ENGINEER DEPARTMENT, Jan. 19th, 1835.

Hon. Lewis Cass, Secretary of War:

SIR:—In obedience to the resolution of the House of Representatives of the 17th instant, I have the honor to hand you the enclosed statement, explaining the difference in the amount of unexpended appropriations on account of the National Road, in the State of Indiana, and furnishing the information called for therein. I beg leave to remark that it is often necessary to close the annual statement of the fiscal operations of the Engineer Department before the returns, &c., from all the work are received. The Department, therefore, can only act on the information before it. This was the case in the present instance, as well as some others included in the same statement.

I have the honor to be, sir, your most obedient servant,

C. GRATIOT, Chief Engineer.

In the tabular statement of the fiscal operations, under the Engineer Department for the year ending the 30th of September,

1834, the unexpended balance of former appropriations is thus stated, relating to the Cumberland Road in Indiana:

Amount undrawn from the Treasury, 30th of September $160,882 00
Amount in the hands of agents, 30th of September 17,631 09
                                                              ──────────
    Total...$178,513 09

Which amount was ascertained from the statement of
    balances from the Treasury, on the 30th of Sept....$160,882 00

And an acknowledged balance in the hands of
    Captain Ogden, on 30th of September....$1,925 79

And from the accounts of Mr. Milroy,
    which had been rendered only to
    the first quarter of 1834, inclu-
    sive, which showed a balance in
    his hands, after deducting......$7,218 38

Paid over to Capt.Ogden, credited in his account
    current for the 3d quarter.of 1834, of....$15,705 30
                                             ──────── $17,631 09
                                                       ──────────
                                                      $178,513 09

Since preparing the annual statement and its transmission to the
    War Department, Mr. Milroy has rendered accounts for the 2d
    quarter, and part of the 3d quarter of 1834, by which he shows
    a balance due him of...... ....$ 1,147 89

So that, had Mr. Milroy's accounts been received to the time of pre-
    paring the statement, the amount in the hands of agents would
    have been, instead of $17,631 09, only..................... 777 90

Which added to the amount in the Treasury,on the 1st of Oct., 1834..$160,882 00

Would make available for the service of the 4th quarter of 1834, and
    the year 1835.. ....$161,659 90

The balance in the Treasury on the 1st of October, 1834, was......$160,882 00

Since which there has been drawn and remitted to the Superinten-
    dent, as follows:
October 21, 1834, to Captain Ogden.....................$ 30,000 00
November 25, 1834, to Captain Ogden................. 17,520 00
January 10, 1835, to Captain Ogden................... 30,000 00
                                                      ──────── $ 77,320 00
                                                                ──────────
Remaining in the Treasury on the 19th of January, 1835.........$ 83,562 00

──────────────────────

The following accounts of two of the old Commissioners are interesting as showing the amount of tolls received and disbursements made for repairs and maintenance at the dates covered, and disclosing the once familiar names of many who had contracts and were otherwise employed on the road:

ACCOUNT OF WILLIAM HOPKINS,

Commissioner of the Cumberland Road in Pennsylvania, from Nov. 10th, 1840, to Nov. 10th, 1841.

EASTERN DIVISION, EMBRACED IN FAYETTE AND SOMERSET COUNTIES, VIZ:

DR.

To cash received from the National Road Stage Co.			$2,378	12	
" " " " Holt & Maltby, supposed			113	94	
" " " at Gate No. 1, Wm. Condon, collector			1,758	87	
" " " " Gate No. 2, Hiram Seaton, "			1,948	24	
" " " " Gate No. 3, Wm. D. Beggs, "			769	27	
" " " " Gate No. 3, Jas. Reynold, "			1,125	29	
" " " a fine collected by Wm. Bradley			5	00	
" " " " " " John Tunsell			5	00	
Total amount received from Nov. 10, 1840, to Nov. 10, 1841					$ 8,103 73

CR.

BY DISBURSEMENTS, VIZ.

Cash paid Thompson McKean, late Superintendent		$ 50	00
" " Henry Woolery in full for work		15	62½
" " Thompson McKean, late Superintendent		40	00
Amount carried forward		$ 105	62½

Cash paid Jackson Brown in full for work			20	75
" " George Hensell ditto			8	22
" " Jesse Sachett ditto			90	00
" " John Smalley, hauling stone			34	20
" " Peter Leonard, quarry leave			8	62½
" " Elijah Crabb, work			197	95
" " Samuel Dean			15	00
" " George Colley, quarry leave			100	00
" " J. & W. W. Woolery, work			242	40
" " Hugh Wilson, "			2	50
" " William Jeffries, "			83	37
" " Isaac Brownfield, "			59	85
" " Thos. McKean, "			300	00
" " John Brownfield, "			41	25
" " John Risler, "			3	90
" " John Dean, "			106	88
" " James Spears, "			23	25
" " Isaac Nixon, "			125	22
" " Elias Gilmore, "			168	20
" " Ephraim Conway, "			20	00
" " A. McDowell, "			94	63½
" " McClean & Emberson, "			28	92
" " C. Rush, "			4	89
" " John Deford, quarry leave			9	04
" " Rich'd Beeson, costs, Com. vs. Stockton			11	83
" " S. D. Skeen, in full for work			4	60
" " Thomas Prentice "			6	00
" " James Amos, "			135	31

"	"	Jno. Hatzman,	"	....	52	84
"	"	William Reynolds,	"	....	982	66
"	"	Michael S. Miller,	"	....	38	37½
"	"	James Watkins,	"	....	2	20
"	"	Jos. M. Sterling,	"	....	60	00
"	"	Samuel Rush,	"	....	881	89
"	"	Hiram Hanse,	"	....	8	00
"	'	Thomas Brown,	"	....	324	00
"	"	Upton Shaw,	"	....	314	37
"	"	John Bennington,	"	....	130	00
"	"	William C. Stevens,	"	....	5	18½
"	"	Hugh Graham, work $300 00				
"	"	" " toll house............ 200 00			500	00
"	"	James Snyder, on account for work...........		235	41½
"	"	same in full..................		28	06
"	"	Charles Kemp, jr.,	"		32	00
"	"	I. & R. Hill,	"	....	39	64
"	"	Wm. H. Graham,	"	....	395	67½
"	"	George Colley,	"	....	80	80
"	"	James Marlow,	"	....	651	70
"	"	John Bradfield,	"	....	1,508	64
"	"	John M. Claybaugh,	"	....	107	63
"	"	Henry G. Brown,	"	....	24	69
"	"	Joseph Dillon,	"	....	49	64
"	"	Charles Rush,	"	....	23	85
"	"	Sam'l McReynolds,	"	....	20	33
"	"	M. H. Jones,	"	....	23	32
"	"	Hiram Hayney,	"	....	50	00
"	"	Morris Mauler	"	....	69	47½
"	"	Huston Todd, hauling stone..................		20	00

————–$ 8,722 41

The foregoing items of expenditures were contracts made by Thompson McKean, Esq., late Commissioner, and paid on his certificate.

Cash paid		Adam Speer, for work on road.................$		5	00
"	"	William D. Beggs, do		1	50
"	"	same do		1	00
"	"	same salary for keeping Gate No. 3.		83	30
"	"	James Reynolds, work on road.............		1	50
"	"	E. Crable, do		2	00
"	"	Rush & McCollough, do		25	00
"	"	E. H. Showalter, on account of work on road...		100	00
"	"	N. Bradley, " " " ...		2	50
"	"	William Milligan, " " "		14	00
"	"	A. L. Pentland, Esq., costs, Com. v. Stockton...		5	00
"	"	Wilson McCandless, Esq., Prof. services.......		20	00
"	"	same " "		30	00
"	"	R. P. Flenniken, Esq., " "		56	62½
"	"	John Irons, for advertising..................		4	00
"	"	Upton Shaw, work on road..................		30	62½
"	"	Samuel McReynolds, work on road...........		1	25
"	"	Samuel Lazure, " "			25
"	"	Robert McDowell......................		20	00
"	"	John Bradfield.....................		67	50
"	"	William Reynolds......................		273	00
"	"	John L. Dawson, Esq.....................		33	62½
"	"	Nicholas Bradley.....................		58	75
"	"	William Condon, Gate No. 1, salary........ ...		200	00
"	"	George Farney, for work on road..........		2	62½
"	"	John Nelson, " " "		1	50
"	"	Jas. Reynolds, Gate No. 3, salary....		116	66
"	"	Hiram Seaton, Gate No. 2, salary.............		200	00

"	"	McCollough & Rush, for work on road........	169	55¾
"	"	Robert S. Brown, " "	169	90½
"	"	Anthony Yarnell, " "	150	00
"	"	Sam'l Dean, " "	50	00
"	"	Henry Showalter, " "	137	50
"	"	Jackson Brown, " "	65	00
"	"	John H. Deford, Prof. services................	20	00
"	"	John Risler, for stone......................	6	40

Total amount of expenditures on Eastern division.... ————$10,847 98¼

WESTERN DIVISION, LYING IN WASHINGTON COUNTY.

To cash received from Good Intent Stage Co.............	$1,246	25
"	"	"	Moore & Henderson...............	512	16
"	"	"	Wm. R. Cope.................	70	00
"	at Gate No. 4, Stephen Phelps, col..............	1,694	23
"	" " No. 5, Wm. Hill...............	1,773	36
"	" " No. 6, David Guinea..............	1,569	44
"	" " No. 5, in Oct., 1840, under R. Quail.	150	41
"	" " No. 6. Sept. and Oct., 1840, R. Quail.......	304	67
"	a fine collected by John Freeman, Esq...........	5	00

Total amount received................................. ————$10,325 52

BY DISBURSEMENTS ON WESTERN DIVISION, VIZ:

Cash paid Egan & Dickey, in full for work on road.......	$1,387	00
"	"	John McDonough " " "	249	22½
"	"	John Dickey, " " "	50	62½
"	"	Henry Murry, " " "	889	04
"	"	same, alleged error in settlement.....	150	00
"	"	Morris Pursell, in full for work on road.......	215	87
"	"	Bradley & Morgan, " " "	234	27
"	"	Daniel Ward, " " "	746	56
"	"	Brown & Valentine, " " "	287	00
"	"	David Guinea, Gate No. 6, salary............	133	18
"	"	Wm. Hill, Gate No. 5..................	66	72

————$ 4 409 40

The above items of expenditure were on contracts made by R. Quail, late Commissioner, and paid on his certificate.

Cash paid T. H. Baird, Esq., Prof. services.............$	5	00
"	"	I. P. Morgan, digging well....................	32	50
"	"	Joel Lamborn, building chimney....	11	00
"	"	William Craven, smith work..................	15	80
"	"	J. T. Rogen, powder......................	5	50
"	"	Amos Griffith, pump......................	40	50
"	"	A. J. Harry, stove pipe	2	96
"	"	Robert Bradley, in full work at well...........	60	12½
"	"	Griffith Taylor, wheelbarrow...............	1	75
"	"	John McMath, in full work on road	8	59
"	"	John Bausman, printing...................	4	00
"	"	Grayson & Kaine, "	10	25
"	"	H. Winten, in full for work on road....	27	00
"	"	Samuel Adams, "	4	50
"	"	James P. Morgan, " "	35	31
"	"	J. Worrell, on account.....................	7	30
"	"	same, in full....................	2	75
"	"	J. McGuire, on account	57	70
"	"	Jacob Shaffer, stove pipe...	1	37

"	"	Robert Sprowl, on account work on road.......	253	00
"	"	Thomas Egan, in full........................	253	68
"	"	Henry Murray, stone........................	36	86
"	"	Jacob Stillwagon, on acct. stone.............	227	00
"	"	Anthony Rentz, " "	59	84
"	"	David Andrews, work........................	128	00
"	"	Joseph Miller, in full, stone.................	62	50
"	"	John Huston, work..........................	42	00
"	"	Joseph T. Rogers, powder....................	5	50
"	"	Isaac Leet, Prof. services...................	10	00
"	"	William Watkins, acct. stone................	15	00
"	"	Stephen Phelps, Gate No. 4, salary...........	200	00
"	"	Robert Bradley, work in full...... .....$122 96		
"	"	same on account............ 81 16	204	12
"	"	William Hill, Gate No. 5, salary.............	200	00
"	"	David Guinea, Gate No. 6, "	200	00
"	"	on acct. book for Superintendent.............	3	00
"	"	counterfeit money received	11	00
"	"	Superintendent, for his services, per account filed, 309 days at $3.00 per day............	927	00
"	"	Auditors, for settling and stating this account, viz:		
		H. Langley.........................$2 00		
		J. K. Wilson...................... 5 00		
		S. Cunningham 5 00	12	00

Total expenditures on Western division.............——————$7,594 09½

RECAPITULATION.   Dr.

To amount received on the Eastern Division........ ..$ 8,103 73
To amount received on the Western Division.......... 10,325 52
————————$18,429 25

                                                  Cr.

By cash paid out on the Eastern Division, per statement.$10,847 98¼
By cash paid on the Western Division, per statement... 7,594 09½
————————$18,442 07¾

Balance due Wm. Hopkins, Esq., Superintendent, on the
    10th Nov., 1841 ....$ 12 82¾

The undersigned, auditors appointed by the Court of Common Pleas for the county of Washington, Pennsylvania, on the 9th day of November, 1841, to audit, settle and adjust the account of William Hopkins, Esq., Commissioner of the Cumberland Road, having carefully examined the accounts submitted to them by said Commissioner (a full statement of which is herewith presented), and having compared the vouchers with said account, do find that the said William Hopkins, Commissioner as aforesaid, has expended up to the 10th day of November, 1841, the sum of twelve dollars and eighty-two ¾ cents more than came into his hands, and that said sum of twelve dollars and eighty-two ¾ cents was due to him on said day.

In testimony whereof, we have hereto set our hands and seals the 22d day of January, A. D. 1842.

        SAMUEL CUNNINGHAM, (SEAL)
        JOHN K. WILSON,   (SEAL) *Auditors.*
        HENRY LANGLY,   (SEAL)

ACCOUNT OF WILLIAM SEARIGHT,

Commissioner of the Cumberland Road in Pennsylvania, from the 1st of May, 1843, to the 31st of December, 1844, inclusive.

DR.

TO TOLLS RECEIVED ON THE EASTERN DIVISION, VIZ:

To tolls received from Thos. Grier, Gate No. 1	....	$ 4,466 24	
" " " " Robert McDowell, Gate No. 2	.....	4,102 70	
" " " " James Reynolds, Gate No. 3	......	4,410 43	
" " " " National Road Stage Co	....	3,200 00	
" " " " Express Co	....	254 00	
Total amount received on Eastern Division	....	————	$16,433 87

TO TOLLS RECEIVED ON THE WESTERN DIVISION, VIZ:

From David Mitchell, Gate No 4	....	$ 3,509 32	
" Wm. Hill, " No. 5	....	3,843 87	
" Wm. McCleary, " No. 6	....	4,105 81	
" Good Intent Stage Co	....	8,447 30	
Cash received from John S. Brady, on account of Quail's securities	....	769 44	
		————	$20,675 74

Total receipts	$37,109 11

CR.

By cash paid Thomas Grier, collector at Gate No. 1	.....	$	333	33
" " Robt. McDowell, " " " No. 2	.....		333	33
" " Jas. Reynolds, " " " No. 3	.....		333	33
" " Dan'l Kaine, for certifying auditors	....		1	00
" " D. Kaine, Wm. P. Wells and Joseph Gadd	..		12	00
" " William Jeffries	....		65	62
" " Geo. Craft, costs	....		6	60
" " Thos. and Robert Brown	....		330	63
" " Wm. Hager.	....		3	00
" " Elias Gilmore	....		2,737	40
" " George Palmer	....		55	25
" " William C. Stevens	....		16	80
" " Peter Kerney	....		1	50
" " James Dougan	....		42	77
" " Thomas Brownfield	....		1,922	98
" " Robert S. Henderson	....		150	00
" " John Malone	....		30	63
" " Sam'l Shipley, admr. of S. Rush	....		216	03
" " Andrew Bryson	....		3	00
" " John McCalpin	....		7	50
" " Thomas McGrath	....		485	94
" " Samuel Harrah	....		4	87
" " John Bradfield	....		1,748	82
By cash paid Robert McDowell	....		1,041	80
" " Calvin Perry	....		44	25
" " Wilson Fee	....		79	93
" " Thomas D. Miller	....		403	66
" " James Dolan	....		92	25
" " Upton Shaw	....		65	75
" " Elijah Crable	....		36	00
" " Samuel Shipley	....		833	38
" " Matthew McNeil	....		107	44
" " Fall & Herbertson	....		24	53
" " James White	....		8	80
" " Jackson Brown	....			50
" " J. L. Wylie & Co.	....		1	44
" " Byers & Gregg	....		35	00

''	''	William Reynolds...........................	698 87
''	''	James Marlow..............	65 15
''	''	Rudolph Brinkman	82 12
''	''	William Spaw....................	99 90
''	''	Sebastian Rush...........	92 75
''	''	John McDowell	809 14
''	''	Edward G. Roddy.............	49 84
''	''	Isaac McLaughlin..................	5 25
''	''	George W. Cass.................	70 00
''	''	John Irons, printing............	21 50
''	''	Samuel McDonald, printing...............	10 00
''	''	J. & G. S. Gideon................	24 00
''	''	James Veech, professional services....... .	100 00
''	''	R. P. Flenniken ''	100 00
''	''	Edward Kerven...........	140 73
''	''	Thomas Hougan............	30 00
''	''	Thomas Dougan................	51 75
''	''	John Powell............	37 75
''	''	George Parmertor...............	71 75
''	''	Daniel Cannon................	329 75
''	''	Hugh Graham................	233 95
''	''	Morris Whalen...............	118 28
''	''	Nicholas Bradley............	91 78
''	''	Perry White..................	116 06
''	''	Simon Deal................	96 39
''	''	William McClean................	73 23
''	''	James Collins	27 37
''	''	James McCartney..............	82 08
''	''	Anthony Yarnell..................	192 65
''	''	William Conard....	1 25
''	''	Thomas McCoy................	33 00
''	''	James Reynolds............	9 47
''	''	John M. Claybaugh.............	20 43
''	'''	Robert McDowell...........	300 44
''	''	Gadd & Henderson..............	2,531 50
''	''	Francis L. Wilkinson.............	12 29
''	''	Kerney & Redfern....	44 62
''	''	Matthias Fry................	442 67
		Depreciated money on hand................	10 00
		Balance due Commissioner on former settlement........	1,580 00
		Salary of Commissioner, from May 1st, 1843, to 31st of December, 1844, being 513 days at $3.00 per day.......	1,539 00
		Whole amount expended on Eastern Division......—————$22,066 53	

BY THE FOLLOWING SUMS EXPENDED ON THE WESTERN DIVISION.

By cash paid David Mitchell, collector Gate No. 4........$					333 33
''	''	William Hill,	''	'' No. 5.	333 33
''	''	Wm. McCleary,	''	'' No. 6	333 33
''	''	E. L. Blaine, for use of Patrick Egan........			34 96
''	''	J. S. Brady, on account of Wm. Paull.......			41 84
''	''	William McCleary......................			7 00
''	''	James Denison........................			213 90
''	''	Henry Masterson			307 87
''	''	Hiram Freeman			1,402 37
''	''	Charles Kern........................			136 72
''	''	Thomas Egan........................			263 32
''	''	John McCollough....................			956 58
''	''	Robert Sprowl.			2,995 38
''	''	Adam Fishburn.......................			1 50
''	''	John Robinson......................			303 07
''	''	Joseph Lawson......................			1,962 50
''	''	Patrick Egan.......................			203 00
''	''	John Bradlley, admr. of R. Bradley........			221 25
''	''	Thomas Hagerty......................			87 95
''	''	John Huston........................			20 25
''	''	George Irvin..........			162 07
''	''	William Hill.......................			2 81

Cr.

"	"	William Paull		161	00
"	"	Samuel Rodgers		3	00
"	"	Michael Monahan		55	00
"	"	Thomas Finley		36	25
"	"	John Curry		6	00
"	"	Michael Dougan		9	00
"	"	McCollough & Gilmore		980	22
"	"	Charles Murphy		70	00
"	"	Charles Stillwagon,		75	00
"	"	Jacob Stillwagon		305	21
"	"	Jacob Daugherty		229	00
"	"	Anthony Rentz		534	25
"	"	Baldwin Miller		3	75
"	"	William Pepper		13	41
"	"	Henry Murry		170	66
"	"	James Thompson		291	17
"	"	James Hurley		280	63
"	"	J. J. Armstrong		58	12
"	"	B. Forester		25	00
"	"	John Mitchell		62	71
"	"	Mark M. Passmore		33	75
"	"	Grayson & Kaine, printing		17	00
"	"	John Bausman "		15	00
"	"	Richard Biddle		60	00
"	"	Michael Price		21	00
"	"	William Scott		15	00
"	"	William Hopkins		52	50
"	"	E. L. Blaine, costs		11	01
"	"	Thomas Sprout		14	94
"	"	John Wheeler		62	87
"	"	Robert Patrick		45	95
"	"	Cornelius Daly		37	85
"	"	James McIntyre		226	50
"	"	William Hastings		125	62
By cash paid		Jacob Dixon		6	10
"	"	Michael Bail		16	00
"	"	Keyran Tolbert		55	52
"	"	David Butts		2	00
"	"	James Redman		160	00
"	"	John Gadd		1,556	53
"	"	Thomas Hagan		34	50
"	"	James Gainer		185	56
"	"	John Whitmire		150	00
"	"	Peter Kerney		51	50
Depreciated money on hand				5	00

Whole amount expended on Western Division.......————$16,655 41

Whole amount expended on Eastern Division....... 22,066 53

Whole amount expended on both divisions $38,721 94

Balance due Commissioner, December 31, 1844......... $ 1,612 83

FAYETTE COUNTY, ss.

We, the undersigned, auditors appointed by the Court of Common Pleas of Fayette county for that purpose, having examined the accounts and vouchers relating to the receipts and expenditures of Wm. Searight, Esq., Superintendent of the Cumberland Road, from the 1st day of May, 1843, to the 31st of December, 1844, inclusive, have found the foregoing statement of the same to be correct and true.

H. CAMPBELL,
JOHN HUSTON,
RICHARD BEESON,
Auditors.

INDEX

INDEX

INDEX

INDEX

INDEX

NATIONAL ROAD

Our first national road; fathered by Albert Gallatin. Begun in 1811 at Cumberland, Md.; completed to Wheeling in 1818. Toll road under State control, 1835-1905. Rebuilt, it is present U. S. Route 40.

PENNSYLVANIA HISTORICAL AND MUSEUM COMMISSION 1948